feminism, theory
and the politics
of difference

feminism, theory and the politics of difference

CHRIS WEEDON

BLACKWELL
Publishers

Copyright © Chris Weedon 1999

The right of Chris Weedon to be identified as author of this work has been asserted in accordance with the Copyright, Designs and Patents Act 1988.

First published 1999

2 4 6 8 10 9 7 5 3 1

Blackwell Publishers Ltd
108 Cowley Road
Oxford OX4 1JF
UK

Blackwell Publishers Inc.
350 Main Street
Malden, Massachusetts 02148
USA

British Library Cataloguing in Publication Data

A CIP catalogue record for this book is available from the British Library.

Library of Congress Cataloging-in-Publication Data

Weedon, Chris.
    Feminism, theory and the politics of difference / Chris Weedon.
        p.   cm.
    Includes bibliographical references and index.
    ISBN 0-631-19823-7 (alk. paper). — ISBN 0-631-19824-5 (pbk. : alk. paper).
        1. Feminist theory.   2. Sex differences—Political aspects.
    3. Sexual orientation—Political aspects.   I. Title.
    HQ1190.W42   1999
    305.42'01—dc21   98-34039
                                                                         CIP

Typeset in 10.5 on 12.5pt Bembo by York House Typographic Ltd, London
Printed in Great Britain by M.P.G. Books Ltd, Bodmin, Cornwall

This book is printed on acid-free paper

contents

List of iLLustrations

pReface

In recent years the *politics of difference* has become increasingly central to both feminist thought and activism. This concern with difference has been driven by the ever-growing complexity of feminism as a political movement, and the struggle for inclusion by groups of women who were marginalized in early second-wave feminism. It has also been fuelled by the theoretical debates about difference that have emerged from the impact on feminist thinking of poststructuralism and postmodernism.

The idea for this book was developed during one month that I spent as a visiting professor in 1994 at the University of Trento in Northern Italy. My task was to give a series of lectures on contemporary feminist theory. It was the absence of a book which I felt covered all that I would want to say about the range and wealth of feminist theory and its political implications that motivated the writing of this book.

In contemporary capitalist societies power is central to the production of difference as both oppressive and hierarchical. Differences between people are the effects of many types of power relations and this book attempts to cover those produced by patriarchy, class, racism and heterosexism. Its focus is the ways in which different types of feminist analysis have addressed these types of power. Chapter 1 offers an introduction to the question of gender difference. Chapter 2 looks in some detail at difference in radical feminism, analysing its inspirational force, its strengths and limitations. Chapter 3 focuses on lesbian feminism and the controversial move into queer theory which radical lesbian feminists see as leading to profoundly regressive ideas of difference and politics. Chapter 4 focuses on the ways in which difference is theorized in feminist appropriations of psychoanalysis. Chapter 5 considers difference in poststructuralist and postmodern feminisms.

In chapters 6, 7 and 8, *Feminism, Theory and the Politics of Difference* shifts focus slightly from the different conceptions of gender in play in feminist theory to other factors which complexify gender difference. Chapter 6 considers class. Chapter 7 looks at questions of whiteness and racism and at the responses of black feminists and other feminists of colour. The final chapter attempts to place Western feminism in a broader global context, taking account of debates in Third World and postcolonial feminist theory. It brings together some concluding thoughts on feminism and the politics of difference as we move into the new millennium.

acknowledgements

I should like to thank those people who have commented on particular drafts of individuals chapters: Gill Boden, Diane Elam, Rhiannon Mason and Alessandra Tanesini. I should also like to thank to Glenn Jordan from whom I have learned much over the last few years, especially about race. Thanks, too, to Jean Verrier for her help in preparing the final typescript, Thelma Gilbert for picture research, Jenny Tyler for copy-editing and Andrew McNeillie for his support.

Earlier versions of parts of chapter 5 appear in the second edition of my *Feminist Practice and Poststructuralist Theory* (Oxford: Blackwell, 1996) and in the Blackwell *Companion to Feminist Philosophy* ed. Alison M. Jaggar and Iris Young (Oxford: Blackwell, 1998).

The author and publishers gratefully acknowledge the following for permission to reproduce copyright material:

Aunt Lute Books, for material from *Making Face, Making Soul: Haciendo Caras,* © 1990 by Gloria Anzaldúa.

The Crossing Press, for material reprinted with permission from *Sister Outside: Essays and Speeches* by Audre Lorde, © 1984. Published by The Crossing Press: Freedom, CA.

Free Association Books for material from © Chapter Nine: 'Situated Knowledges: The Science Question in Feminism and the Privilege of the Partial Perspective' from Donna Haraway's book *Simians, Cyborgs and Women: The Reinvention of Nature* © 1991 Donna J. Haraway. First published in Great Britain by Free Association Books in 1991, represented by the Cathy Miller Foreign Rights Agency, London, England.

ACKNOWLEDGEMENTS

St Martin's Press, Incorporated, for material copyright © 1987 by Charlotte
Bunch; from *Passionate Politics* by Charlotte Bunch. Reprinted by permission
of St. Martin's Press incorporated.

The extract reprinted on pages, 30–34 from *Gyn-Ecology* by Mary Daly
published in Great Britain by The Women's Press Ltd, 1979, 34 Great Sutton
Street, London EC1V 0DX, is used by permission of The Women's Press.

The publishers apologize for any errors or omissions in the above list and
would be grateful to be notified of any corrections that should be incorporated in the next edition or reprint of this book.

CHapteR 1
The Question of Difference

In recent years difference has become a key concept in political, social and cultural theory. There are many reasons for this. They range from the changing composition of Western societies and the increasing diversity of the postmodern market place, to the impact of new social movements on society, with feminism at the forefront. Important, too, has been the impact of poststructuralist theory, with its critiques of traditional approaches to meaning, identity and difference. In Britain, the last three decades have witnessed changing perceptions of the nature of society in institutions as important and diverse as the political parties, schools, the churches and the arts councils. Multiculturalism and cultural diversity have become accepted frameworks for social and cultural policies.[1]

The decades since the Second World War have seen a wide-ranging expansion and transformation of the political sphere. No longer centred on traditional forms of trades unionism and parliamentary democracy, politics today includes areas previously deemed private, personal or simply natural. New forms of political action, focused on gender, sexuality, race, post-colonialism, poverty, peace, animal rights and the environment have developed, often with strong cultural dimensions which involve music, drama, literature and the visual arts (see figure 1.1).

Since the late 1960s second-wave feminism has placed a wide range of previously marginalized issues on the political agenda. Beginning as loose networks of consciousness-raising and campaigning groups, the women's movement attempted to develop new forms of political organization which aspired to non-hierarchical structures and aimed to empower all women whatever their background. It initiated a wide range of political campaigns directed at issues as diverse as equal pay, pornography, sexshops, lesbian

1.1 Women's peace movement protest at Greenham Common air base, 1984.
Photographs: Alison Jackson

rights, nuclear weapons and abortion (see figures 3.1 and 3.2). As the
movement developed, it encouraged women to take an active part *as women*
in other struggles, ranging from campaigns in Northern Ireland including the
development of cross-community women's peace groups, (see figures 1.2
and 1.3) to women's support groups in the miners' strike of 1985 (see figure
6.1). Like other new social movements, feminism has given rise to new forms
of social and cultural theory.

Recent changes in the political sphere and in social and cultural theory are
often seen as part of a broader set of changes affecting all areas of life. These
shifts and transformations tend to be grouped together under the general

1.2 Women's picket outside Armagh gaol on International Women's Day, March 1983. Photograph: Joanne O'Brien/Format

heading of 'postmodernity'. Variously linked to multi-national, global capitalism (Jameson 1984), changes in the nature and status of knowledge (Lyotard 1984) and the proliferation of previously marginalized voices via alternative social movements, postmodernity has a number of identifiable characteristics.[2] These include what Jean-François Lyotard calls a scepticism towards metanarratives (that is the questioning of theories which make universalist claims, such as liberalism, Marxism or radical feminism) and the fragmentation of liberal humanist notions of unified subjectivity. In postmodernity, subjectivity is often theorized as an effect of culture which produces not unified identity, but a subjectivity which is fragmented, contradictory and which comprises multiple identities. Postmodernity is further characterized by the development of new technologies and the relativization of truth claims.

Social and cultural theory have been further transformed by radical forms of politicized knowledge produced by social movements such as second-wave feminism, black power, Third World liberation movements, gay liberation, and the peace and environmental movements. These new forms of knowledge have, in their turn, been radically affected by a range of postmodern theories, which can be loosely grouped together under the heading of poststructuralism and which draw on the work of Derrida, Lacan, Foucault, Deleuze, Irigaray and Kristeva. Focusing on issues of language,

1.3 Belfast mural, 1995. Photograph: Chris Weedon

subjectivity, the unconscious, the body, discourse and power, poststructuralism questions the givenness of the world, the transparency of language, the
nature and status of the individual subject, subject–object relationships, the
nature of power and the possibility of accessing truth.[3] It has queried the
status and explanatory power of general theories (metanarratives) such as
liberal humanism and Marxism and produced a discursive shift which – it it
is often argued – opens up space for alternative voices, new forms of
subjectivity, previously marginalized narratives, and new interpretations,
meanings and values. Radical appropriations of this space, particularly in
feminist and postcolonial theory, see it as somewhere where difference can
be realized in positive ways and respected.[4]

Differences between individuals and groups – between sexes, classes, races, ethnic groups, religions and nations – become important political issues when they involve relations of power. Power takes many forms, affecting access to material resources as well as questions of language, culture and the right to define who one is. Power relations of class, sexism, heterosexism and racism have ensured that it has been largely white, Western, middle- and upper-class men who have defined meaning, controlled economies and determined the nature of relations between East and West and North and South. In the process, women, all people of colour and non-Western nations have been defined as different and implicitly or explicitly inferior. Differences can be categorized in various ways, for example as social, political, cultural or natural. How differences are defined has implications for whether they are seen as desirable, changeable or fixed.

TRADITIONAL IDEAS OF GENDER DIFFERENCE

The man who fights for two or more in the struggle for existence, who has all the responsibility and the cares of tomorrow, who is constantly active in combating the environment and human rivals, needs more brain than the woman he must protect and nourish, than the sedentary woman, lacking any interior occupations, whose role is to raise children, love and be passive. (Topinard 1888: 22, quoted in Gould 1981: 104)

Ideas of difference such as the above, which are grounded in a mixture of biology and nineteenth-century, middle-class views of femininity, have not disappeared from contemporary Western culture. We need only think of images from popular culture: Tarzan and Jane, and the heroes of westerns, science fiction or James Bond films. Man is the provider in a hostile world, who fights to preserve our values and way of life. Woman is the vulnerable sexual partner or passive nurturer. Gender difference, a central issue in popular culture and the practices of everyday life, is also a key dimension of social and cultural theory, the law, religion, psychology and the life sciences. Gender difference (like sexuality in Foucault's work) is not naturally given but is an effect of relations of knowledge and power which permeate all areas of life. Moreover, the ways in which gender difference is defined are far from neutral.[5] They involve interests which construct the meanings of difference in competing and often contradictory ways.

The assumption that women are naturally different from men is fundamental to the history of Western civilization. From biblical accounts of the creation, to Darwinism and modern science, stress has been laid on women's intrinsic difference from men. This difference is most often grounded in

5

biology. In Western thought gender tends to be conceptualized as a set of polarized binary oppositions in which one term is privileged over the other, a point made forcefully in 1975 by the radical French writer Hélène Cixous in her well-known essay 'Sorties':

Father/Mother
Head/Heart
Intelligible/Palpable
Logos/Pathos
Form, convex, step, advance, semen, progress.
Matter, concave, ground – where steps are taken, holding and dumping ground.

Man

Woman

Always the same metaphor: we follow it, it carries us, beneath all its figures, wherever discourse is organized. If we read or speak, the same thread or double braid is leading us throughout literature, philosophy, criticism, centuries of representation and reflection.
Thought has always worked through opposition,
Speaking/Writing
Parole/Écriture
High/Low
Through dual, hierarchical oppositions. (Cixous 1987: 63–4)

Such hierarchically structured discourses of gender value aspects defined as male over those defined as female, for example, reason over emotion, or activity over passivity. Moreover, theories of gender difference have most often been written from perspectives that assume the white male to be the norm against which all others should be measured and which see all women as deviating from this norm in ways that fit them for domesticity and motherhood. Their supposed natural attributes both contrast with and complement those of men.

Biological theories of difference, from Darwin to contemporary sociobiology, tend to focus on women's and men's different reproductive roles. Motherhood as the essence of woman's being was central to nineteenth- and early twentieth-century scientific accounts of gender. It surfaced, for example, in biology, psychology and medicine, and in a popular form in advice and conduct books. Here is an example from the widely read 'Self and Sex Series' of books, published in English by the Vir Publishing Company in the USA in 1901 and translated into nine other language. The series was marketed as 'Pure Books on Avoided Subjects' and included four titles for boys and men and four for girls and women. The target audiences were divided by age and gender, so that there were books for girls or boys, young women or young men, wives or husbands, and women or men over forty-five. This extract is from *What A Young Wife Ought to Know*.[6]

> Let us consider a little, [woman's] peculiar adaption, and the suitability of each part to the purpose intended by the all-wise Creator. The nervous system is a little more highly organised than in man; the heart and blood vessels adjusted to swifter work; the brain quicker, the muscles not so hard and tense. In place of the logical, she possesses the intuitive mind, which makes her capable of reaching a conclusion while man is thinking about it. She has less strength, but greater endurance; less daring in achievement, but more patience; less force-fulness, but more quiet insistence; less practicability, but more of the aesthetic; less ambition to assume the great responsibilities of life, but more painstaking in the little and no less important things which go so far towards making the days sweet and peaceful. All these differences from man, her companion, but make her the more desirable and attractive to him.
>
> Unlike man in her physical form, her departure from his type, was to fit her for motherhood. Narrower shouldered and less muscular, because not needing the brawn for lifting and laboring with her hands in the harder coarser ways; she is broader through the hips to give ample room for cradling her children. (Drake 1901: 27–8)

This text identifies differences between women and men which encompass physical, emotional and intellectual characteristics, and grounds them in biology. While the tone of the book – aimed as it is at women – is positive, it suggests that women are both fundamentally different from men and complementary to them. Their strengths – intuition, endurance, patience – fit them for domesticity and motherhood rather than professional or public life. Their weaknesses include illogicality and lack of strength, daring, forcefulness and ambition.

Similar and related views of gender difference can be found throughout the biological and social sciences in the nineteenth and early twentieth centuries. Scientific theories of difference were used to justify women's exclusion from higher education and public life. Biologically based classificatory sciences sought to define 'natural' differences through empirical studies of bodies – in particular of skulls. Both white women and women and men of colour were said to possess smaller brains than white men, a factor taken to signify their lesser powers of reasoning. For example, the psychologist Gustave Le Bon, who is regarded as a founder of social psychology and who was part of Paul Broca's French school of craniometry, drew the following conclusions from his study of brain sizes:

In the most intelligent races, as among the Parisians, there are a large number of women whose brains are closer in size to those of gorillas than to the most developed male brains. This inferiority is so obvious that no one can contest it for a moment; only its degree is worth discussion. All psychologists who have studied the intelligence of women, as well as poets and novelists, recognize today that they represent the most inferior forms of human evolution and that they are closer to children and savages than to an adult civilized man. They excel in fickleness, inconstancy, absence of thought and logic, and incapacity to reason. Without doubt there exist some distinguished women, very superior to the average man, but they are as exceptional as the birth of any monstrosity, as, for example, of a gorilla with two heads; consequently we may neglect them entirely. (Le Bon 1879: 60–1, quoted in Gould 1981: 104–5)

At the beginning of the new millennium in the wake of two significant waves of feminist activism, such ideas seem both extreme and outdated, yet many of the gender stereotypes which Le Bon grounds in biology still pervade popular images of women today.

Nineteenth-century theories of gender difference often drew parallels between black men and white women in which black men's inferiority was grounded in their similarity to white women: 'Men of the black races have a brain scarcely heavier than that of white women' (Hervé 1881: 692, quoted in Gould 1981: 103). Black women – subject to both racist and sexist exclusions – barely figured in the debate. Racial science was very extensive in this period and claimed to prove a hierarchy of races and civilization.[7] Like scientific studies of women, which measured body and brain sizes, racist science used shape of skull and brain size, as well as skin colour and phenotype, to define people of colour as naturally different and inferior to white people.

The influence of nineteenth-century scientific discourses of gender was not restricted to the realm of theory: these discourses formed the ideological basis and justification for a range of social policies towards women which materially affected their lives. While the adequacy of the techniques, methods and assumptions of nineteenth-century science – particularly phrenology, craniology and the various forms of sociobiology – does not stand close scrutiny, this science was widely accepted at the time and was used to justify the exclusion of women from suffrage, higher education and public life.

In the case of race, science was used to legitimate colonialism and extreme brutal practices such as slavery and segregation. Pro-slavery campaigners in the southern United States in the 1840s, for example, drawing on the craniology of Samuel Morton, argued that the natural differences of African people meant that they were biologically suited to slavery.[8] Emancipation, they argued, meant a shorter life span as could be seen from the fate of black people in the northern states. Quoting an article published in the *Boston Medical and Surgical Journal* of 1843, the popularizer of racial science and apologist for slavery Josiah C. Nott MD argued:

> That the mortality of the free people of color is more than a hundred per cent greater than that of slaves. . . .

	New York	Philadelphia	Baltimore
Whites	1 in 14	1 in 31.82	1 in 42.29
Free blacks	1 in 18	1 in 19.91	1 in 32
Slaves			1 in 77

> (Nott 1844: 30–1)

According to Nott's figures, slaves are by far the most long-lived group.

This type of scientific racism and similar work on gender set the terms of the debates about difference well into the twentieth century. Indeed, the negative qualities consistently attributed to sexual and racial difference from a white, middle-class, male norm by the institutions of science, medicine, philosophy and the law made it very difficult to see questions of difference in positive terms.

Difference as lack and inferiority has remained a key aspect of many influential twentieth-century theories of sexual difference. In Freudian psychoanalysis, for example, which is discussed in detail in chapter 4, we find a theory which takes the male as the norm and defines women as different from and inferior to this norm:

> The first step in the phallic phase . . . is not the linking up of masturbation with the object cathexes of the Oedipus complex, but a momentous discovery which little girls are destined to make. They notice the penis of a brother or playmate, strikingly visible and of large proportions, at once recognise it as the superior counterpart of their own small and inconspicuous organ, and from that time forward fall a victim to envy for the penis. (Freud 1975a: 31; original 1925)

In psychoanalysis the penis/phallus is the primary signifier of difference and women are defined in terms of lack. For Freud, lack of a penis leads to penis envy which has further profound psychological consequences for women's character, endowing them with the traits of jealousy and a lesser sense of justice. Summarizing his conclusions about the psychical consequences of the anatomical differences between the sexes, Freud writes:

I cannot evade the notion (though I hesitate to give it expression) that for women the level of what is ethically normal is different from what it is in men. Their super-ego is never so inexorable, so impersonal, so independent of its emotional origins as we require it to be in men. Character-traits which critics of every epoch have brought up against women – that they show less sense of justice than men, that they are less ready to submit to the great exigencies of life, that they are more often influenced in their judgements by feelings of affection or hostility – all these would be amply accounted for by the modification in the formation of their super-ego which we have inferred above. We must not let ourselves be deflected from such conclusions by the denials of the feminists, who are anxious to force us to regard the two sexes as completely equal in position and worth. (1975a: 36; original 1925)

In a similar vein, sex-role psychology has long categorized certain qualities as masculine and others as feminine. In such studies the feminine pole tends to be identified with a long list of predictable characteristics including lack of aggression, lack of independence, emotionality, subjectiveness, submissiveness, passivity, illogicality, indecisiveness and lack of confidence, stereotypical traits which continue to surface in popular representations of gender difference.[9]

THE FEMINISTS' RESPONSE

Throughout its history feminism has taken issue with the hegemonic meanings ascribed to women's biological and anatomical differences from men. The meanings given to femaleness and femininity assumed political importance for women because they were used to determine and limit the social and economic spheres to which women had access. In Britain in the 1790s, Mary Wollstonecraft, inspired by the French Revolution, argued that women were different from men not for any innate 'natural' reasons, but as a result of an inadequate education which privileged sensibility over reason:

Women, commonly called ladies, are not to be contradicted, in company, are not allowed to exert any manual strength; and from them the negative virtues only are expected, when any virtues are expected – patience, docility, good humour, and flexibility – virtues incompatible with any vigorous exertion of intellect. . . .

In the regulation of a family, in the education of children, understanding, in an unsophisticated sense, is particularly required – strength of body and mind; yet the men who, by their writing, have most earnestly laboured to domesticate women, have endeavoured, by arguments dictated by a gross appetite, which satiety had rendered fastidious, to weaken their bodies and cramp their minds. (Wollstonecraft 1975: 148 and 155; original 1792)

In answer to this Wollstonecraft argued for an equal education which would prepare women for family life, the professions and public life. Education was a theme to which feminists would return again and again over the next two centuries. Indeed the debate over girls' and women's education has remained a key aspect of feminist politics to the present day and currently feminists in Britain find themselves faced with calls for positive action for boys who now achieve less at school than girls.

Whereas Mary Wollstonecraft and many nineteenth-century women writers stressed unequal education as the key factor determining the differences between women and men, some first-wave feminists at the turn of the nineteenth-century, particularly in Germany, embraced ideas of women's intrinsic difference and special feminine cultural mission. Instead of arguing that women were, like men, essentially rational beings, they attempted to use arguments about difference in the battle for access to education and the professions. If women were intrinsically different, they urged, their special qualities lay in their natural capacity for motherhood which required cultivation through education. Motherhood was, in this discourse, much more than a biological capacity. Feminist activist Helene Lange, for example, argued that in society at large,

> Instead of regarding motherhood as a quality of woman which determines her being, colours it in a special way, shapes her endeavours, securing for mankind a unique dimension of culture, physical motherhood was seen as the only purpose of woman, for which she must wait, for which she must live exclusively, without which her life would be a failure – without considering that this meant removing her from the ranks of rational beings. ...
>
> ... We, too, start from the proposition that the woman's whole being is determined by motherhood. But we conceive of it, where psychological questions are concerned, as a quality, as a certain essence of being; not as an impediment to intellectual development. ... This determining role of motherhood can be seen – irrespective of individual deviations from the norm – in the whole genus. It constitutes the specifically feminine; it is the source of psychological altruism, pity and love which, in its spiritual forms, too, bears the traits of woman. It contrasts with the more abstract, speculative disposition of man which is directed towards the systematic and impersonal. The intellectual processes take the same form in both men and women; but in many cases they stimulate different centres, triggering different connections. This different direction taken by their interests, their feelings, *but not the structure of their brains as such*, constitutes, in fact, something resembling a spiritual boundary between the sexes. It guarantees precedence to the one sex here, the other sex there. (Lange 1977: 49–50; original 1899; my emphasis)

11

The argument – widespread in Germany between 1880 and 1914 – that women possessed special mothering qualities which should be extended to the rest of society was used by German feminists in their campaigns for equal rights in a range of areas.[10] Many German feminists argued that to accept the assumption that women and men are intrinsically different should not necessarily imply that women are inferior. Their platform was the familiar one of suggesting that women and men are equal but different.

This type of argumentation, with its fixing of difference as natural, was rejected by most Anglo-American feminists of the period, who campaigned for suffrage and access to education and the professions on the basis of women's sameness to men. While the right to be different without being seen as inferior is a key theme of present-day feminist thought, historically it has more often than not led to legitimation of separate spheres for women and men. The effect of privileging certain ideas of difference – for example women's natural and intrinsic mothering nature – has been to limit women's value, whatever their individual circumstances, to discourses of motherhood with which most women did not fully or even partly identify.

The problem of conceiving difference in ways which are not restrictive but liberating remains a key theoretical and political question for contemporary feminism. Second-wave rejections of women's traditional role in the patriarchal nuclear family, for example, were countered by women who choose motherhood and domesticity over a career and public life. Indeed the need to recognize the domestic sphere as a place of work for women has been a consistent theme of recent feminism from the wages for housework campaigns of the 1970s onwards.[11] The issues of women's dual role as domestic and paid worker and of motherhood and family responsibilities pointed to the need to move beyond the binarism of either/or thinking. It was not just a question of respecting different individual choices where family versus work was concerned; the structure of the world of work, the sexual division of labour and the nuclear family all needed rethinking in ways which would transform men's as well as women's roles and expectations.

The need to respect differences and choices and to re-evaluate traditional hierarchies of what counts as important remains a key dimension of feminism. It is particularly strong in the ecological feminist movement where lifestyle politics is linked to fundamental questions about the future viability of the planet. Ecofeminist critiques of wasteful, consumer-oriented societies and the attempt to live differently are part of a fundamental concern for the environment and, in many cases, the radically unequal distribution of resources between First and Third World countries.

The idea of lifestyle politics has gained increasing importance in wealthy, First World, postmodern societies. It is a significant dimension, for example, of gay, lesbian and queer critiques of heterosexuality. The queer movement, with its insistence that nothing is intrinsically normal or natural, can be seen as both quintessentially postmodern in its assumptions and libertarian in its politics. Indeed, it is one of the most quoted strengths of postmodernity that it allows for, indeed celebrates, difference and creates the conditions in which respect for difference can thrive. Yet the history of both gender and race relations clearly demonstrates that discourses of sexual and racial difference – which take bodies as their referent and guarantee – continue to be implicated in relations of power which both assume and produce structural relations of privilege and disadvantage. These issues are taken up throughout this book.

THE ESCAPE FROM THE BODY INTO 'SAMENESS'

From the beginnings of liberalism in the West in the eighteenth century until the advent of the contemporary Women's Liberation Movement in the late 1960s, feminism in the Western world was predominantly liberal in character. Since its inception, liberal feminism, like liberalism more broadly, has been concerned with the rights of the individual to political and religious freedom, choice and self-determination. Until the advent of second-wave feminism, liberal discourse consistently spoke of 'man'. The French Revolution proclaimed 'Liberty, Equality and *Fraternity*' while the American Declaration of Independence of 4th July 1776 insisted that 'all *men* are created equal, that they are endowed by their Creator with certain inalienable Rights, that among these are Life, Liberty and the pursuit of Happiness' (my emphasis). Until recently the rights of the individual were coterminous with the rights of man; at best man was said to include woman. In theory, the individual for whom liberalism legislates is an abstract individual untouched by social relations of class, gender or race. In practice, in the last quarter of the eighteenth-century, the 'man' of the American declaration of independence signified a relatively small group of property-owning, mainly white males. All women and most men of colour were excluded. Indeed it was not until the 1960s that black people in the United States were guaranteed full civil rights, and even today, endless studies show that many people in Western countries who are not white, male and middle-class do not enjoy equal access to the things that make for 'Life, Liberty and the Pursuit of Happiness'.

Liberal ideas of the individual are founded on a dualist mode of thinking in which the mind is conceived as distinct from the body and superior to it. The defining feature of the abstract individual of the liberal tradition is rational consciousness. Rationality is placed in binary opposition to the body.

Indeed, it was the meanings ascribed to the bodies of pre-twentieth-century liberalism's 'Others' – all women and men of colour – which were used to justify their exclusion from universal human rights. Until well into the twentieth century all women and most men of colour in the West were forced to fight against their exclusion from the rights and duties of liberalism. Inclusion, they argued, was essential to the development of a more enlightened and humane society:

> We take our stand on the solidarity of humanity, the oneness of life, and the unnaturalness and injustice of all special favoritisms, whether of sex, race, country or condition. . . . The coloured woman feels that woman's cause is one and universal; and that . . . not till race, colour, sex and condition are seen as accidents, and not the substance of life; not till the universal title of humanity to life, liberty and the pursuit of happiness is conceded to be inalienable to all; not till then is woman's lesson taught and woman's cause won – not the white woman's nor the black woman's, not the red woman's but the cause of every man and of every woman who has writhed silently under a mighty wrong. (Cooper 1976, 330–1; original 1893).

The feminist battle for inclusion within liberalism has been waged for 300 years. From Mary Astell's appeal in the 1700s for women's education and emancipation from the patriarchal family to the present, liberal feminists have fought to extend the benefits of liberalism to women and to achieve for them suffrage, education, access to the professions and property rights. In this struggle they have argued for women's equality with men on the basis of their *sameness*. They argue that women are equally rational and equally capable of holding public office and administering property. To make these arguments, liberal feminists have inevitably played down women's differences from men, however these differences are understood (as biologically determined or as socially produced). Thus, for example, in his essay 'On the Subjection of Women', the nineteenth-century advocate of women's rights, John Stuart Mill, argued:

> [Women] have always hitherto been kept, as far as regards spontaneous development, in so unnatural a state, that their nature cannot but have been greatly distorted and disguised; and no one can safely pronounce that if women's nature were left to choose its direction as freely as men's, and if no artificial bent were attempted to be given to it except that required by the conditions of human society, and given to both sexes alike, there would be any material difference, or perhaps any difference at all, in the character and capacities which would unfold themselves. (Mill 1984: 305; original 1869)

Mill's speculation that, given equality of education and opportunity, men

14

and women would be alike helped strengthen the liberal feminist argument for equal rights and opportunities. Indeed, from the birth of liberalism to the present day, liberal feminists have argued that sexual difference should not determine how one is regarded as a human being.

Liberal feminism in the West today has achieved the extension of most civil rights and duties to women. However, the liberal strategies of arguing from the perspective of abstract individuals and playing down the differences which result from women's role as child bearers and carers led to the burdens of women's dual role and what became known in the 1980s as the ideology of the 'superwoman'. A superwoman was expected to participate fully in all spheres – the domestic, the workplace and public life – while raising a family, looking good and engaging in a mutually satisfying sex life, without any fundamental structural changes to society. Similarly, in Britain in the late 1990s, New Labour's policy of facilitating paid employment for women through the provision of childcare and after school clubs, leaves the structures of work intact, while increasing the casualization of labour. In Eastern Europe under socialism, women found themselves in a similar position. Supposedly freed from patriarchal oppression by the socialization of the means of production and access to a world of work organized according to socialist principles, they found themselves expected to manage family life, paid work and public life without any fundamental changes in the structure of work or the sexual division of labour.[12]

Liberal feminism has tended to focus on choice and equality of opportunity within existing social relations:

> The true liberator can always be recognized by her wanting to increase the options open to the people who are to be liberated, and there is never any justification for taking a choice away from a group you want to liberate unless it is demonstrable beyond all reasonable doubt that removing it will bring other, more important options into existence. To give women freedom we must give them more choice, and then if they really do not want the things they are choosing now, like homes and families, those things will just die out without our having to push them. (Radcliffe Richards 1982: 100)

The failure of much liberal feminism up to 1968 to problematize categories such as the individual, freedom and choice or to challenge the deep-rooted structures of contemporary capitalist societies – particularly the sexual division of labour and the public/private divide – meant that relatively little progress was made in transforming either the sexual division of labour or dominant norms of femininity and masculinity. Indeed the tendency within liberal feminism to perpetuate the definition of the private sphere as an area of individual choice led to a failure to politicize specific areas of women's oppression within the family and sexual relations. The perceived limitations of liberal feminism provided an important impetus for the development of more radical forms of feminism over the last thirty years. These include radical feminism, lesbian feminism, new forms of socialist and materialist feminism, black and Third World feminisms and poststructuralist and post-modern feminisms.

More than anything else, second-wave feminist critiques of liberal feminism have taken issue with its failure to challenge that normative dualism which defines the essence of humanity solely in terms of rationality.[13] Such views of human beings tend to be at the expense of bodies and emotions. To ignore the social significance of bodies for both patriarchy and racism is to fail to address many aspects of women's lives and the structural power relations which continue to govern them. Insofar as women's oppression is grounded in views of female difference which see the body as their guarantee, this body and its meanings cannot be ignored by feminists. Moreover, many of the key areas in which patriarchal power is focused, for example, sexuality and procreation, have the body at their centre.

The liberal feminist disregard for bodies and emphasis on sameness has been compounded by another aspect of modern liberal societies: the public/private divide. This divide took on new significance with industrialization and the growth of modern capitalist states. Whereas in the pre-modern period paid work and politics were seen as part of the public domain, the family and interpersonal relationships were confined, at least in theory, to the private. Since the aim of liberal theory is to guarantee the rights of the individual, liberal politics tends to argue for as little state involvement in the lives of individuals as is compatible with guaranteeing individual freedom and choice. For many liberal feminists, choice within the domestic sphere is guaranteed only if women have an income which enables them to pay other women to carry out domestic labour and child care.

THE SOCIALIST ALTERNATIVE

From the nineteenth century until the 1960s, the main alternative to liberalism in the West was socialism. Attitudes to the 'woman question' in the labour movement and in social democratic and Marxist political organizations varied from the overtly hostile to the argument that women's equality would follow automatically from a socialist revolution. Frederick Engels, for example, in his influential book *The Origin of the Family, Private Property and the State* (1972; original 1884) argued that the emancipation of women would follow from their free and full involvement in a socialist labour market.

Until the advent of second-wave feminism, gender politics was seen by the British labour movement either as a non-issue or a harmful deviation from the class struggle. Moreover, not only industrial relations and politics, but also education, were long seen as a male preserve. Women's role was to fundraise and service male activists' domestic needs. This can be seen in the practice of even the most radical organizations. Like much of the labour movement, the Marxist Plebs League in the first half of the twentieth century saw education as central to working-class struggle and emancipation, yet even as late as 1928, women had to argue for inclusion:[14]

> I've washed up for peace, I've washed up for socialism, I've washed up for disarmament, but I am not going to wash up for education, because I want to be in the class and not at the sink. (*The Plebs* 1928, 20 (1): 13)

The tendency to restrict women to a domestic support role was reinforced within trades unionism by the idea of the family wage. The hegemonic nineteenth-century, bourgeois model of the nuclear family in which women did not have to work outside the home (or were not allowed to do so) but could dedicate themselves to motherhood and homemaking had much ideological appeal for working-class families. However it could only be realized by the achievement of a living family wage. One important side effect of this was the tendency to see women as at most secondary wage-earners working for 'pin money' and to pay them less. While the Marxist Left, following Engels, regarded women's access to the labour market as central to their liberation from patriarchy, this tended to be seen as something which would follow naturally from a socialist revolution and the abolition of private ownership of the means of production.[15] Thus first-wave feminism was identified by Marxists as a bourgeois deviation from the class struggle for a socialist revolution.

The effects of Marxist theories of women's liberation can be seen in Eastern Europe between 1945 and 1989, where socialism was officially regarded as having solved the 'woman question'. What did this socialist solving of the woman question mean in practice? Clearly it varied widely between the different socialist states. In Poland, for example, fundamental changes in women's traditional social role and in gender norms were hindered by the continued influence of the Catholic church. In secular states like the German Democratic Republic, however, which suffered from a shortage of labour and a low birthrate, considerable efforts were made to bring women into the workforce and to enable them to combine full-time

17

paid work with motherhood and child care. These included extensive maternity leave and child care facilities, positive discrimination for women with children in work and education, a day's paid leave each month for housework, and government promotion of the image of the working mother. Yet even after forty years of socialism in the GDR, there was little evidence that fundamental changes in the sexual division of labour either at work or in the home, or in social and cultural norms of femininity and masculinity, followed automatically from the socialization of the means of production. Official discourse propagated by the Socialist Unity Party and the official women's organization rendered such issues invisible and sexual politics remained limited to a narrowly sanctioned public domain. Western feminism was widely regarded, even by women, as irrelevant to the GDR, though many of the issues around sexuality and femininity which were central to Western feminism came to the fore in women's fictional writing of the 1970s and 1980s.[16]

In the West, second-wave feminism saw the birth of new forms of socialist feminism which – inspired in part by radical feminism – challenged the public/private divide and placed issues of domesticity, reproduction and sexuality on the political agenda. Early radical feminists who had links to the Left adapted Marxist language to develop a theorization of patriarchy. Shulamith Firestone, for example, theorized women as a class defined by their sex:

> Historical materialism is that view of the course of history which seeks the ultimate cause and the great moving power of all historic events in the dialectic of sex: the division of society into two distinct biological classes for procreative reproduction, and the struggle of these classes with one another; in the changes in the modes of marriage, reproduction and childcare created by these struggles; in the connected development of other physically-differentiated classes (castes); and in the first division of labour based on sex which developed into the (economic-cultural) class system. (Firestone 1972: 12; original 1970)

This approach involved the privileging of patriarchal oppression over all other types of oppression, a move which socialist feminists – with their commitment to class analysis – did not support. The main feature of second-wave socialist feminism from the early 1970s onwards was the desire to hold together class and gender as social factors which constitute difference in oppressive ways. Gradually, in response to critiques from women of colour and lesbian women, race and sexuality were added to class and gender. A key feature of socialist feminism when contrasted with traditional Marxism was that attempts were made to resist subsuming one category of oppression under another, for example, making gender or racist oppressions effects of the capitalist mode of production. (Socialist feminist approaches to difference are discussed in detail in chapter 6.)

THE LIMITS OF SAMENESS: REINSTATING THE BODY, RADICAL CRITIQUES

> No matter how empathetic you are to another's oppression, you become truly committed to radical change only when you realise your own oppression – it has to reach you on a gut level. This is what has been happening to American women, both in and out of the New Left. (Morgan 1993: 15; original 1968)

Second-wave feminism, which developed in the late 1960s, fundamentally transformed the domain of the political. Its most famous principle, 'the personal is political', was symptomatic of an opening up to public and political scrutiny of areas previously seen as personal. Second-wave feminism challenged the public/private divide and in the process reinstated the importance of the body in sexual politics. Women's exploitation and oppression were seen as all-pervasive and intrinsic to all elements of contemporary society. Writing on the occasion of the first major Women's Liberation demonstration in the United States at the Miss America Pageant in Atlantic City on 7 September 1968, Robin Morgan explained:

> The pageant was chosen as a target for a number of reasons: it is patently degrading to women (in propagating the Mindless Sex-Object Image); it has always been a lily-white, racist contest (there has never been a black finalist); the winner tours Vietnam, entertaining the troops as a mascot of murder; the whole gimmick of the million-dollar pageant corporation is one commercial shill-game to sell the sponsors' products. Where else could one find such perfect combination of American values – racism, militarism, capitalism – all packaged in one 'ideal' symbol: a woman. (Morgan 1993: 25–6; original 1968)

Much of the early theoretical and political impetus in second-wave feminism came from radical feminism. Radical feminism turned its attention to the body as the site of women's difference and oppression. It reinstated the centrality of the body in politics, attempting to both expose and counteract the exploitation of women's bodies and to give new, positive meanings to female difference.

Radical feminism rejects the theoretical frameworks and political practice of both liberalism and traditional Marxism. It argues, on the one hand, against liberalism, that women's liberation cannot be achieved by a theory and practice which make provisions for the rights of abstract individuals, irrespective of social class, race and gender relations. On the other hand, radical feminists argue that women's oppression cannot be reduced to class oppression and made an epiphenomenon of the economic and social structures of the capitalist mode of production. In opposition to Marxism, radical feminism regards women's oppression as the primary and fundamental form of oppression. Gender is seen as an elaborate system of male domination of women's minds and bodies which is at the basis of all social organization. The term used to signify this universal system of oppression is *patriarchy*:

> Patriarchy is the power of the fathers: a familial-social, ideological, political system in which men – by force, direct pressure, or through ritual, tradition, law, and language, customs, etiquette, education, and the division of labor – determine what part women shall or shall not play, and in which the female is everywhere subsumed under the male. It does not necessarily imply that no woman has power, or that all women in a given culture may not have certain powers. Among the matrilineal Crow, for example, women take major honorific roles in ceremony and festival, but are debarred from social contacts and sacred objects during menstruation. Where women and men alike share a particular cultural phenomenon, it implies quite different things according to gender. 'Where men wear veils – as among the North African Tuareg – this remoteness serves to increase the status and power of an individual, but it hardly does so for women in purdah.' 'Ultimately the line is drawn' [Ortner 1971], as it is drawn, albeit differently in every culture. (Rich 1977: 57)

While all forms of feminism use the term patriarchy, in radical feminism it refers to a system of domination which pervades all aspects of culture and social life and which is to be found in all cultures and at all moments of history. Thus, for example, quoting and expanding upon Kathleen Gough's eight characteristics of male power, Adrienne Rich shows how male power permeates every aspect of women's lives. She argues, for example, that male sexuality is forced on women by institutions and practices as different as sexual violence, literature and psychoanalysis. It is enforced by means of:

> rape (including marital rape) and wife beating; father–daughter, brother–sister incest; the socialization of women to feel that the male sexual 'drive' amounts to a right; idealization of heterosexual romance in art, literature, media, advertising, and so forth; child marriage; arranged marriage; prostitution; the harem; psychoanalytic doctrines of frigidity and vaginal orgasm; pornographic depictions of women responding pleasurably to sexual violence and humiliation (a subliminal message being that sadistic heterosexuality is more 'normal' than sensuality between women). (Rich 1984: 218)

These examples span different cultures and different historical moments. They are part of global patriarchy and in this analysis gender oppression is seen as the primary form of oppression. (Radical feminism is discussed in detail in chapter 2.)

Since the publication of the influential radical feminist texts of the late 1960s and 1970s, there has been a fundamental shift in much feminist theory and criticism. One of the early objectives of radical criticism was the unmasking of the patriarchal colonization of women's minds and bodies. A key early target was patriarchal discourse. Thus, for example, Kate Millett argues in her seminal text of 1971, *Sexual Politics*, that patriarchal meanings and values pervade all aspects of culture, from myth and literature to social and psychoanalytic theory. Millett presents in detail how a range of male writers, including Freud, D. H. Lawrence, Henry Miller, Norman Mailer and Jean Genet, reinforce patriarchal meanings, values and forms of female subjectivity. Implicit in the project of decolonization was the assumption that women, freed of patriarchal oppression, would be different. Decolonizing women's minds and bodies would lead to the realization of a true undistorted feminine.

As feminist criticism expanded and developed, female difference soon became a primary object of feminist analysis in a wide range of feminist projects from feminist psychoanalysis to woman-centred approaches to history, society, literature, philosophy and culture. In psychoanalysis, for example, Luce Irigaray has attempted to contest Freudian and Lacanian theories of female subjectivity based on lack by theorizing a distinct positive feminine which Western culture has marginalized and which might serve as the starting point for fundamental challenges to the patriarchal order. Here the mother–daughter relationship, unsymbolized in the patriarchal order, has a crucial role to play:[17]

> The culture, the language, the imaginary and the mythology in which we live at the moment . . . I say to myself . . . let's have a look . . . this edifice that looks so clean and subtle . . . let's see what ground it is built on. Is it all that acceptable? . . . In a sense we need to say goodbye to maternal omnipotence (the last refuge) and establish a woman-to-woman relationship of reciprocity with our mothers, in which they might possibly also feel themselves to be our daughters. In a word, liberate ourselves along with our mothers. That is an indispensible precondition for our emancipation from the authority of fathers. In our societies, the mother/daughter, daughter/mother relationship constitutes a highly explosive nucleus. Thinking it, and changing it, is equivalent to shaking the foundations of the patriarchal order. (Irigaray 1991b: 47–50)

Whereas, traditionally, psychoanalysis has defined women in terms of lack, in

Irigaray's theory the feminine becomes a positive oppositional term, banished by Western thought, which might be realized by the coming into being of a feminine imaginary and symbolic. This is discussed further in chapter 4.

In woman-centred approaches to history, society and culture, work has focused on recovering the history of women and lost or marginalized traditions of female cultural production. Woman-centred research aims to establish alternative traditions of women's cultural production and to (re)write women's history. Having started as an undifferentiated project which claimed to take women as its subject, it soon diversified to encompass work on the history and cultural production of a range of specific groups of women who found themselves excluded from the predominantly white, middle-class, heterosexual and Western focus of initial works of recovery.[18]

Woman-centred feminist cultural politics finds its strongest expression in cultural feminism. Cultural feminism developed the tendency to view women's creativity as something different from male culture to the point where there could be no overlap between the two cultures. It took a path that initially involved eluding patriarchy by having nothing to do with men and it diversified, particularly in the USA, into a range of forms including a separatist social movement based on the celebration of difference and the assertion of women's natural superiority to men.

The focus on difference in woman-centred research and writing led among other things to the exploration of the question of whether women artists and writers show evidence of a specifically female aesthetic. The idea that women might have intrinsically different modes of expression has led to a focus on three related questions:

1   Do women *naturally* have languages and modes of expression that are different from men?
2   Do women use different modes of representation for social and historical reasons?
3   How can women use existing language to resist patriarchal forms of subjectivity?

In addressing these questions, writers and artists fall into two main groups: (1) those concerned with history and social change and (2) those concerned with essentially female modes of expression. The first group tends to concentrate on historically specific forms of writing and visual representation by women and the constructions of femininity that go with them. In producing new representations, they work with existing language and forms, attempting to subvert them. They see differences in women's and men's language as historically produced.

The second group seeks to identify essentially feminine modes of representation. They assume the existence of a naturally different female or feminine language. This language is often rooted in female biology or a female imaginary and it is thought to enable women to articulate an identity freed from patriarchal colonization. In feminist writing influenced by psychoanalysis, for example, this includes the work of Luce Irigaray on the feminine imaginary and Hélène Cixous' theory of feminine writing, *écriture feminine*, which offers a challenge to the patriarchal symbolic order (Cixous 1987). Black feminist critics are also concerned with the question of female aesthetics. Their approach has been predominantly historical. They look to the history of black women since slavery and the influence of transplanted and partially transformed West African cultural forms in their work. Here difference – positively valued and historically produced – is central. This is discussed further in chapter 7.

DECONSTRUCTING DIFFERENCE: POSTMODERN APPROACHES

Whereas liberalism has tended to ignore biological difference, and radical and woman-centred feminisms to reinstate ideas of positive female difference, poststructuralist and postmodern approaches to difference seek to deconstruct its various meanings. They argue that difference is cultural rather than natural, and analyse its role in the constitution of gendered subjectivity. Deconstructive approaches to gender tend to draw on the Derridean theory of textuality and reading which lays bare the binary oppositions which structure texts:

> Derrida adopts a strategy of reading which questions the assumptions and limitations of textual meaning by revealing how the polarities and certainties a text has proposed have actually been constructed through a series of preferences and repressions which have privileged certain ideas values and arguments above others. Derrida's point is that what has been presented as a dichotomy in Western thought, such as man/woman, is in fact merely a difference which has been manipulated into a hierarchy. (Norcross 1996: 136)

This method of reading does not do away with oppositions but shows their cultural and therefore changeable status.

The other main poststructuralist approach to gender takes its lead from the work of Foucault on subjectivity, the body, discourse and power. Feminists who draw on Foucault have suggested, for example, that biological theories constitute discursive fields of competing discourses which seek to define the natural, including the meaning of womanhood. These discourses structure institutional practices and shape the bodies and subjectivities of women and men. In doing so they produce and reproduce power relations which, from a feminist perspective, are patriarchal. Moreover, biologically based theories influence a broad range of other social practices. Thus theories of female sexuality – often influenced by Freud – which see it as passive and masochistic are reflected in much pornography and advertising and in sex manuals. Foucauldian poststructuralists would argue that these are powerful discourses which help shape sexual identities and sexual practices in profound ways which liberal feminism does not address. The liberal individual who can use her reason to makes choices about pornography, for example, is (from a poststructuralist perspective) shaped by discourses of gender and sexuality which preclude objective free choice.

In poststructuralist forms of feminism, differences are discursively produced. Modern ideas of race and gender, for example, were produced in part by the classificatory sciences of natural history and anthropology from the eighteenth century onwards. The idea that differences are produced within discourse does not, however, mean that they do not take material forms which have material effects. In the case of femininity, for example, middle-class, nineteenth century codes of femininity shaped not only women's minds but also their bodies, as they were encouraged to conform to norms of female beauty – eighteen-inch waists and pale complexions – which involved the denial of access to physical exertion that might produce stronger, healthier bodies. In an autobiographically based novel, published in 1899, German feminist Hedwig Dohm has her narrator recall her girlhood in the mid-nineteenth-century.

> I know why we girls did not learn anything. Little more than the most basic knowledge was taught in girls' schools at that time.
> The boys were lucky. They did gymnastics, they exercised. They were allowed to romp around freely in the streets and squares. Snow and ice was theirs in the winter, the lake in the summer.
> We girls didn't do gymnastics, we didn't swim, we didn't row. We weren't allowed to have snowball fights, not even to skate. Remember, the knitted sock was still in its heyday. (Dohm 1988: 24; original 1899)[19]

In the novel, restricted intellectual and physical education are shown to take their toll on the minds, bodies and emotions of middle-class women of the period. The effect of poststructuralist theory is to see difference as material, as produced, but as ungrounded in any fixed nature. Some postmodern

24

feminism has taken this idea further to see gender as a question of performance.[20] These ideas are discussed further in chapter 5.

Many important political and theoretical questions have preoccupied
second-wave feminism since the late 1960s. Practical political issues have
included quintessentially liberal questions such as equal rights under the law,
equal access to education and work, and equal pay. After 1968 issues
previously seen as belonging to the domain of private life were added to this
agenda: domestic and sexual violence, pornography, contraception, abortion, reproductive technology, child care provision, the rights of women to
define their own sexuality and lesbian rights. Issues of race and anti-colonial
struggle, of peace and the environment subsequently became important
feminist issues.

As the political questions which feminists addressed became more complex so, too, did the theoretical issues. To the question of women's difference
from men has been added the question of differences between women, and
the recognition of difference has become an important political question in
its own right. Over the last thirty years feminist theory has addressed itself to
numerous theoretical questions which are themselves integrally related to
practical politics. These have included theories of difference, the nature/
culture opposition, the invisibility of women in history and scholarship, the
importance of writing women's history/herstory, heterosexism, class, identity politics, Eurocentrism, racism, postmodernism, postcolonialism and the
politics of location. Shifts in feminist theory and politics have been brought
about by both external social and political factors and by the efforts of
previously marginalized groups of women to make their voices heard. The
chapters that follow look at these developments, mapping the conceptions of
difference in play.

CHAPTER 2
Challenging Patriarchy, Decentring Heterosexuality: Radical and Revolutionary Feminisms

But the fear and hatred of our bodies has often crippled our brains. Some of the most brilliant women of our time are still trying to think from somewhere outside their female bodies – hence they are still merely reproducing old forms of intellection. There is an inexorable connection between every aspect of a woman's being and every other; the scholar reading denies at her peril the blood on the tampon; the welfare mother accepts at her peril the derogation of her intelligence. These are issues of survival, because the woman scholar and the welfare mother are both engaged in fighting for the mere right to exist. Both are 'marginal' people in a system founded on the traditional family and its perpetuation. (Rich 1977: 285).

Women are a colonized people. Our history, values, and (cross-cultural) culture have been taken from us – a gynocidal attempt manifest most arrestingly in the patriarchy's seizure of our basic and precious 'land': our own bodies. (Morgan 1993: 76; original 1974)

The late 1960s and early 1970s are unequalled in second-wave feminism for their radicalism. These years saw the development of global theories of patriarchy as the fundamental form of oppression which was thought to unite women throughout the world. In Robin Morgan's words, written in 1969, 'Women have been subjugated longer than any other people on earth. Empires rose and fell but one constant remained, except in a few civilized tribal pockets of the world: everyone could stomp on women. This knowledge is carried, even if only semi-consciously, by every woman' (1993: 42; original 1969) This idea of shared oppression, irrespective of class, race or culture, became the basis for oppositional notions of *sisterhood* through which women everywhere could unite in the struggle against patriarchy. In radical feminist analysis patriarchy itself is founded on a fundamental polarization between men and women in which men exploit women for their own interests.

Radical and revolutionary feminist politics transformed traditional conceptions of the political which encompassed the state and public life, placing emphasis on areas beyond those traditionally seen as political. They breached the public/private divide, focusing on the personal as a key site for political action. The personal for women under patriarchy was inevitably bound up with the meaning, status and control of their bodies, issues which soon became the unifying focuses in radical feminist analyses. Radical feminism theorizes patriarchy as an all-encompassing set of power relations aimed at securing male control of women's bodies: our sexuality, procreative power and labour. From the early radical and revolutionary texts of the late 1960s and 1970s through to the present, radical feminists have privileged issues of women's sexuality, control of fertility, violence against women and sexual exploitation as never before:

> The first and fundamental theme is that women as a social group are oppressed by men as a social group and that this is the primary oppression for women. Patriarchy is the oppressing structure of male domination. Radical feminism makes visible male control as it is exercised in every sphere of women's lives, both public and private. So reproduction, marriage, compulsory heterosexuality, and motherhood are primary sites of attack and envisaged positive change. (Rowland and Klein 1996: 11)

Issues of sexuality, motherhood, abortion, contraception and lesbianism had been raised by European and North American feminists at the turn of the nineteenth-century but in a much more repressive and illiberal climate.[1] By 1970 the legacies of 1960s' 'sexual liberation' and improved methods of birth control had created the conditions for sustained and radical oppositional politics focused on women's bodies. In the first instance this meant getting to know one's body:

> We must begin, as women, to reclaim our land, and the most concrete place to begin is with our own flesh. Self-and-sister education is a first step, since all that fostered ignorance and self-contempt dissolve before the intellectual and emotional knowledge that our female bodies are constructed with beauty, craft, cleanliness, yes, holiness. Identification with the colonizer's standards melts before the revelations dawning on a woman who clasps a speculum in one hand and a mirror in the other. She is demystifying her own body for herself, and she will never again be quite so alienated from it. (Morgan 1993: 77; original 1974) (see figure 2.1)

A radical feminist politics meant learning to see one's body differently and

From *Sister, the Newspaper of the Los Angeles Women's Center*
(July 1973)

2.1 Wonder Woman from *Sister*, July 1973. Los Angeles Women's Center

decolonizing one's mind of the patriarchal meanings traditionally ascribed to female bodies. This project rapidly became central to feminist critique from early works like Kate Millett's *Sexual Politics* (1971) to substantial historical research in a wide range of disciplines which has recovered both mainstream and oppositional discourses defining the female body. In feminist politics it has given rise to a broad-ranging women's health movement which challenges male-defined medical approaches to the female body, as well as campaigns on issues of sexuality, pornography, violence and reproduction.

In early radical feminist thought, women's bodies are given a foundational status: they are both the focus of women's oppression and the basis of women's positive difference from men:

> Patriarchal thought has limited female biology to its own narrow specifications. The feminist vision has recoiled from female biology for these reasons; it will, I believe, come to view our physicality as a resource, rather than a destiny. In order to live a fully human life we require not only control of our bodies (though control is a prerequisite); we must touch the unity and resonance of our physicality, our bond with the natural order, the corporeal ground of our intelligence. (Rich 1977: 39).

Yet although radical feminism stresses the positive nature of women's difference, its true meanings have to be uncovered since patriarchy has consistently defined and moulded women's bodies and minds in the interests of men.

The emphasis on the body, procreation and sexuality helped to make radical feminist theory and politics one of the most powerful forces shaping contemporary feminism. Whereas liberal feminism tended to ignore women's bodies, focusing its attention on equal rights for women as abstract individuals, and Marxist feminism privileged class and the transformation of the capitalist mode of production, the impact of radical feminist thought and politics expanded these agendas for the wider women's movement and focused feminist attention firmly on issues connected with the body.

With its emphasis on the female body, early radical feminism placed the question of difference in sharper focus than previously. Endorsing the binary oppositions between female and male, woman and man, radical feminists sought to transform and revalue the meaning of the terms 'female' and 'woman', celebrating the female body as a site of strength, endurance, creativity and power. In her powerful and poetic text *Woman and Nature: The Roaring Inside Her* (1984; original 1978), for example, Susan Griffin exposed how man has used science and religion over the centuries to colonize both woman and nature and to shape them in his own interests. Man, she argues, has sought to gain ascendancy over woman and nature by separating himself off from them and cultivating forms of rationality denied to women. The themes of Griffin's work have subsequently become central to a broad-based ecofeminist movement which takes issue with many of the assumptions and practices of modern science. In the second half of *Woman and Nature*, Griffin explores a range of non-patriarchal meanings of both woman and the female body which she sees as rooted in the natural world rather than separate from it: 'This earth is my sister; I love her daily grace, her silent daring, and how

29

loved I am, how we admire this strength in each other, all that we have lost, all that we have suffered, all that we know: we are stunned by this beauty, and I do not forget: what she is to me, what I am to her' (Griffin 1984: 219; original 1978).

Taking as role models marginalized figures such as witches, mystics, goddesses, Amazons, wise women and healers, radical feminists have created a discourse of strong and resistant women throughout history. These are women who refused to submit to the power relations of an all-pervasive patriarchy. These inspirational figures who elude patriarchal control are seen to embody strength, wildness and self-determination, together with traits more usually ascribed to women such as intuition, emotion and fertility. In radical feminist discourse, traditional female traits and values are given a new and positive status which challenges the supremacy of traditionally male traits such as reason and objectivity. The devalued qualities which are central to traditional ideas of femininity are seen as necessary to the wholeness of both women and men. To reinstate their importance is a first step towards radically transforming patriarchal understandings of reason and emotion.

Radical feminism does not only reclaim positive, traditionally female qualities, but also patriarchal terms of abuse such as 'hags', 'crones', 'harpies', 'furies' and 'spinsters':

> The functioning of the word *spinster* to contort women's minds into double-think is clear. It has been a powerful weapon of intimidation and deception, driving women into the 'respectable' alternative of marriage, forcing them to believe, against all evidence to the contrary, that wedlock will be the salvation from a fate worse than death, that it will inevitably mean fulfilment. The alternatives, traditionally, have been the roles of prostitute, nun or mistress. In more recent times, another alternative is the lifestyle of 'swinging single', euphemistically called 'bachelor girl'. The process of reclaiming the meaning of *spinster* does not follow the route of affirming the 'freedom' of the 'swinging' bachelor girl, which is simply a variation on the theme of prostitute/mistress/wife. Instead it begins with reversing the reversal, seeing the basic unfreedom in all these feminine roles. . . .
>
> In essence, the Spinster is a witch. She is derided because she is free and therefore feared. Since derision is not powerful enough to stop her spinning, she is the object of attack by propaganda. Any cursory reading of a typical children's fairy tale gives overwhelming evidence of the campaign against witches, which includes mothers, stepmothers, wicked queens, ogresses. It is not accidental that in the story of Sleeping Beauty, the princess is cursed to prick her finger on a spindle which causes her to fall asleep for one hundred years, until she is awakened by her prince. More adept spinsters are not falling asleep, not waiting to be awakened, but awakening and waking each other by our Presence. (Daly 1979: 393–4)

For Mary Daly, Spinsters becomes a metaphor for women involved in creating new meanings and a new culture beyond patriarchy. Although often inspirational, the effect of radical feminist celebrations of long-established but traditionally devalued ideas of female difference is twofold. It both revalues the female and the feminine and tends to leave old binary oppositions intact. Like their patriarchically defined sisters who were confined to the domestic sphere, the strong women of the radical feminist tradition tended to remain outside of mainstream society and politics in a separatist sphere.

The radical feminist emphasis on women's bodies as the locus of both patriarchal power and women's difference has often been read as essentialist, particularly in those influential texts – such as the work of Susan Griffin and other ecofeminists – which link women to nature rather than culture.[2] Yet degrees of essentialism within radical feminism vary from analyses which root patriarchy in biology – most often in the male capacity to dominate through rape and physical violence – to those which stress the social (as opposed to biological) nature of femininity and masculinity:

> It is possible that differences between women and men arise out of a biological base but in a different way to that proposed by a reductivist determinism. The fact that women belong to the social group which has the capacity for procreation and mothering, and the fact that men belong to the social group which has the capacity to, and does carry out, acts of rape and violence against women, must intrude into the consciousness of being female and male. But this analysis allows for *change* in the sense that men themselves could change that consciousness and therefore their actions. It also allows women to recognise that we can and must develop our own theories and practices and need not accept male domination as unchangeable. (Rowland and Klein 1996: 34)

Radical feminist theories of patriarchy, which developed in the late 1960s and 1970s, stressed its universal structures and effects, and its global status. A classic example of this approach, which captures both the radical critique and emotional power of radical feminism, is Mary Daly's *Gyn/Ecology* (the source of the above quotation on spinsters). In *Gyn/Ecology* Daly looks at how the status of women in language, myth and religion shifted with the consolidation of patriarchy in Ancient Greece and subsequently with the growing hegemony of the Judeo-Christian tradition in the West. In this process, Daly argues, the realm of goddesses is increasingly taken over by male gods until the female presence is totally eradicated – as in Christianity – and replaced by what Daly calls 'male femininity':

> The adequate androcratic invasion of the gynocentric realm can only be total erasure/elimination of female presence, which is replaced by male femininity.

31

Thus in the christian myth the divine son is reborn again and again without even the vestigial presence of the 'Virgin Mother'. One of his rebirths is his baptism by John the Baptist, at which time the Paternal Voice from heaven booms: 'This is my beloved Son, in whom I am well pleased' (Matt. 3: 17). This is later followed by the supreme rebirth, namely his resurrection from the dead. This theme of descent to the Underworld and emerging from the earth had of course been present in myths concerning the Goddess. Thus, for example, Persephone, Demeter's daughter and Self, was obliged to spend three months of each year in the underworld realm of her husband Hades, who had raped and abducted her. Although this earlier myth was male-manipulated and functioned to legitimate the transition to patriarchal control, it still contains remnants of the theme of the Goddess rising/emerging from the depths. In the Christian tale, however, the feminine male god, the 'Son of God' who has replaced the Daughter/Self of the Goddess, descends into 'hell' (the earth's womb) and emerges on his own. There is no female presence involved in this Monogender Male Auto-motherhood. (1979: 87)

With the establishment of Christianity as the dominant religion in the West, God becomes exclusively male and pre-Christian goddesses who symbolize fertility, sexuality and power are replaced by the image of the virgin mother, an image which denies women's sexuality, power and fecundity. This type of critique of Christianity has been taken up within the feminist theology movement which, among other things, looks to feminize the godhead. It is also a theme of feminist fictive rewritings of the Christian tradition, for example, Michèle Robert's novel about Mary Magdalene, *The Wild Girl* (1984). This novel traces the exclusion of women and femininity from early Christianity. Narrated by Mary Magdalene:

The Wild Girl is a fifth gospel. Mary Magdalene's account of the life and death of Jesus – but an account that differs markedly from the other four. Mary's is in fact a book of revelation – a source of complete reappraisal – for it suggests another Christianity and another Jesus. Here is a Jesus open to sexuality, a Christianity that embraces the female equally with the male, a Mary Magdalene who is the wellspring of womanhood – all lost to us now. (Roberts 1984, book jacket)

Gyn/Ecology analyses examples of the oppression of women from a range of cultures and historical periods and looks at the ways in which these practices have been treated by male scholarship. Daly takes the examples of European witch burning, Chinese footbinding, Indian *sati*, African genital mutilation, Nazi medicine and American gynaecology to show the global nature of patriarchy and the male conspiracy in scholarship which has hidden the true nature of these practices. Writing of *sati*, for example, Daly gives several illustrations of how patriarchal scholarship seeks to hide the real issues at stake in the practice:

> Writing in 1960, David and Vera Mace masterfully muddied the issues illustrated in the rite of *suttee* for anyone searching in their book for insight. They wrote:
>
>> Although *custom* and *duty* left many widows in the East no alternative but to suffer and even to die, it would be a grave *injustice* to explain all their sacrifices in these terms. In many, many cases the widow walked into the fire *proudly* and by *deliberate choice*. This was her way of showing the depth of her *affection*, her *devotion*, her *fidelity*. It was a strange way, and to us a gravely *mistaken* one. But leaving aside the *inappropriateness* of the action and looking at the motive, dare we say that these women of the east knew less of *true love* than their Western sisters? [emphasis Mary Daly's]
>
> The authors erase such obvious questions as: Why did not widowers walk 'proudly' into the fire? And what does 'proudly' mean? At times, hundreds, even thousands, of women die in *suttee* for *one* royal male. Who could speak of 'pride' in dying for such godmen? How could anyone continue to use such language in the face of such frank admissions as the following statement of a Hindu, cited by Mayo:
>
>> We husbands so often make our wives unhappy that we might well fear that they would poison us. Therefore did our wise ancestors make the penalty of widowhood so frightful – in order that the woman may not be tempted.   (Daly 1979: 124)

Daly argues that:

> Scholarly mystification continues to dull all sense of the unrightness of such rites as *suttee*, regarding them with detached interest and making them appear isolated and unrelated to 'our' culture. It thus keeps minds/imaginations in a state of readiness to accept similar or comparable practices which carry out the same programme – the killing of female divinity – ultimately requiring the extinction of female life and will to live. (pp. 123–4)

For Daly, the killing of female divinity and independent creativity is the ultimate goal of patriarchy everywhere. In Daly's analyses, as in much radical feminism, men and masculinity figure as an undifferentiated oppressor. It is assumed that patriarchal practices work unambiguously in the interests of men. Patriarchal masculinity is not, however, natural. It is acquired through processes of socialization which teach boys and men that 'their collective strength depends upon a colossal commitment to covering up their own individual weakness' (Daly 1979: 379). Given the global nature of patriarchy in radical feminist analysis, and the relatively simple model of exploitative

2.2 Monica Sjoo, *Goddess at Avebury*, 1978. 8' × 4', oil on hardboard

and repressive masculinity that it implies, it is not surprising that separatism should be seen as at least the short-term answer to patriarchy. *Gyn/Ecology*, for example, ends with a romantic set of images of strong and independent women close to Nature, self-defined and able to see through patriarchy:

> As we feel the empowerment of our own Naming we hear more deeply our call of the wild. Raising pairs of arms into the air we expand them into shells, sails. Splashing our legs in the water we move our oars. Our beautiful spiral like designs are the designs/purposes of our bodies/minds. We communicate these through our force-fields, our auras, our O-Zones. We move backwards over the water, towards the Background. We gain speed. Argonauts move apart and together, forming and reforming our Amazon Argosy. In the rising and setting of our sister the sun, we seek the gold of our hearts' desire. In the light of our sisters the moon and the stars we rekindle the Fore-Crones' fire. In its searing light we see through the snarls of the Nothing-lovers. (p. 424)

The radical feminist reclaiming of women's sexuality and capacity for motherhood as the source of potential strength and resistance to patriarchy, and the themes of mothers and goddesses, have had a powerful influence on feminist art and literature (see figure 2.2). They have encouraged women to produce work which places women's different experience at its centre and to develop new language and other forms of representation. Thus, for example, previously repressed and tabooed aspects of women's lives and experience become the subject of art as, for example, in Judy Chicago's controversial

34

exhibition *The Dinner Party* (1979), which was installed at the San Francisco Museum of Modern Art in 1980. The exhibition takes the theme of the Last Supper and transforms it using women and imagery based on female sexuality. It attempts 'to show the contribution of women to Western civilization using a triangle banqueting table strewn with altar cloths, 39 place settings representing 999 women grouped together according to a common experience, achievement, historic period or place of origin within the context of a sacramental celebration . . . the representation of each group of women by a plate crafted as a vagina . . .' (Woodley 1987: 97). In Britain controversy was similarly caused in the art world by Mary Kelly's *Post Partum Document* (1976, published in book form in 1983), which focuses on 'motherhood, with all the deeply traumatic emotion and unrecognised elements involved . . . which have been almost taboo as a subject for art in male dominated culture' (Mulvey 1987: 100). Although dealing with a subject placed centre-stage by radical feminism, Kelly's exhibition was framed by psychoanalytic theory. It included objects not usually displayed within the context of art:

> The objects in the work – the stained nappy-liners, the scribblings, the hand imprints, the insect specimens, and in the recent work the inscriptions of Kelly's pre-writing – all these constitute a strand of extra-linguistic discourse within the *Document*. They're recognition points, particularly for mothers, but at some level for everyone in their relationship with the mother. (Kelly 1987: 75)

Writing of *Post Partum Document* Laura Mulvey comments: 'A painting of a mother changing her baby's nappy would be easily overlooked as kitsch, but not so with dirty nappy liners annotated and placed within a discourse that needs work to be unravelled, and refuses to place the figure of the mother on view' (Mulvey 1987: 100).

SEPARATISM

Degrees of separatism vary in radical feminism. At minimum, early second-wave feminists insisted on setting up an autonomous radical Women's Liberation Movement which, in Robin Morgan's words, could offer 'sisters in counterleft captivity . . . somewhere to turn, to use their power and rage and beauty and coolness on their own behalf for once, on their own terms, on their own issues, in their own style' (Morgan 1993: 67; original 1970). More radical were the refusal to have anything to do with men and a move by heterosexual women into what became known as 'political lesbianism', a position which was the logical consequence of radical and revolutionary feminist critiques of heterosexuality:

> ... any woman who takes part in a heterosexual couple helps to shore up male supremacy by making its foundations stronger. ... Every act of penetration for the woman is an invasion which undermines her confidence and saps her strength. For a man it is an act of power and mastery which makes him stronger, not just over one woman but over all women. So every woman who engages in penetration bolsters the oppressor and reinforces the class power of men. (Leeds Revolutionary Feminist Group 1981: 6; original 1979)

Political lesbianism – while controversial among many lesbian women – has had a long-lasting effect on second-wave feminism.[3] For example, at a grass roots level in the Women's Liberation Movement in Britain from the mid-1970s to the mid-1980s, a heterosexual lifestyle was often regarded as incompatible with feminism. To relate sexually to men was to consort with the enemy. This radical version of separatism implied having nothing to do with men, the first step in the process of freeing oneself from patriarchal power structures. This process involved a decolonization of patriarchally defined female consciousness, body image and ways of living. The result, it was thought, would be the discovery of a truly woman-defined woman-hood. Important effects of this politics were to taboo heterosexuality, to instil guilt in heterosexually-defined women and to discourage them from engaging in critiques and analyses of their own sexuality:

> Because our heterosexuality is not *felt* as a political identity (who would want to mobilize around being straight?!), and because in many ways lesbianism appears to be the most appropriate political identity for feminists, we feel guilty. (Gill and Walker 1993: 71)

Susan Ardill and Sue O'Sullivan argue that:

> The rise of revolutionary feminism [in Britain] in the late 1970s claimed a certain place for our sexuality on the feminist agenda – firmly in the centre. Men's sexuality was the key problem, but in a different way from the view of many radical feminists. In revolutionary feminism, male sexuality was, for the foreseeable future, irredeemable. Feminists' struggle was against male sexuality, not with it; they mobilized against it in WAVAW [Women Against Violence Against Women] and anti-pornography groups. Woman's sexuality was the key to both her oppression and liberation.
>
> Suddenly everyone was grappling with compulsory heterosexuality and political lesbianism, separatism, non-monogamy, lesbian lifestyle, lesbianism as the practice of feminism. Where was socialist-feminism in all this? Despite the

brief existence of Lesbian Left, the terrain around lesbianism seems to have been left wide open for revolutionary and radical feminism to claim as their own. In the late 70s and early 80s heterosexual socialist-feminists, confronted with the growing divisions in the autonomous women's movement, not the least of which were accusations of consorting with the enemy, dropped out in droves. (Ardill and O'Sullivan 1987: 286)

For a long time heterosexuality remained an unspoken and barely examined norm for many women, and it would take interventions by lesbian women in the late 1980s and 1990s to put it back on the theoretical and political agenda.[4]

THE CENTRALITY OF EXPERIENCE

A central tenet of radical feminist thought is that existing theory and scholarship, like the academy more generally, is both male-defined and patriarchal. It is male-defined in its norms, values and objects of study which exclude women's history, experience and interests. It is patriarchal in the meanings and values which it both produces and reproduces. As such it cannot serve as a source of useful knowledge for women. To develop useful and self-affirming knowledge, women need to start from their own experience, both of their personal lives and of politics:

> [Theory] is not an academic exercise but 'a process based on understanding and advancing the activist movement' (Bunch 1983: 248). To this end, radical feminist theory is not an objective exercise disengaged from women themselves. A theory which begins with women, places women and women's experience at the centre, and names the oppression of women, involves a holistic view of the world, an analysis which probes every facet of existence for women. It is not, as Bunch indicates, a 'laundry list of women's issues', but 'provides a basis for understanding every area of our lives ... politically culturally, economically and spiritually' (250). (Rowland and Klein 1996: 13)

In the 1970s this type of argument led to a widespread rejection of mainstream (malestream) social theories. At a grass roots level in Britain it encouraged a scepticism towards existing theories which were seen as male-defined modes of thinking. It also legitimated a widespread anti-intellectualism within large sections of the women's movement. At this time other types of feminist analysis which engaged with the malestream were in their early stages. Marxist and socialist feminisms and early post-structuralist and psychoanalytic feminisms were all rejected by radical feminists as male-defined. For the women concerned, the experience of finding their feminism questioned on account of their interest in 'great men', while often painful, was also useful. Radical feminist critique was both important and productive in so far as it strengthened the commitment of many socialist and poststructuralist feminist theorists and writers to developing new types of theory which could be accessible and politically useful. Moreover, it motivated thoroughgoing feminist critiques of existing scholarship, its exclusions and the methods by which it was produced. The rejection of feminist theories which have been developed via an appropriation and critique of existing male-authored texts remains a strong feature of contemporary radical feminism. The most often attacked targets are the psychoanalytic, poststructuralist and postmodern forms of feminism discussed in chapters 4 and 5.

THE ETHNOCENTRIC LIMITS OF RADICAL FEMINISM

The oppression of women knows no ethnic nor racial boundaries, true, but that does not mean that it is identical within those differences. Nor do the reservoirs of our ancient power know these boundaries. To deal with one without even alluding to the other is to distort our commonality as well as our difference. (Lorde 1984: 70)

In a private and then open letter to Mary Daly about her book *Gyn/Ecology*, the black American lesbian feminist theorist and poet Audre Lorde welcomed Daly's cross-cultural exposure of women's oppression throughout the ages. However, her endorsement of Daly was severely tempered by Daly's one-sided treatment of African and other non-white women. Lorde points out that whereas *Gyn/Ecology* includes many inspirational white, European examples of female power, the examples that it uses which are taken from Africa are restricted to the oppression of women, specifically genital mutilation:

When I started reading *Gyn/Ecology*, I was truly excited by the vision behind your words and nodded my head as you spoke in your First Passage of myth and mystification. Your words on the nature and function of the Goddess, as well as the ways in which her face has been obscured, agreed with what I myself have discovered in my searches through African myth/legend/religion for the true nature of old female power.

So I wondered, why doesn't Mary deal with Afrekete as an example? Why are her goddess images only white, western european, judeo-christian? Where

38

was Afrekete, Yemanje, Oyo, and Mawulisa? Where were the warrior goddesses of the Vodun, the Dahomeian Amazons and the warrior-women of Dan? Well, I thought, Mary has made a conscious decision to narrow her scope and deal only with the ecology of western european women.

Then I came to the first three chapters of your Second Passage, and it was obvious that you were dealing with non-european women, but only as victims and preyers-upon each other. I began to feel my history and my mythic background distorted by the absence of any images of my foremothers in power. Your inclusion of African genital mutilation was an important and necessary piece in any consideration of female ecology, and too little has been written about it. To imply, however, that all women suffer the same oppression simply because we are women is to lose sight of the many varied tools of patriarchy. It is to ignore how those tools are used by women without awareness against each other. . . .

Mary, I ask you to be aware of how this serves the destructive forces of racism and separation between women – the assumption that the herstory and myth of white women is the legitimate and sole herstory and myth of all women to call upon for power and background, and that non-white women and our herstories are noteworthy only as decorations, or examples of female victimization. I ask you to be aware of the effect that this dismissal has upon the community of black women and other women of color, and how it devalues your own words. (Lorde 1984: 67–9)

At issue here is the question of difference. Daly's emphasis on the universal nature of patriarchy and her failure to challenge a Eurocentric view of women of colour as victims leads to the denial of the positive aspects of other women's cultures and their resistance to patriarchy. Her studies of patriarchal practices from non-white cultures are reduced to illustrations of a general thesis about global patriarchy. In the process, not only positive dimensions of non-European cultures but also the other factors affecting the lives of women of colour – in particular colonialism and racism – are rendered invisible.

A similar critique of Daly's chapter on *sati* has been made by Uma Narayan in her book *Dislocating Cultures* (1997). Narayan demonstrates in detail how Daly reproduces what Narayan terms 'colonial modes of representation' in her depiction of *sati*. Daly's analysis, she suggests, reinforces the Eurocentric perspective developed in the colonial era which views Indian culture and religion in undifferentiated terms as unchanging, timeless tradition and fails to do justice to the detailed history of *sati* and the material conditions under which it occurred. This is discussed in more detail in chapter 8.

More recent radical feminist writing, for example many of the essays in the anthology *Radically Speaking: Feminism Reclaimed* (Bell and Klein (eds) 1996), stresses radical feminism's attention to questions of class and race. The Bell and Klein anthology includes essays by a wide range of women of different classes and colours and attempts to bring together the specific and the global:

> We need to listen to many women: working-class women, lesbian women, Indigenous women, Black women, women who took on the hard issues and stayed with them. The brave, prophetic voices of the late 60s and early 70s are still speaking. We need to hear them, more than ever joined by new ones. Do you see the violence against women getting any less?
>
> We need to make it plain that radical feminism is global and that it is and always has been driven by issues; that the theory arises from the practice; and that it is women of all classes, creeds, colours and dispositions that are the basis of the movement. (Bell and Klein (eds) 1996: xix)

Despite the tendency towards Eurocentrism, ideological commitment to inclusiveness has been an important feature of radical feminist politics since its inception. The radical feminist stress on the global nature of patriarchy and sisterhood is indicative of this. The central issue raised by women of colour has been the terms on which they are included and the actual class and racial interests represented in particular strategies and campaigns. Thus, for example, Audre Lorde questions the terms on which women of colour are included in *Gyn/Ecology*. Like other feminists, radical feminists have learned from these critiques and now take more account of race and class. How far the insistence on privileging patriarchy as the fundamental and primary form of oppression for women remains a stumbling block for feminists of colour, working-class women and feminists from the Third World will be examined in chapters 7 and 8.

HETEROSEXUALITY AS AN INSTITUTION

> The assumption that 'most women are innately heterosexual' stands as a theoretical and political stumbling block for many women. It remains a tenable assumption, partly because lesbian existence has been written out of history or catalogued under disease; partly because it has been treated as exceptional rather than intrinsic; partly because to acknowledge that for women heterosexuality may not be a 'preference' at all, but something that has to be imposed, managed, organized, propagandized, and maintained by force is an immense step to take if you consider yourself freely and 'innately' heterosexual. (Rich 1984: 226–7)

If radical feminism reinstates the female body as the primary site of women's difference from men and the focus of patriarchal power, it also raises

40

fundamental questions about heterosexuality. As the quotations from Robin Morgan and Adrienne Rich earlier in this chapter suggest, patriarchy flourishes through the expropriation by men of women's sexuality and their procreative and labour power. It is male need to control these aspects which motivates the elaborate social and cultural practices of patriarchal societies. For many radical feminists patriarchy is centred on the reproduction of the patriarchal family and the institution of heterosexuality. To see heterosexuality as an institution is to move away from positions which assume that it is a natural preference and to stress its social nature.

In her influential essay, 'Compulsory Heterosexuality and Lesbian Existence', American lesbian feminist and poet Adrienne Rich writes of the 'bias of compulsory heterosexuality, through which lesbian experience is perceived on a scale ranging from deviant to abhorrent, or simply rendered invisible' (1984: 212). The questions which Rich sets herself in this essay include 'how and why women's choice of women as passionate comrades, life partners, co-workers, lovers, tribe, has been crushed, invalidated, forced into hiding and disguise' (p. 212) and why even feminist scholarship has neglected lesbian existence. This neglect, she argues, has weakened the accuracy and transformative power of feminist scholarship. Writing of recent feminist books, Rich suggests that 'each one might have been more accurate, more powerful, more truly a force for change, had the author felt impelled to deal with lesbian existence as a reality, and as a source of knowledge and power available to women' (p. 213).

In Rich's analysis, feminist writing has failed to ask the fundamental question: 'whether in a different context, or other things being equal, women would *choose* heterosexual coupling and marriage?' (p. 213). In other words, feminists have failed to address heterosexuality as an institution rather than a natural preference. In doing so, they have failed to analyse heterosexuality as the cornerstone of patriarchy. Rich develops an analysis which starts from the proposition that far from being innate, heterosexuality is systematically imposed on women via wide-ranging forms of mental and physical violence. As we saw in chapter 1, Rich quotes and expands on the eight characteristics of male power defined in Kathleen Gough's essay 'The Origin of the Family' (Gough 1975). These forms of male power are, Rich argues, used to enforce heterosexuality. The first concerns female sexuality under patriarchy. Male power denies women their own sexuality:

by means of clitoridectomy and infibulation; chastity belts; punishment, including death, for female adultery; punishment, including death, for lesbian sexuality; psychoanalytic denial of the clitoris; strictures against masturbation; denial of maternal and postmenopausal sensuality; unnecessary hysterectomy;

pseudo-lesbian images in media and literature; closing of archives and destruction of documents relating to lesbian existence. (Rich 1984: 218)

The varied list of social practices which Rich invokes all work to ensure that female sexuality is expressed only in the interests of male pleasure and reproduction. Gough's second point is the forcing of male sexuality on women. Rich identifies the mechanisms by which this occurs as ranging from rape to art and literature (see chapter 1 above, p. 20). Heterosexuality is imposed, Rich argues, by means of both physical and psychological violence as well as the ideological construction of heterosexual sex as natural and normal.

Men also exercise control over women's procreative and labour powers which they exploit for themselves through marriage and the sexual division of labour. They exploit and coerce women via 'the horizontal segregation of women in paid employment; the decoy of the upwardly mobile token woman; male control of abortion, contraception, and childbirth; enforced sterilization; pimping, female infanticide, which robs mothers of daughters and contributes to generalized devaluation of women' (Rich 1984: 218–19). Men even define and control women's access to their children, seeking to 'control or rob them of their children by means of father-right and "legal kidnapping"; enforced sterilization; systematized infanticide; seizure of children from lesbian mothers by the courts; the malpractice of male obstetrics; use of the mother as "token torturer"' (p. 219). Under patriarchy women are restricted in their movements. Men 'confine them physically and prevent their movement by means of rape as terrorism, keeping women off the streets; purdah; foot-binding; atrophying of women's athletic capabilities; haute couture, "feminine" dress codes; the veil; sexual harassment on the streets; horizontal segregation of women in employment; prescriptions for "full-time" mothering; enforced economic dependence of wives' (p. 219). Women become objects of exchange in the patriarchal order. Thus men 'use them as objects in male transactions: use of women as "gifts", bride-price; pimping; arranged marriage; use of women as entertainers to facilitate male deals, for example, wife-hostess, cocktail waitress required to dress for male sexual titillation, call girls, "bunnies", geisha, *kisaeng* prostitutes, secretaries' (p. 219).

Rich's argument shares much with other radical feminism. It offers a global account of the institution of patriarchy which is both cross-cultural and trans-historical, drawing on examples from a range of cultures and historical moments. As in Mary Daly's work, this strategy results in male power appearing monolithic and all-encompassing. Yet, unlike much radical feminist writing, Rich's does not limit the female and the feminine to those areas traditionally so defined. Indeed, she argues that it is patriarchy itself which limits women to the traditionally feminine. Thus men seek to cramp women's creativeness through mechanisms such as:

> witch persecution as campaigns against midwives and female healers and as pogrom against independent, 'unassimilated' women; definition of male pursuits as more valuable than female within any culture, so that cultural values become the embodiment of male subjectivity; restriction of female self-fulfilment to marriage and motherhood; sexual exploitation of women by male artists and teachers; the social and economic disruption of women's creative aspirations; erasure of female tradition. (Rich 1984: 219)

And finally Rich suggests that it is the patriarchal practices which support and reproduce heterosexuality as the norm which restrict women's access to education, the professions and public life. Male power seeks to:

> withhold from them large areas of the society's knowledge and cultural attainments by means of non-education of females (60 percent of the world's illiterates are women); the 'Great Silence' regarding women and particularly lesbian existence in history and culture; sex-role stereotyping that deflects women from science, technology, and other 'masculine' pursuits; male social/professional bonding that excludes women; discrimination against women in the professions. (p. 219)

In this analysis of the institution of heterosexuality, women's bodies, sexuality and minds are shaped by physical coercion, brutality and restriction of access to knowledge and experience so as to ensure their compliance with and endorsement of heterosexuality. Heterosexuality itself is seen as the cornerstone of patriarchy. The heterosexual organization of female sexuality and reproduction guarantees male control of women and their labour power both in the domestic arena and beyond.

As in much radical feminist analysis of heterosexuality's role in securing the global institution of patriarchy, questions of how class, race and cultural difference affect the meaning and materiality of patriarchal practices are not addressed. Social practices are interpreted only in terms of their role in the reproduction of heterosexuality as the basis of patriarchy. In the process the cultural specificity of particular practices is rendered invisible. For example, few postcolonial feminists now would accept interpretations of arranged marriages, purdahs and the veil as simple expressions of patriarchal power. Their functions are much more complex and context-specific. To read them simply as forms of oppression is to negate both possible positive meanings and the possibility of resistance and transformation which might be undertaken from within the patriarchal order. What Rich's analysis does make clear, however, is the role of these practices in upholding norms of heterosexual marriage which reinforce patriarchal power.

CONTESTING THE DOMINANT, THEORIZING HETEROSEXUALITY

> Those of us who identify ourselves as both in some sense 'really' heterosexual and in some sense politically feminist, come up against a feminist consciousness which is both critical of our most intimate being and entails at least some resistance to close relationships with our nearest and dearest men. (Wilkinson and Kitzinger (eds) 1993: 59)

In Adrienne Rich's analysis of heterosexuality as an institution, many aspects of women's lived difference from men are seen as socially imposed via the institutionalized practices of heterosexuality. Underpinning Rich's approach is the assumption that women's true difference lies not in the polarized, patriarchally defined binary opposition man – woman, but in a woman-identified lesbian sexuality. Heterosexuality is seen only as a tool of patriarchy and in consequence heterosexual women are by definition its colonized subjects. This perspective leaves little room for a more positive engagement with heterosexuality, reinforcing heterosexual feminists' tendency to silence on the question of their sexuality.

Serious theoretical engagement with the question of heterosexuality outside of radical feminism is a relatively recent phenomenon. Whereas classic radical feminist readings of heterosexuality as the foundation of global patriarchy leave no space for reclaiming heterosexuality as a viable way of living, recent writing has begun to look at what heterosexuality means for heterosexual women who are also feminist. Yet, even here, it has been mostly radical lesbian writers and theorists who have begun the difficult task of deconstructing and theorizing heterosexuality.

The problems which heterosexual women face in theorizing their sexuality begin with the very question of self-identification. The year 1993 saw the publication of *Heterosexuality: A Feminism and Psychology Reader* (Wilkinson and Kitzinger (eds) 1993) a book which includes twenty-one personal statements by feminists and feminist psychologists on the question 'How does your heterosexuality contribute to your feminist politics (and/or feminist psychology)?'[5] One of the most striking things to emerge from the personal statements is the unwillingness of heterosexual feminists to describe themselves as such:

How does my heterosexuality contribute to my feminist politics? That is an impossible question for me to answer because, although I have lived monogamously with a man I love for over 26 years, I am not now and have never been a 'heterosexual'. But neither have I ever been either a 'lesbian' or a 'bisexual'. What I am – and have been for as long as I can remember – is someone whose gender and sexuality have just never seemed to mesh very well with the available cultural categories, and *that* – rather than my presumed heterosexuality – is what has most profoundly informed my feminist politics. (Wilkinson and Kitzinger (eds) 1993: 50)

A key issue here is the desire of heterosexual feminists to mark themselves off from a category that has almost always been associated within feminism with oppression. Moreover, most mainstream theories of heterosexuality have little to offer feminists, since they assume that traditional gender differences are natural. Another important issue is the question of who defines whom. Oppositional identities are often formed in a relation of differentiation from hegemonic categories. It is much easier to define what one is not, rather than what one thinks one is. It is only in oppositional forms of identity politics that women tend consciously to embrace particular forms of categorization with which they attempt, as a group, to define themselves.

The difficulties that individual women have with the category 'heterosexual' do not, however, obviate the need to theorize it. However much a heterosexual woman may disidentify with the category, she still benefits from its privileged status in society. One productive approach would be to move away from monolithic views of heterosexuality as merely a tool of patriarchy and to begin from the different ways in which it is materially produced through a variety of discursive practices. All those discourses – medical, psychological, religious, demographic, familial and cultural, to name but a few – which from a Foucauldian perspective can be seen as constituting the domain of sexuality, privilege heterosexuality as the natural way to be.[6] In the process they define the differences between women and men in specific ways. The institutions and practices which produce the discursive context into which we are born also produce individuals with particular expectations about women and men and how they should relate. The privileging of heterosexuality as natural, to the point at which it becomes an invisible, unmarked category, render other ways of being (lesbian, gay, bisexual or even celibate) seemingly deviant or not quite natural.

A differentiated approach to heterosexuality which assumes that it does not have a single, natural meaning but is discursively produced, allows one to raise questions of power as a relationship and ask in historically grounded ways whether or not heterosexuality is necessarily patriarchal. Heterosexuality works on the basis of the eroticization of gender difference. For feminists this difference is structured by relations of power, but these relations do not have to be seen as all alike. Heterosexuality is much more complex than such an approach suggests. It offers women forms of power as well as subjection, and produces forms of pleasure. If these are seen as cultural rather than natural, then they can be transformed. Such an approach would also question the foundational status of sexuality as a key to the subjectivity of the individual. It allows one to ask how important sex need be and to what extent sexual orientation determines broader modes of relating. It also allows one to distinguish between heterosexuality as a sexual practice, as a set of institutions and practices, and as a socially produced and imposed identity which may be accepted, negotiated or refused.

Heterosexuality with its widely accepted status as 'normality' is not usually lived as a political identity by heterosexual feminists in the way that lesbianism is lived as a political identity by many lesbian feminists. It is the hierarchization of difference in heterosexist societies which makes lesbianism a political issue. In patriarchal and heterosexist societies the terms 'heterosexual' and 'lesbian' can never be symmetrical. To be defined or even to define oneself in terms of them will have different material consequences according to which term is in question. Whereas self-naming can be an affirmative act, labelling and categorization are forms of subjection to the power of others. Given the role that patriarchally defined heterosexuality plays in the reproduction of power relations between women and men, one key problem for heterosexual feminists is how to develop non-patriarchal forms of heterosexuality which empower women and bring them both sexual and emotional fulfilment free from an already prescribed sexual division of both labour and gender roles. From a radical feminist perspective this would require the transformation of patriarchy and the establishment of non-patriarchal societies.

ECOFEMINISM

> I know I am made from this earth, as my mother's hands were made from this earth, as her dreams came from this earth and all that I know, I know this earth, the body of the bird, this pen, this paper, these hands, this tongue speaking, all that I know speaks to me through this earth and I long to tell you, you who are earth too, and listen *as we speak to each other of what we know: the light is in us.* (Griffin 1984: 227; original 1978)

In the late 1970s and early 1980s, radical feminist ideas, with their celebration of women's affinity to nature and pre-Christian goddess cultures, fed directly into the development of ecofeminism. As already signalled, Susan Griffin's

Woman and Nature was of key importance in this context. Written after Griffin was asked to deliver a lecture on women and ecology, it identifies the root of the world's ecological crisis as man's separating of himself from nature and placing himself above it:

> The fact that man does not consider himself a part of nature, but indeed considers himself superior to matter, seemed to me to gain significance when placed against man's attitude that woman is both inferior to him and closer to nature. (1984: xv; original 1978)

Ecofeminism stresses the analogies to be drawn between the treatment of women and the natural world under patriarchy, focusing on concepts of domination. For example, Carolyn Merchant, in her influential book *The Death of Nature* (1982), describes how the rise of science led directly to the development of the present agenda faced by ecofeminists. Merchant posits a pre-modern 'organic cosmology . . . undermined by the Scientific Revolution and the rise of a market-orientated culture in early modern Europe' (1982: xvi). She examines 'the transition from the organism to the machine as the dominant metaphor binding together the cosmos, society and the self into a single cultural reality – a world view' (p. xviii). It was precisely the normative dualism of rationalist thought with its privileging of mind over body, man over nature and male over female which, ecofeminists argue, led to the exploitation of women and nature and the need to transform attitudes to the natural world, to the body and to the non-rational dimensions of human beings. The overcoming of this dualism is a central objective of ecofeminism:

> Making the connection between feminism and ecology enables us to step outside the dualistic, separated world into which we were all born. From this vantage point, this new perspective, we begin to see how our relations with each other are reflected in our relations with the natural world. The rape of the earth, in all its forms, becomes a metaphor for the rape of woman, in all its many guises. In layer after layer, a truly sick society is revealed, a society of alienated relationships all linked to a rationalization that separates 'man' from nature. (Plant 1989: 5)

Ecofeminism is explicitly holistic in its view of women, politics and the environment:

> Cultivating the female mind, acknowledging the female source of wisdom and harmony – these practices must extend beyond our own bodies and our own circles. Of all the patriarchal outrages – racism; harassment of homosexuals; increasing violence against women; forced prostitution; pornography; non-

47

personhood for women in legal, educational, and medical areas; economic oppression – it is nuclear power and weaponry that promises irreversible effects. But our activism is not a matter of 'either this issue or that;' all of the above stem directly from our society's acceptance of patriarchal values. As we work in each area, we will voice the connections among the issues. (Spretnak 1989: 131)

From an ecofeminist perspective, political and social issues ranging from AIDS to nuclear weapons and Third World poverty are seen as related and this holistic approach encourages new forms of spirituality. In their account of ecofeminism, Maria Mies and Vandana Shiva describe how, for example, 'As women in various movements – ecology, peace, feminist and especially health – rediscovered the interdependence and connectedness of everything, they also rediscovered what was called the spiritual dimension of life – the realization of this interconnectedness was itself sometimes called spirituality' (Mies and Shiva 1997: 500). It is not a conventional form of Western spirituality:

> Ecofeminism is a movement with an implicit and sometimes explicit spiritual base. Yet to use the term 'spirituality' is itself almost misleading, for the earth-based spirituality that influences ecofeminism has nothing to do with systems of thought which divide 'spirit' from matter. . . . What we are doing . . . is attempting to shift the values of our culture. We could describe that shift as one away from battle as our underlying cultural paradigm and toward the cycle of birth, growth, death, and regeneration, to move away from a view of the world as made up of warring opposites toward a view that sees processes unfolding and continuously changing. (Starhawk 1989: 174)

Moreover spirituality is not limited to human beings:

> If divinity is multiple and diverse, it is also diffused throughout the world. It is not something only 'out there' and 'above.' Divinity is inherent in all nature. This world, the here and now, the body, the mind, sexuality, all are holy. And a spiritual path that is not stagnant ultimately leads one to the understanding of one's own divine nature and the divine nature of all life. (Adler 1989: 154)

In the political arena ecofeminists have been very active in the environmental, anti-nuclear and peace movements as well as in debates about technology, especially reproductive technology. Here they have tended to argue against reproductive technology as an unwarranted male-controlled set of interventions into what should be a natural process:

> One powerful theoretical approach sees in these new techniques a means for men to wrest 'not only the control of reproduction, but reproduction itself'

from women. Following O'Brien [1981], it is suggested that men's alienation from reproduction – men's sense of disconnection from their seed during the process of conception, pregnancy and birth – has underpinned through the ages a relentless male desire to master nature, and to construct social institutions and cultural patterns that will not only subdue the waywardness of women but also give men an illusion of procreative continuity and power. New reproductive technologies are the vehicle that will turn men's illusions of reproductive power into a reality. By manipulating eggs and embryos, scientists will determine the sort of children who are born – will make themselves the fathers of humankind. By removing eggs and embryos from some women and implanting them in others, medical practitioners will gain control over motherhood itself. Motherhood as a unified biological process will be effectively deconstructed: in place of 'mother' there will be ovarian mothers who supply eggs, uterine mothers who give birth to children and, presumably, social mothers who raise them. Through the eventual development of artificial wombs, the capacity will arise to make biological mothers redundant. Whether or not women are eliminated, or merely reduced to the level of reproductive prostitutes, the object and effect of the emergent technologies is to deconstruct motherhood and to destroy the claim to reproduction that is the foundation of women's identity. (Stanworth 1997: 483–4)

This radical appraisal of the patriarchal nature of reproductive technology is, of course, highly controversial. Feminists critics of this position have argued that wholesale rejections of technology tend to be regressive and unhelpful and do not do justice to the sometimes positive role of technology in women's liberation – particularly in the area of contraception and fertility.[7]

REFLECTIONS

Despite those limitations arising from the universalist claims of radical feminist theory, it was and remains an important branch of feminist thought and activism which has had transformative effects on society and on other forms of feminism, and which has fed directly into the contemporary ecological feminist movement. In the 1970s, radical feminist discourse attempted to develop a universally valid and trans-historical account of women's oppression under global patriarchy which could be the basis for a universal sisterhood. In doing so it privileged a particular interpretation of gender relations over all other forms of power. Differences of class, race and ethnicity became less significant or sometimes invisible. Founded on theories of female difference which were often grounded in women's biology, radical feminism, particularly in the 1970s, proved both inspirational and empowering for many women. It celebrated what had previously been denigrated:

women's bodies, sexuality, traditionally feminine qualities and women's capacity for motherhood. Subsequent critiques of the failure of much radical feminism to pay attention to differences of class, race and culture were both necessary and appropriate and have led to greater attention to these issues on the part of contemporary radical feminist writers. Even where women do not identify or only partly identify with radical feminism's analysis of patriarchy, celebration of womanhood and separatist programme, the emotional appeal of much radical feminist writing continues to offer an inspirational dimension which is lacking in much other feminist writing. In the next chapter, which looks at lesbian difference, many of the issues raised by radical and revolutionary feminists will recur, since lesbian feminists played a very important part in the development of radical and revolutionary critiques of patriarchy.

CHAPTER 3
Lesbian Difference, Feminism and Queer Theory

The year was 1969.

The women's movement was picking up steam. NOW was picking up members. Consciousness-raising groups were springing up all over the country.

I was a clinical psychologist in private practice.

And I was in the closet.

I joined a counselling collective, really a support group, of local feminist therapists. For the first time in my life, it was all right for adult women to sit together in a room, no men allowed, and talk about being women. For the first time in my life, it was right for women to *like* each other.

One night, some area lesbian activists came to our meeting to conduct a workshop. As part of an exercise, they instructed us to divide into two groups – lesbians on one side of the room, 'straight' women on the other. A moment of panic. I looked around. Everyone else was going to her place. Any minute now, I would be very conspicuous, standing in the middle of the floor with my face the color of chalk and my heart pounding out of my chest. I thought about fainting, but didn't know how. I thought about lying, but guilt stopped me.

Time was passing. The centre of the room was clearing.

I took a deep breath and went to join my sisters.

After more than thirty years of fear and hiding, more than thirty years of loneliness and self-hatred, I walked from one side of the room to another and changed my life. (Dreher 1993: 110)

Until the event of gay liberation and second-wave feminism, lesbianism in the West remained largely closeted. While there have been moments when lesbianism was fashionable in particular class and social circles, for example in the Berlin of the Weimar Republic, this has only rarely been the case. For the most part lesbians have been forced to lead a subcultural or closeted existence, or to deny their own sexuality. Lesbian sex was neither condoned nor tolerated by mainstream society. When visible at all, the lesbian was portrayed in popular culture as depraved, a threat both to decency and to other women and girls. Moreover, the fear of unnatural femininity – embodied by the independent, educated lesbian – played a cautionary role in the socialization of girls into patriarchal heterosexuality. Inadequate femininity, it was suggested, would mean failure to gain male approval and love and to marry well and happily.

In her comprehensive study of lesbian life in twentieth-century America, Lillian Faderman traces the range of class-specific ways in which lesbian women negotiated their lives in a homophobic environment. She tells of how older, middle-class lesbians in the 1950s and 1960s tended to remain closeted while their younger and working-class sisters participated in a bar-based subculture governed by strict butch/femme role play. This precarious lifestyle was subject to persistent police harassment and physical attacks on the streets, but it enabled the women concerned to affirm a positive identity based on difference:

> But perhaps the most important function of the roles was that they created a certain sense of membership in a special group, with its own norms and values and even uniforms. The roles offered lesbians a social identity and a consciousness of shared differences from women in the heterosexual world. Through them outsiders could be insiders. And those who were not familiar with roles, rules and uniforms were the outsiders on butch/femme turf. (Faderman 1991: 174)

Much twentieth-century thinking about lesbianism has its roots in the sexology of the late nineteenth and early twentieth centuries; indeed, sexology played a crucial role in the pathologization of lesbianism. Accounts of the history of lesbianism in the West suggest that it became an object of knowledge and classification relatively recently and that this process was linked in part to perceived threats posed by first-wave feminism.[1] Among the late nineteenth- and early twentieth-century attempts to describe and theorize lesbianism systematically were the works of Krafft-Ebing (1882), Forel (1908), Bloch (1909) and Havelock Ellis (1934). These writers identified lesbianism not just as a mode of sexual behaviour but as a way of being that profoundly affected – indeed undermined – the femininity of women. For example, in 1882 the German sexologist Richard Krafft-Ebing wrote of lesbians in his *Psychopathia Sexualis:*

> For female employments there is manifested not merely a lack of taste, but often unskillfulness in them. The toilette is neglected and pleasure found in a

coarse boyish life. Instead of an inclination for the arts, there is manifested an inclination and taste for the sciences. Occasionally there may be attempts to drink and smoke. Perfumes and cosmetics are abhorred. The consciousness of being born a woman and therefore of being compelled to renounce the University, with its gay life, and the army, induces painful reflections. (Krafft-Ebing 1882: 34)

Krafft-Ebing stressed that lesbian women were not only driven by their sexual orientation to reject all the trappings of femininity but were actually incapable of feminine behaviour and lacked the ability to carry out female tasks. This biologically determined difference manifest in the tendency towards 'boyishness' and masculine pursuits was thought to have profound psychological and social effects on individual lesbian women. However, precisely because this theory of lesbianism was grounded in biology, it offered a platform from which lesbian women could argue for civil rights. Since they could not change the way they were, the argument ran, lesbians should be tolerated by heterosexual society. This position, however, was never uniformly adopted by all lesbian activists, even in the early twentieth century.

Sexology was the framework for the best-known lesbian novel of the early twentieth century, Radclyffe Hall's *The Well of Loneliness* (1982; original 1928), which for decades offered lesbian women and girls particular role models:

Hall's book, although it was published in the late 1920s, remained important into the '50s and '60s in providing an example of how to be a lesbian among the young who had no other guide. Stephen Gordon's butch role in relation to the totally feminine Mary in the novel could be a plausible image to any homosexual female who grew up in a heterosexual milieu. (Faderman 1991: 173)

The Well of Loneliness offers a vivid and powerful fictive account of the life of a lesbian depicted in terms of the sexological discourse of 'inversion' according to which lesbianism is a masculine reversal of normal heterosexual femininity. Born female, but named Stephen by her father who had wanted a son, the protagonist of the novel betrays all the characteristics of lesbians as defined by sexology:

At seventeen Stephen was taller than Anna, who had used to be considered quite tall for a women, but Stephen was nearly as tall as her father − not a beauty this in the eyes of the neighbours. . . .

But in spite of all this Stephen's figure was handsome in a flat broad-shouldered and slim-flanked fashion; and her movements were purposeful,

having fine poise, she moved with the easy assurance of the athlete. . . . A fine
face, very pleasing, yet with something about it that went ill with the hats on
which Anna insisted – large hats trimmed with ribbons or roses or daisies, and
supposed to be softening to the features.

Staring at her own reflection in the glass, Stephen would feel just a little
uneasy: '*Am* I queer looking or not?' (Hall 1982: 70; original 1928)

Lesbianism in *The Well of Loneliness* is much more than a sexual practice: it is
an inborn feature which affects physical, emotional and intellectual characteristics, making the woman in question more like a man. Stephen not only
looks masculine – just like her father – but shares his conventionally male
passion for learning and physical pursuits such as hunting. She lacks all the
attributes considered feminine in this period. Gender in the novel is implicitly grounded in sex. 'Deviant' sexuality leads to 'deviant' femininity; yet, the
text argues, society should tolerate lesbian women, since they themselves
have no choice about how they were born.

The Well of Loneliness clearly shows how in societies which privilege
heterosexuality, lesbian difference is defined against a dominant set of
assumptions which see heterosexuality as the only normal and natural mode
of sexuality. Moreover, patriarchal societies link femininity to particular
versions of heterosexuality in which women are regarded as different from
and subordinate to men. Lesbian sexuality is seen as a deviation from the
heterosexual norm and, as such, abnormal.

In her book *The Social Construction of Lesbianism*, Celia Kitzinger argues
that the sexologists at the turn of the nineteenth century were responding to
an agenda set, in part, by first-wave feminism:

> Firstly through the 'discovery' of women as sexual beings and the glorification
> of heterosexuality . . . and secondly through the morbidification of lesbianism.
> This latter strategy relied on the construction of 'the lesbian' as someone
> defined by a specific and potentially describable 'essence' which sets her apart
> from normal women. (Kitzinger 1987: 41–2)

This pathologization of lesbianism within heterosexual culture was used to
discredit independent women with intellectual aspirations and reinforce the
ideologies of domesticity and motherhood as the natural spheres for women.
Indeed more recently lesbian feminists have pointed to the continued
policing function of heterosexist definitions of lesbianism:

> Lesbianism is the word, the label, the condition that holds women in line.
> When a woman hears this word tossed her way, she knows she is stepping out
> of line. . . . Lesbian is a label invented by the Man to throw at any woman who
> dares to be his equal, who dares to challenge his prerogatives (including that of

54

all women as part of the exchange medium among men), who dares to assert the primacy of her own needs. (Radicalesbians 1988; original 1970)

Heterosexist images of lesbianism here become a tool in maintaining the institution of patriarchal heterosexuality.

Essence and Identity

The theories of lesbianism developed within sexology at the turn of the last century posited a biological essence which determined both the nature of the lesbian, her sexuality and her femininity, and, by implication, 'normal' heterosexuality. Sexology worked with traditional binary oppositions between male/female and masculine/feminine accounting for lesbianism as a form of masculinization. A similar model of lesbianism is to be found in Freudian psychoanalysis where it is seen as arrested development on the path from initial polymorphous perversity to mature adult heterosexuality:

> Quite different are the effects of the castration complex in the female. She acknowledges the fact of her castration, and with it, too, the superiority of the male and her own inferiority, but she rebels against this unwelcome state of affairs. From this divided attitude three lines of development open up. The first leads to a general revulsion from sexuality. The little girl, frightened by the comparison with boys, grows up dissatisfied with her clitoris, and gives up her phallic activity and with it her sexuality in general as well as a good part of her masculinity in other fields. The second line leads her to cling with defiant self-assertiveness to her threatened masculinity. To an incredibly late age she clings to the hope of getting a penis some time. That hope becomes her life's aim; and the phantasy of being a man in spite of everything often persists as a formative factor over long periods. This 'masculinity complex' in women can also result in a manifest homosexual choice of object. Only if her development follows the third, very circuitous, path does she reach the final normal female attitude, in which she takes her father as her object and so finds her way to the feminine form of the Oedipus complex. (Freud 1975b: 77–8; original 1931)

The rejection by lesbian feminists of these heterosexist accounts of lesbianism opened up the question of what it meant to be lesbian, raising a range of questions and possibilities.

Within lesbian theory there is a range of approaches to the question of lesbian identity and difference. These include both perspectives which view lesbianism as an effect of a biological imperative and theories of lesbianism as a form of sexuality and identity which is socially and historically constructed.

They further include positions which see lesbianism as the result of a successful attempt to evade the oppressive institutions of heterosexuality; that is, as a question of social and political choice. All these possibilities imply either acceptance or rejection of a lesbian essence.[2] Differences in sexual orientation can be seen as natural, cultural or political. Yet even where sexual orientation is seen as something lesbian women are born with, culture plays an important role in shaping identities and lifestyles. For some the terms 'lesbian' (or 'gay' and 'homosexual') denote forms of sexual practice necessarily affecting identity in heterosexist and homophobic societies but not constituting the essence of individual subjectivity and identity. For others lesbianism signifies a woman-identified mode of living which implies values different from those of the male world. For others again, lesbianism signifies a true form of subjectivity, describing identities, subjectivities and lifestyles that are radically other to those of heterosexuals. Alternatively lesbianism can be understood as a dimension of an individual which becomes central to identity precisely because of the real and felt need to hide lesbian sexuality in societies which discriminate against lesbian women. Important, too, is the fact that lesbians are women and, as such, come up against the full force of patriarchal as well as heterosexist power. This factor – often forgotten in male gay theory and politics – has been important in the development of lesbian feminism and in the current lesbian feminist critique of queer theory.

Commenting on lesbian identity, Bonnie Zimmerman suggests that:

> The process of developing a lesbian or gay perspective is not so clear, partly because women become lesbians any time from puberty to old age. Furthermore, there is little agreement among lesbians as to whether or not one is born gay, as one is born female or black. Lesbian writers of retrospective narratives often claim to have felt themselves to *be* lesbian from birth, or age two, or certainly from puberty, and thus always to have a lesbian perspective. Many claim that there is an 'essential' lesbian vision, marked by strong attractions to another girl or woman, feelings of difference, or perhaps rejection of traditional female socialization.
>
> But fictional and autobiographical accounts of lesbian identity formation are retrospective, products of the very perspective that they purpose to explain. They tend to isolate factors that create a sense of continuity within the self, while ignoring factors that clash with current identity. For example, a woman might focus on the fact that she was intimate friends with Sally at age six and fail to note that so were a dozen other girls, none of whom became lesbians. (Zimmerman 1993a: 135–6)

Whereas Zimmerman comes out against essential identities stressing the role of culture and society in forming subjectivities, radical and revolutionary lesbian feminists of the 1980s turned the tables on mainstream theories of lesbianism by defining it as the 'normal' way to be a woman:

> A lesbian is the rage of all women condensed to the point of explosion. She is a woman who . . . acts in accordance with her inner compulsion to be a more complete and free human being than her society . . . cares to allow her. . . . She has not been able to accept the limitations and oppressions laid on her by the most basic role of her society – the female role. (Radicalesbians 1988; original 1970, quoted in Faderman 1991: 206)

This position was the basis for ideas of political lesbianism which were a powerful force in the women's movement in the 1980s.

LESBIANISM AND FEMINISM

Despite feminism's liberating dimensions, lesbians have long had an uneasy relationship with the women's movement. In both first- and second-wave feminism there has been a tendency on the part of heterosexual feminists to ignore or pay lip service to questions of sexual orientation and heterosexist oppression. As Celia Kitzinger points out, lesbian rights were not taken up by mainstream first-wave feminism. She quotes A. Ruhling speaking at the annual meeting of the Scientific Humanitarian Committee in 1904:

> When we consider all the gains that homosexual women have for decades achieved for the Women's Movement, it can only be regarded as astounding that the big and influential organisations of this movement have up to now not raised one finger to secure for their not insignificant number of Uranian [lesbian] members their just rights as far as the state and society are concerned, that they have done nothing – and I mean not a thing – to protect so many of their best known and most devoted pioneers from ridicule and scorn as they enlightened the broader public about the true nature of uranianism. (Kitzinger 1987: 43)

The Scientific Humanitarian Committee mobilized sexology to campaign for rights for homosexuals and welcomed both gay men and lesbians within its ranks. At the turn of the century, as in the 1960s, it had been left to a homosexual rights movement to campaign for the interests of lesbians and to lesbians to make links between gay liberation and feminism:

> I connect gay rights to feminism most closely around the question of the individual's right to control one's own body, including the right to control

one's sexuality, and therefore to have self-determination at the most basic human level. (Bunch 1987: 65; original 1982).

In the 1970s, as second-wave feminism increased in visibility and influence, lesbian feminists articulated similar concerns to Ruhling's, pointing to the failure of heterosexual feminists to take heterosexism and its negative effects on lesbian women seriously:

> There are many lesbians still who feel that there is no place in socialist-feminist organizations in particular, or the women's movement in general, for them to develop that politics or live that life. Because of this I am still, in part, a separatist; but I don't want to be a total separatist again. . . to unify the lesbian feminist politics developed within the past four years with socialist-feminism requires more than a token reference to queers. It requires an acknowledgement of lesbian-feminist analysis as central to understanding and ending women's oppression. (Bunch 1987: 175–6; original 1975)

The effects of heterosexism were felt in all areas of life, for example in discrimination in the workplace, in verbal and physical attacks on lesbians and in the problems lesbians faced in obtaining the custody of their children. Writing to the feminist monthly *Spare Rib* in June 1981, Sara Hardy explained how 'lesbian mothers are never safe as long as their husbands are alive. Lesbian mothers never actually win custody for keeps. That's the way the law works. . . . There are a lot of lesbian mothers freaking out over custody around the country, they need support, they need recognition' (quoted in Kanter et al. 1984: 138). It took constant campaigning on the part of lesbian women for their needs to be addressed within the wider movement (see figures 3.1 and 3.2).

LESBIAN FEMINISM

> The heart of lesbian-feminist politics, let me repeat, is a recognition that heterosexuality as an institution and an ideology is a cornerstone of male supremacy. Therefore, women interested in destroying male supremacy, patriarchy and capitalism must, equally with lesbians, fight heterosexual domination – or we will never end female oppression. This is what I call 'The heterosexual question' – it is *not* the lesbian question. (Bunch 1987: 176; original 1975)

Since the early years of second-wave feminism, radical lesbian feminists have argued forcefully that their sexuality; social position and politics are crucial to

3.1 Lesbian Strength march, 1984. Photograph: Brenda Prince/Format

undermining the basis of patriarchy by challenging its cornerstone: hetero-sexuality. Moreover, the institution of heterosexuality is the central political question for *all* women. Lesbian women stand in a position of radical otherness *vis-à-vis* heterosexuality. Lesbian feminists argue that whereas patriarchal power structures have much to offer men, whether gay or straight, and heterosexuality positions straight women within patriarchy, lesbianism is not easily co-opted by a patriarchal heterosexual culture. For example, cultural icons such as male pop and film stars can engage both heterosexual women and gay men as objects of desire and heterosexual men as role models, yet they have little to offer lesbian women. From a lesbian feminist perspective it is the non-dependence of lesbian women on men which makes lesbian feminism potentially so radical. (This is not to say that all lesbian feminists reject either male friendships or political alliances with men.) Lesbianism, in its ability to do without men, can be variously viewed as a real challenge to the patriarchal order or as of little relevance to it. Yet any lack of relevance is only a question of numbers. It would soon be transformed were large numbers of women to come out as lesbians or political lesbians and refuse to service men's needs.

From its early years, lesbian feminism has sought to move beyond narrow conceptions of lesbianism as merely a form of sexual practice to develop a 'woman-identified' perspective which might serve as the basis for the radical social and political transformation of society:

3.2 Kathy Sells and son Daniel on Positive Images march in Haringay, protesting against the ban of books about homosexuality in schools. Photograph: Brenda Prince/Format

> Lesbianism, like heterosexuality, is more than just whom you sleep with. Being woman-identified, giving space and support to women, are parts of the things it means to be a lesbian. It is also about our life-styles. (Bellos 1984: 95)

It is precisely this broader political definition of lesbian difference that radical lesbian feminists have stressed.

In her essay 'Compulsory Heterosexuality and Lesbian Existence' which was discussed in part in chapter 2, Adrienne Rich attempts to define what it might mean to be woman-identified. Starting from the position that hetero-sexuality is imposed on women by patriarchy, Rich counterpoises new definitions of woman to those depicting a patriarchally and heterosexually defined subject of patriarchal power. She uses two terms to identify these new definitions of woman's nature: *lesbian existence* and *lesbian continuum*. She is anxious to move beyond a limiting definition of lesbianism as merely a form of sexual practice: 'As the term lesbian has been held to limiting, clinical associations in its patriarchal definition, female friendship and comradeship have been set apart from the erotic, thus limiting the erotic itself' (Rich 1984:

228). To move beyond this limiting definition is to open up the possibility of the female erotic, not defined or constrained by patriarchy:

> But as we deepen and broaden the range of what we define as lesbian existence, as we delineate a lesbian continuum, we begin to discover the erotic in female terms: as that which is unconfined to any single part of the body or solely to the body itself, as an energy not only diffuse but, as Audre Lorde has described it, omnipresent in 'the sharing of joy, whether physical, emotional, psychic', and in the sharing of work, as the empowering joy which 'makes us less willing to accept powerlessness, or those other supplied states of being which are not native to me, such as resignation, despair, self-effacement, depression, self-denial' (Rich 1984: 228)

Rich uses the term 'lesbian existence' to suggest that there have always been lesbians, even though the term itself is relatively recent. What it has meant to be lesbian has varied in different cultures and changed historically. Rich's second term, 'lesbian continuum', is used to expand the meaning of being lesbian beyond sexual relations between women to encompass what Rich calls 'woman-identified experience', which can include heterosexually oriented women. As part of the lesbian continuum, all women can share a rich inner life. They bond against oppression, supporting each other practically and politically.

In lesbian feminism, to become woman-identified is a question of political choice:

> Male society defines lesbianism as a sexual act, which reflects men's limited view of women: they think of us only in terms of sex. The also say lesbians are not real women, so a real woman is one who gets fucked by men. We say that a lesbian is a woman whose sense of self and energies, including sexual energies, center around women – she is woman-identified. The woman-identified-woman commits herself to other women for political, emotional, physical and economic support. Women are important to her. She is important to herself. Our society demands that commitment from women be reserved for men.
>
> The lesbian, woman-identified-woman, commits herself to women not only as an alternative to oppressive male/female relationships but primarily because she *loves* women. Whether consciously or not, by her actions, the lesbian has recognized that giving support and love to men over women perpetuates the system that oppresses her. If women do not make a commitment to each other, which includes sexual love, we deny ourselves the love and value traditionally given to men. We accept our second-class status. When women do give primary energies to other women, then it is possible to concentrate fully on building a movement for our liberation.

> Woman-identified lesbianism is, then, more than a sexual preference; it is a political choice. It is political because relationships between men and women are essentially political: they involve power and dominance. Since the lesbian actively rejects that relationship and chooses women, she defies the established political system. (Bunch 1987: 161–2; original 1972)

The radical lesbian feminist insistence on political lesbianism, that is, on lesbianism as a political choice for all women which includes sexuality, is much more uncompromising that Rich's lesbian continuum. Thus, whereas many heterosexual feminists have welcomed the concept of a woman-identified lesbian continuum as a liberating and affirming way of thinking about their own relationships with other women, Rich's concept of a lesbian continuum has been criticized by lesbian writers because it is open to appropriations which marginalize sexuality and implicitly deny the specificity and difference of lesbian women:

> The women's liberation movement has taken lesbianism and joined it to itself in theory and practice so that in some explanations the justification of lesbianism was feminism and vice versa. ... The process of constructing yourself primarily from sexual and erotic experiences or desires is not the same as constructing a woman-identified lesbian woman. Some women do argue that there is intrinsically little difference and that has been obscured by the women's liberation movement. My criticism of men does not equal lesbianism. My desires and my sexual practice are not predicated on a dislike of men and my lesbian identity is not to be equated with an anti-male stance. Women who feel they are lesbians have a right to call themselves lesbians but what is in contention is the way they 'explain' their lesbianism and the way new explanations have subverted previous experience. (Clark 1987: 206)

Here sexual desire and practice are the key issues and, as Catherine Stimpson argues, that 'desire must be there and at least somewhat embodied' (1981: 364). Bonnie Zimmerman also warns that to use lesbianism as an inclusive category, as both Adrienne Rich and radical and revolutionary lesbian feminists do, is to 'risk blurring the distinctions between lesbian relationships and nonlesbian female friendships, or between lesbian identity and female centred identity. ... By so reducing the meaning of "lesbian", we have in effect eliminated lesbianism as a meaningful category' (Zimmerman 1993a: 38):

> As I have stated, many if not all heterosexual feminists now see women in the lesbian way. Patriarchs know this to be true. They insist that all feminists are lesbians ('You're taking a women's studies course? But they're all dykes over there!') and suspect that all lesbians are feminists. The key point made by

Adrienne Rich in 'Compulsory Heterosexuality and Lesbian Existence' is that no firm line can be drawn between lesbian experience and other female experience. But many lesbians know – or believe we know – that we see women differently than do even the most feminist of heterosexual women. What is the distinctiveness of, to paraphrase Djuna Barnes, this vision with a difference? [Barnes 1972: 26]

The most immediate and self-evident (to a lesbian) answer is that lesbians include sexuality – desire and passion – as a possibility in women's relationship with each other. Lesbians not only *see* women, but desire and feel passion for them. This is certainly one part of the discord that often exists between lesbians and heterosexual women, whether feminist or not. Heterosexual women may fear that lesbians will see them as sexual objects, as men do. Indeed, many lesbians, particularly those who come out as a result of feminist awakening, avoid the use of sexual imagery in their writing as a reaction to patriarchal reification of both heterosexual women and lesbians. But this is a futile avoidance. Lesbian being-in-the world is sexual; it is largely our sexuality that distinguishes us from other women. But not sex alone – lesbians also feel romantic and passionate about women. Thus a lesbian reader of literature will note women relating to each other, but see and emphasize the sexual, romantic, and/or passionate elements of this relation. Furthermore, a lesbian perspective focuses on the primacy and duration of the female friendship.
. . .

Finally, lesbians look beyond individual relationships to female communities that do not need or want men. (Zimmerman 1993b: 138–9)

Zimmerman endorses Lillian Faderman's definition in *Surpassing the Love of Men*:

'Lesbian' describes a relationship in which two women's strongest emotions and affections are directed towards each other. Sexual contact may be a part of the relationship to a greater or lesser degree, or it may be entirely absent. By preference the two women spend most of their time together and share most aspects of their lives with each other. (Faderman 1981: 17–18)

In Zimmerman's view, 'broader than the exclusive definition of lesbianism – for Faderman argues that not all lesbian relationships may be fully embodied – but narrower than Rich's "lesbian continuum", this definition is both specific and discriminating' (Zimmerman 1993b: 139).

The lesbian feminist strategy of extending lesbianism as a political and sexual choice to all women and insisting that heterosexuality equals consorting with the enemy did not only create resistance from lesbians who defined themselves in terms of a different desire and sexuality. It was not easily accepted by many heterosexually defined feminists. Susan Ardill and Sue O'Sullivan recount its effects on the women's movement in Britain:

63

In the mid-70s lesbianism and/or separatism were first presented within the [British] women's liberation movement as possibilities for all women to take up as part of their political struggle. For many feminists the printing of the CLIT statement from the USA in issue after issue of the London Women's Liberation Workshop newsletter was shocking, frightening and led to the first significant withdrawal of women from under the umbrella of sisterhood. (We are aware that many, particularly Black and working-class women never got under it in the first place.) In the CLIT statement all heterosexual women were named as untrustworthy dupes at best, or, at worst, as active collaborators with the enemy. Given that, the only feminist choice was withdrawal from men and bonding with women. (Ardill and O'Sullivan 1987: 284)

Also writing at the time, Wendy Clark suggests that heterosexual feminists failed to respond adequately to the radical lesbian feminist challenge:

Many heterosexual feminists have colluded with the way lesbianism and feminism have come to mean one and the same thing. Feminists have found themselves unable to rebut adequately the view that to engage in heterosexuality and therefore heterosexual sex was to co-operate with the oppression of women and this made them feel guilty. Conveniently so too, as there was something obviously 'wrong' with being turned on by men. They are now the new deviants while lesbian feminists were in the vanguard of feminism. (Clark 1987: 211)

The effect of this was to silence both other positions on lesbianism and any attempt to analyse more adequately the practice of heterosexuality.

SEPARATISM AND CULTURAL FEMINISM

Lesbian feminism developed in the context of both gay liberation and women's liberation, addressing what were seen as the blind spots of each movement: indifference to heterosexism in the women's movement and to patriarchy in the gay liberation movement. In some cases the separatist impulse of lesbian feminism in the 1970s fed into what became known in the 1980s as cultural feminism:

In their idealism [lesbian feminists] resembled the cultural feminists of the beginning of the century, such as Jane Addams, but instead of hoping to transform patriarchal institutions as the earlier women often did, they wanted to create entirely new institutions and to shape a women's culture that would embody all the best values that were not male. It would be nonhierarchical, spiritual, and without the jealousy that comes of wanting to possess other human beings, as in monogamy and imperialism. It would be nonracist, nonagist, nonclassist, and nonexploitative – economically or sexually. It would be pro-women and pro-children. These women believed that such a culture could only be formed if women stepped away from the hopelessly corrupt patriarchy and established their own self-sufficient, 'women-identified-women' communities into which male values could not infiltrate. Those communities would eventually be built into a strong Lesbian Nation that would exist not necessarily as a geographical entity but as a state of mind and that might even be powerful enough, through its example, to divert the country and the world from their dangerous course. Their visions were utopian. (Faderman 1991: 216–17)

Ironically it was precisely the uncompromising ways in which lesbian feminism defined women's difference and a separatist women's culture which prevented the realization of a Lesbian Nation since it excluded those women who were unwilling to conform:

There were rules for everything, even acceptable dress. Makeup, skirts, high heels, or any other vestiges of the 'female slave mentality' would arouse suspicion in the community and were shunned. The uniform was usually jeans and natural fibre skirts. Expensive clothing suggested conspicuous consumption and was inappropriate in a community where downward mobility was 'p.c.'. ... the goal was to appear strong and self-sufficient, rather than masculine: no matriarchy could function if its inhabitants had to run or fight in high heels and tight skirts. (Faderman 1991: 230–1)

Not only was role play politically incorrect, so too were pornography and forms of sexual practice which depended on power. As in radical feminism more widely, pornography was regarded as integral to the global patriarchal exploitation of women: 'pornography is not just symbolic violence against women. It is part of an international slave traffic in women that operates as a multinational effort, where our bodies are the product, often procured unwillingly and usually abused' (Bunch 1987: 207; original 1977). Faderman argues that this culture led to a de-eroticization of lesbian feminists in the broader context of societies in which eroticism tends to be constructed around difference. She recounts how research in the 1970s showed that sex played a much reduced role in lesbian relationships and was often regarded by lesbian feminists as something whose importance was exaggerated by men (Faderman 1991).[3] This stance, however, inevitably provoked strong reactions and resistance among many lesbians who considered themselves feminists, paving the way for the current debate on feminism and queer politics discussed below.

Yet it was not only questions of lifestyle and modes of sexual practice which prevented the realization of lesbian feminist conceptions of a Lesbian Nation. Class, too, was important, and above all race and ethnicity. While not all lesbian feminists were ethnocentric or insensitive to the realities of racism,[4] there was a widespread tendency among white lesbian feminists to stress the primacy of the institution of heterosexuality in the oppression of women which had the (often unintended) effect of alienating black women and other women of colour for whom racism was often a more brutal and visible oppression. A critique and rejection of heterosexuality implied for many women a critique and rejection of the family. Yet for black feminists the family was often experienced as a refuge from the harsher world of racism:

> We would not wish to deny that the family can be a source of oppression for us but we also wish to examine how the black family has functioned as a primary source of resistance to oppression. We need to recognize that during slavery, periods of colonialism and under the present authoritarian state, the black family has been a site of political and cultural resistance to racism. (Carby 1982: 214)

The importance of not separating heterosexism from racism and class is a repeated theme in the writing of black lesbians and other lesbians of colour and gradually it had its effects. Faderman describes how in the 1980s, as the influence of early radical lesbian feminism waned, more women joined the visible lesbian community and it became 'more racially and ethnically diverse' (1991: 285):

> By the end of the '80s minority lesbians usually felt most comfortable working and socializing with each other when possible; however they were also willing to offer their input to the larger lesbian community on issues they felt were pertinent. . . . Minority lesbians preferred to call themselves 'lesbians of color' in the '80s. . . . it was not uncommon by the end of the '80s for there to be not only 'lesbians of color' groups but also organized groups of Latina lesbians, Chicana lesbians, Asian lesbians, South Asian lesbians, Japanese lesbians, black lesbians. . . . (p. 286)

LESBIAN CULTURAL CRITICISM

It was not only in the realm of sexual politics that questions of the nature of lesbian difference were central. They were equally important in lesbian cultural politics. In her 1981 overview of lesbian feminist criticism, Bonnie Zimmerman recounts how:

In the 1970s a generation of lesbian feminist literary critics came of age. Some, like the lesbian professor in Lynn Strongin's poem, 'Sayre', had been closeted in the profession; many had 'come out' as lesbians in the women's liberation movement. As academics and as lesbians, we cautiously began to plait together the strands of our existence by teaching lesbian literature, establishing networks and support groups, and exploring assumptions about a lesbian-focused literary criticism. Beginning with nothing, as we thought, this generation quickly began to expand the limitations of literary scholarship by pointing to what had been for decades 'unspeakable' – lesbian existence – thus phrasing, in the novelist June Arnold's words, 'what has never been' (Arnold 1976: 28). (Zimmerman 1993a: 33)

Since the early 1970s lesbian cultural criticism has been concerned with questions similar to those addressed in other areas of woman-centred feminist criticism. The first task was to uncover and create lesbian traditions in literature. Once a body of text had begun to be made available the critics could begin to ask questions about the specificity of lesbian writing, lesbian aesthetics and their place in education. Zimmerman summarizes these questions as follows:

Does a woman's sexual and affectational preference influence the way she writes, reads and thinks? Does lesbianism belong in the classroom and in scholarship? Is there a lesbian aesthetic distinct from a feminist aesthetic? What should be the role of the lesbian critic? Can we establish a lesbian 'canon' in the way in which feminist critics have established a female canon? Can lesbian feminists develop insights into female creativity that might enrich all literary criticism? (1993a: 33–4)

The main concerns of lesbian cultural criticism have included the work of recovering lost lesbian texts, reclaiming lesbian history, creating positive images and traditions and exploring the specificity of lesbian creativity and aesthetics. All these objectives have contributed to positive self-affirmation, creating lesbian language and traditions where there was only silence and invisibility or negative images. Yet all these tasks constantly raised the central question of the meaning of lesbianism and involved defining lesbian difference in its historical specificity as it changed over time and in different social contexts:

Lesbian criticism begins with the establishment of the lesbian text: the creation of language out of silence. The critic must first define the term 'lesbian' and then determine its applicability to both writer and text, sorting out the relation of literature to life. Her definition of lesbianism will influence the texts she identifies as lesbian, and, except for the growing body of literature written from an explicit lesbian perspective since the development of a lesbian political movement, it is likely that many will disagree with various identifications of lesbian texts. It is not only *Sula* that may provoke controversy,[5] but even the 'coded' works of lesbian writers such as Gertrude Stein. The critic will need to consider whether a lesbian text is one written by a lesbian (and, if so, how do we determine who is a lesbian?); one written about lesbians (which might be by a heterosexual woman or by a man); or one that expresses a lesbian 'vision' (which has yet to be satisfactorily described). But, despite the problems raised by definition, silence, and coding, and absence of tradition, lesbian critics have begun to develop a critical stance. Often this stance involves peering into shadows, into the spaces between words, into what has been unspoken and barely imagined. It is a perilous critical adventure, with results that may violate accepted norms of traditional criticism, but it may also transform our notions of literary possibility. (Zimmerman 1993a: 41)

Similar projects have been undertaken by black lesbian critics, for example, Barbara Smith who in her path-breaking essay of 1977, 'Towards a Black Feminist Criticism', described the immense task facing black women:

> I do not know where to begin. Long before I tried to write this I realized that I was attempting something unprecedented, something dangerous, merely by writing about Black women writers from a feminist perspective and about Black lesbian writers from any perspective at all. These things have not been done. Not by white male critics, expectedly. Not by Black male critics. Not by white women critics who think of themselves as feminists. And most crucially not by Black women critics, who, although they pay the most attention to Black women writers as a group, seldom use a consistent feminist analysis or write about Black lesbian literature. All segments of the literary world – whether establishment, progressive, Black female or lesbian – do not know that Black women writers and Black lesbian writers exist. (Smith 1986: 168; original 1977)

The inevitably plural definitions of lesbianism which have emerged in the course of recovering lost literary traditions – black, white or of colour – are not unlike those carefully traced by Lillian Faderman in her *Odd Girls and Twilight Lovers: A History of Lesbian Life in Twentieth-Century America*. Here recognition and respect for diversity are of the utmost importance:

> Even in 1964 [the year in which Donald Webster Cory published a book entitled *The Lesbian in America*] lesbians and lesbian communities were extremely diverse.[6] They have metamorphosed to be even more so as more women have dared in a relatively liberal society to accept a lesbian identity and a broader spectrum of women has publicly claimed a place in the community. More than ever they challenge the notion that lesbians can be described as a

whole, as writers have tried to do since the sexologists first formulated the concept. (Faderman 1991: 307–8)

This diversity is increasingly taking account of other factors which affect the forms taken by heterosexism, lesbian identity and lifestyle, particularly, class, race and ethnicity.

FROM LESBIAN FEMINISM TO QUEER THEORY: DIFFERENCES WITHIN LESBIAN THEORY AND POLITICS

In her account of the social construction of lesbianism, Celia Kitzinger argues that:

> Since the mid-1970s research on lesbianism has, increasingly, moved away from the earlier pathological models towards conceptualizations which represent lesbianism in terms of individual choices and lifestyles or private quests for self-fulfilment and loving interpersonal relationships: the lesbian and gay man are no longer a species apart, but human beings of equal worth and dignity to heterosexuals, contributing to the rich diversity of humankind. (Kitzinger 1987: 44)

This shift in emphasis reflects the achievements of the gay and lesbian liberation movements. As in other movements with their roots in the 1960s, civil and human rights were an important part of the political rhetoric and aspirations of the gay liberation movement. The movement, which came into being in 1969 following the Stonewall rebellion in New York, focused initially on issues of visibility, positive identity and human rights. (The Stonewall rebellion developed when gays and lesbians, provoked by repeated police harassment and arrests, defended the Stonewall bar in Greenwich Village against a police raid.) In addition to events such as gay pride parades, the movement called for an end to the closet and to the many forms of discrimination which gay and lesbian men and women experienced and continue to experience on a day-to-day basis, ranging from physical and verbal attack to discrimination in housing and at work. Many lesbian activists were involved in both gay liberation and women's liberation where lesbian politics were profoundly affected by feminism. As has been argued above, radical lesbian feminist theory and politics were and are guided by a radical critique of patriarchy and their aims go far beyond civil and human rights, a politics which Kitzinger, for example, terms liberal humanist. They are not interested in inclusion within the existing system but in transforming patriarchy.

The implications of a shift away from a radical lesbian feminist political agenda into a liberal politics of lifestyle and choice can perhaps be seen most clearly in the case of lesbian sexual practice. For revolutionary lesbian feminist writer and theorist Sheila Jeffreys, writing in the lesbian feminist tradition, same-sex relationships can embody either heterosexual or truly lesbianism/homosexual forms of desire. Heterosexuality for Jeffreys is characterized by 'power difference' and lesbian difference by 'sameness of power, equality and mutuality':

> Once the eroticizing of otherness and power difference is learned, then in a same sex relationship, where another gender is absent, otherness can be reintroduced through differences of age, race, class, the practice of sadomasochism or role playing. So it is possible to construct heterosexual desire within lesbianism and heterosexual desire is plentifully evident in the practice of gay men. The opposite of heterosexual desire is the eroticizing of sameness, equality and mutuality. It is homosexual desire. (Jeffreys 1990: 301)

True lesbian difference, according to Jeffreys, thus involves sexual relationships which are fundamentally other than heterosexual models. Neither role playing nor sadomasochism can be part of a lesbian feminist practice. The narrowness of this position created schisms among radical lesbians who saw themselves as feminists. In the early 1980s the question of lesbian sexual practice came to the forefront in lesbian feminist circles in Britain:

> So, 'woman-identified' ruled OK. Then *Sex Heresies* came along, published in the Spring of 1981. This issue of an American feminist periodical was an attempt to combat the latent feminist assumptions about how we, hets or dykes, 'should' express sexuality. With a paucity of feminist writings around on sex, and after a few years of *The Joy of Lesbian Sex* and others of that ilk, it was definitely exciting. And shocking to some – with articles on butch–femme relationships, sadomasochism, masturbation and celibacy, prostitution, fag hags and feminist erotica. Whatever else, *Sex Heresies* signalled a move to put the erotic back into sex. Whereas the British revolutionary feminists appeared to see sex as a pleasant possibility between women who had withdrawn from men, *Sex Heresies* underlined the deep and confusing currents of desire between women. (Ardill and O'Sullivan 1987: 286–7)

Writing in *Feminist Review* in summer 1986, Susan Ardill and Sue O'Sullivan traced the history of confrontations around the question of sadomasochism as they affected the London Lesbian and Gay Centre in the 1980s. The protracted battle was over whether SM (sadomasochism) lesbian groups should be allowed to meet there. At issue was the meaning of lesbianism. Was it, as Jeffreys contends, incompatible with any sexual practice which did not restrict itself to the 'eroticizing of sameness, equality and mutuality', or was it wrong to reduce lesbian difference to a narrow lesbian feminist definition in which no space was given to the possibility that other forms of sexual practice could mean something different in a lesbian as opposed to heterosexual context? Positions critical of 1980s lesbian feminism have repeatedly stressed the need to allow for difference:

> It is my contention that as far as lesbianism is concerned feminists may well have allowed rhetorical and theoretical stances to influence their view of lesbian practice and activity. *As an example*, consider the terms 'active/passive' and the synonymous linking with the given roles of 'butch and fem'. Because a certain core of lesbian self-identity does have to do with the sexual activity between women (or the possibility thereof) then some examination of actual sexual practice needs to take place. By means of a crude assumption the passive/active of heterosexual sex is passed on to lesbian sex. Whereas in heterosexual sex, because of the present influence of social relations between women and men and the history of those relations, active = taking = men, while passive = receiving = women, in lesbian sexual practice the reality of active/passive can be experienced differently. In lesbian sex the active is the one *giving* pleasure to the other as well as possibly obtaining pleasure from the act as well. Even the passive is in a way active. Having pleasure can be an active thing, even though its heterosexual meaning is not that. Because of the way the active partner has always been seen as the man our feminist use and meaning of active/passive has been severely restricted to embody a critique of sex where the man uses the woman for his own pleasurable ends. But in lesbian sex (except for extreme role-playing behaviour) the basic actions of the active and passive are different. Hence it is incorrect to take the meanings of active passive in a heterosexual sense and just apply them as if they were the same to a sexual practice which is quite different. (Clark 1987: 209)

The revolutionary lesbian feminist rejection of diversity within lesbian sexual practice, founded as it is on a narrow doctrine of mutuality, has been rejected as constricting and moralistic by many lesbians writing in the 1980s and 1990s. Moreover, it is seen as undermining the possibility of alliances between lesbians and gay men, since it is ultimately founded on a rejection of men as the agents of patriarchal power:

> Most of us – some of us to our great personal distress – are familiar with the attempts revolutionary and radical feminists have made to purify sexual practices within the British and North American women's movement. These have included hostility to butch/femme relationships, the systematic defaming of lesbians who do sado-masochism coupled with efforts to excommunicate them from the movement, attempts to hinder political alliances between lesbians and gay men, and a pointedly suspicious attitude towards feminists

who sleep with men. The resemblance to past social purity practice is, once more, striking. It can be seen most readily in the revolutionary feminist insistence that only a very few kinds of sexuality are acceptable, and that even a suggestion of other kinds whether via the printed word or by other sorts of representations including the clothes one wears, poses a clear and present danger to women. (Hunt 1990: 38–9)

At issue in this disagreement is the meaning of particular modes of relating and forms of dress and sexual practice. Whereas Jeffreys assumes that butch/femme roles in lesbian relationships mirror the power structures of patriarchal heterosexuality, other lesbian writers see them rather differently:

> Butch–femme relationships, as I experienced them, were complex erotic statements, not phoney heterosexual replicas. None of the butch women I was with, and this included a passing woman, ever presented themselves to me as men; they did announce themselves as tabooed women who were willing to identify their passion for other women by wearing clothes that symbolized the taking of responsibility. (Nestle 1987: 100)

If butch/femme role playing is problematic for lesbian feminism, the issue of sadomasochism is even more controversial since it raises questions of power in a very immediate sense. For its lesbian supporters, for example Gayle Rubin (1992), it is a question of the right to free sexual expression versus the attempts of an unholy alliance between lesbian feminists and the religious Right to impose censorship. Whereas Rubin's politics are libertarian, for lesbian feminists sadomasochism is a clear example of a mode of relating governed by those forms of power and subordination which are characteristic of patriarchal heterosexuality. Jeffreys, for example, argues that sadomasochism reintroduces power and exploitation into the intimate realm of personal life. The move towards diversity and away from lesbian feminist critiques of patriarchal power both in relation to sexual practices and the social position of lesbians more generally has gained momentum with the development in the 1990s of queer theory.

Queer Theory and Politics

In April 1990 a group of New York ACT-UP [Aids Coalition to Unleash Power] lesbians and gay men who were interested in doing direct action around broader lesbian and gay issues formed Queer Nation. (Faderman 1991: 300)

The choice of the word 'queer' was important both for its inclusiveness and as part of a political project to shift meanings based on traditional homophobic views of difference:

> In recent years, the word 'queer', long used as a term of insult and self-loathing, has been reclaimed by lesbians, gay men, bisexuals, transvestites, transsexuals – and even some heterosexuals – as a proud declaration of non-conformist sexualities: 'we're here, we're queer; get used to it!'. In place of the medicopsychiatric 'homosexual', or the euphemistic and self-justificatory 'gay', the word 'queer' is seen as confrontational and as underscoring the fact that we are 'queer' ('deviant' and 'abnormal') to a world in which normality is defined in rigid and suffocating terms. (Wilkinson and Kitzinger 1996: 375)

Before the advent of queer politics and theory and the founding of the Queer Nation, the gay and lesbian liberation movements had concentrated on extending the civil rights enjoyed by heterosexuals to gay men and lesbian women. These include, for example, the right not to be discriminated against on the basis of one's sexual orientation, the right of gay couples to the same financial and social benefits as heterosexual couples and the right to have and bring up children. This predominantly liberal strategy aimed at inclusion and acceptance, implying that gay and heterosexual ways of living are equally valid.

If lesbian feminists criticized this strategy for its failure to address the deep and all-pervasive structures of patriarchy, queer theory has focused on its implicit endorsement of the normality of heterosexuality. Refusing hegemonic notions of what is normal or natural, the queer movement challenges the very ideas of normality which underpin social institutions and practices. From a queer perspective nothing is natural, nothing is normal. Everything is a social and cultural construct and gender identities are acquired, at least in part, through performance. Indeed much queer cultural politics is aimed at exposing the cultural nature of gender. Thus queer demonstrations tend to stress the arbitrariness and unnaturalness of traditional signifiers of gender difference.

In theoretical terms queer theory is in many ways postmodern, since it renounces any fixed notions of difference; in particular, fixed distinctions between masculine and feminine, maleness and femaleness. Binary oppositions are replaced by a proliferation of differences which queer theory and politics refuses to hierarchize. Gender ceases to express anything fundamental about women and men. For some queer theorists, gender becomes a question of performance. Transgender practices, such as drag, are seen as fundamentally transgressive. As Judith Butler argues in *Gender Trouble*, once the centrality, obviousness and naturalness of heterosexuality is questioned it is no longer clear that gender has any natural meaning, and drag is one way of acting out this political point. Indeed, little or no distinction can be drawn between drag and so-called 'normal' femininity:

> Is drag the imitation of gender, or does it dramatize the signifying gestures through which gender itself is established? Does being female constitute a 'natural fact' or a cultural performance or is 'naturalness' constituted though discursively constrained performative acts that produce the body through and within the categories of sex? Divine notwithstanding, gender practices within gay and lesbian cultures often thematize 'the natural' in parodic contexts that bring into relief the performative construction of an original and true sex. What other foundational categories of identity – the binary of sex, gender, and the body – can be shown as productions that create the effect of the natural, the original, and the inevitable? (Butler 1990: xiii–ix)

Butler, whose work is discussed more fully in chapter 5, argues for a move away from the distinction – long used by feminists – between sex and gender, suggesting that there is only gender.

In recent years the most controversial issues within the lesbian-queer community have been the questions of transgender behaviour and transsexuality.[7] Pre-queer approaches to these issues were strongly influenced by Janice Raymond's *The Transsexual Empire: The Making of the Shemale* (1982; original 1979), which theorized them as expressions of male envy, particularly of women's capacity to give birth. Other writers, for example Sheila Jeffreys, have interpreted transsexuality and transgender as forms of internalized homophobia. It is only since the arrival of queer theory that increasing numbers of feminists have ceased to view transsexuality, transgender practices and bisexuality as betrayals of both feminism and lesbianism. Yet attitudes to transgender behaviour and transsexuality differ radically. Whereas queer readings of transgender tend to see it as inherently transgressive, transsexuality is often regarded as regressive. Unlike those who practice transgender behaviour, transsexuals attempt to become the other sex and pass as male or female, refixing the binary oppositions that structure conventional norms of gender.

THE EVACUATION OF POWER

> If all is artifice, simulation and performance, if 'sex' is only a passing fashion, there is no point in opposing this by looking for some underlying reality of truth about 'men' and 'women'; rather the strategy becomes actively to participate in the artifice precisely in order to underscore the fragility of 'sex'

and 'gender' *as artifice*. This strategy is described as 'gender play' (Schwichten-berg 1993), 'gender bending' (Braidotti 1991), or, most popularly, as 'genderfuck' (Reich 1992) or 'fucking with gender'. The gender-fuck is supposed to 'deprive the naturalising narratives of compulsory heterosexuality of their central protagonists: 'man' and 'woman' (Butler 1990: 146) and to illustrate the social constructedness of 'sex' in all its multiple meanings.

This key queer strategy, the gender-fuck, is about parody, pastiche, and exaggeration. It replaces resistance to dominant cultural meanings of 'sex' with carnivalesque reversals and transgressions of traditional gender roles and sexualities, which reveal their own artificiality. Media figures like Prince, Boy George and Annie Lennox have been cited as gender benders (Braidotti 1991: 122–3). (Wilkinson and Kitzinger 1996: 377)

From a radical lesbian feminist perspective, the key point to be examined in any evaluation of queer theory and politics is its power to transform patriarchy. In their discussion of queer theory, Wilkinson and Kitzinger comment on the attractiveness of queer theory's apparent power to dena-turalize and subvert essentialist links between sex and gender and its challenge to heterosexual norms. However, they reject its political implica-tion for feminism:

While superficially attractive for its vigour, wit, sense of possibility and transformative potential, the move towards queer is, in fact, a conservative one – and one that is deeply dangerous for radical feminism.

Within queer, radical feminist analyses are ignored or marginalised at best, subverted or derided at worst. Despite its 'denaturalising' potential, queer theory is centrally antagonistic to feminism. This is partly because queer theorists see feminism as a totalising 'grand narrative', whose meanings and values must be subverted and thrown into question, along with the other explanatory frameworks in politics, science and philosophy – mere fodder for deconstruction in the post-modern age. More than this, however, queer politics is often expressed in terms explicitly oppositional to feminism – especially radical feminism, characterised as 'moralistic feminist separatism' (Smyth 1992: 36). Lyndall MacCowan (1992: 323) wants to 'reclaim the right to fuck around with gender' but also insists that 'we need to take back "lesbian" as a sexual definition disburdened of any political justification'. Within queer theory, there is no attempt to problematise pleasure, much less to engage with radical feminists' attempts to do so (see Jeffreys 1990; Wilk-inson and Kitzinger 1993; Kitzinger 1994), other than to characterise these as repressive, restrictive and totalitarian in effect or intent. Queer functions as apologia or justification for much behaviour seen by radical feminism as damaging to women and – especially – to lesbians. The queer critique not only ignores, but sometimes reverses, key feminist critiques, particularly radical feminist critiques: of sadomasochism; of gay male culture; of transsexuality/

75

transvestism; of bisexuality; and of heterosexuality. (Wilkinson and Kitzinger 1996: 379–80)

Wilkinson and Kitzinger reject what they see as queer theory's endorsement of forms of gay male culture (including camp, drag and sadomasochism) and of pornography, all of which work through heterosexual models of sex as 'eroticised dominance and submission' (p. 381). In queer theory, heterosexual patriarchal power no longer figures as the central object of lesbian struggle. The effect of this is to legitimize heterosexuality, suggesting that it is 'unimportant, based on transitory and provisional attribution' rather than the profoundly oppressive effect of a network of patriarchal institutions (Wilkinson and Kitzinger 1996: 381). Power relations within and between heterosexuality and homosexuality become invisible, allowing for a liberalism which hides oppression.

> The queer elision of heterosexuality and homosexuality as sexually – and hence politically – equivalent or interchangeable is not as radical as queer theorists would have us believe.
>   The presentation of lesbianism and heterosexuality as equivalent betrays the underlying liberalism of queer theory – a liberalism which negates both the political force of lesbianism as a refusal of the heteropatriarchal order, and the radical feminist analysis of heterosexuality as the key site of women's oppressions. As the meanings of heterosexuality and homosexuality become blurred within a fantasy world of ambiguity, indeterminacy and charade, the material realities of oppression and the feminist politics of resistance are forgotten. (Wilkinson and Kitzinger 1996: 382)

For radical lesbian feminists, queer is ultimately part of the growing backlash against feminism, particularly radical feminism. Not only does an untransformed heterosexuality become acceptable, but even the specific nature of lesbian oppression is rendered invisible. In the queer prioritizing of pleasure over political analysis, the specificity of lesbian oppression, shaped as it is by patriarchy, is lost. If anything goes in the realm of queer sexuality, this does not do away either with lesbian oppression as women or the negative implications of heterosexuality for women in general. A liberatory queer politics of sexuality would, lesbian feminists argue, need to address the institution of heterosexuality as it affects women.

CHAPTER 4
Psychoanalysis and Difference

Since the 1970s feminists working in many areas of social and cultural theory have turned to psychoanalysis in order to theorize sexual difference and gendered subjectivity. Psychoanalytic categories and theories of difference have been widely used in literary and film criticism, in work on subjectivity and identity and even in postcolonial theory.[1] The appeal of psychoanalysis for feminists lies in its claims to see gender as a psychic and social construct rather than as the natural expression of biological differences between the sexes. This chapter outlines the assumptions about gender difference which underpin psychoanalysis and form the basis for feminist appropriations of Freud and Lacan. It also looks at the development of feminist object relations theory in the United States. The work of Lacan has become central to a number of feminist theories of sexual difference, in particular to French feminist rewritings of psychoanalysis, such as the work of Julia Kristeva and Luce Irigaray. Language plays a central role in these theories where it is often a site of resistance to patriarchy, for example, poetic language in Kristeva and *écriture feminine* in the work of Hélène Cixous. This chapter further examines how feminist rewritings of psychoanalysis privilege the significance of the body of the mother in the acquisition of gender difference and its centrality in feminist attempts to move beyond patriarchal versions of psycho-sexual development. Finally, the chapter looks at more recent developments in psychoanalytic feminism outside France and considers the strengths and limitations of psychoanalytic approaches in the politics of difference.

PSYCHOANALYSIS AND DIFFERENCE

In his controversial essays of 1925, 'Some Psychical Consequences of the Anatomical Distinction Between the Sexes' (1975a; original 1925) and 'Female Sexuality' (1975b; original 1931), Sigmund Freud laid out the implications – as he saw them – of his theory that gender difference is based on the psychical effects of the presence or absence of the penis. As we saw in chapter 1, once she notices a boy's penis, the little girl falls victim to penis envy, recognizing 'the fact of her castration and with it, too, the superiority of the male and her own inferiority' (1975b: 75; original 1931). Whereas the realization of anatomical difference forces boys 'to believe in the reality of the threat' of castration, a belief which is strong enough to destroy the Oedipus complex, in girls it can have a variety of effects. According the Freud these include the development of a masculinity complex which hinders the acquisition of healthy femininity; disavowal of difference, that is, refusal to 'accept the fact of being castrated'; the development of a sense of inferiority; 'the character-trait of *jealousy*'; 'a loosening of the girl's relation with her mother as a love object'; the rejection of masturbation and 'the elimination of clitoral sexuality' which is for Freud, by definition a 'masculine activity' (1975a: 32–3; original 1925). Summarizing his theory, Freud notes:

> I cannot evade the notion (though I hesitate to give it expression) that for women the level of what is ethically normal is different from what it is in men. Their super-ego is never so inexorable, so impersonal, so independent of its emotional origins, as we require it to be in men. Character-traits which critics of every epoch have brought up against women – that they show less sense of justice than men, that they are less ready to submit to the great exigencies of life, that they are more often influenced in their judgements by feelings of affection or hostility – all these would be amply accounted for by the modification in the formation of their super-ego which we have inferred above. (1975a: 36; original 1925)

The fundamental Freudian assumptions that the male body is the desirable norm, and that women's lack of a penis is the key factor determining their intellectual and moral differences from men, were central to early second-wave feminist debates on femininity both within psychoanalysis and beyond. Attempts to reclaim Freud for feminism, for example Juliet Mitchell's ground-breaking book *Psychoanalysis and Feminism* (1975a), tended not to read the penis in biological terms – grounded in the species' need to reproduce itself – but rather as a symbol of the powerful position occupied by men under patriarchy. Commenting on 'Some Psychical Consequences of the Anatomical Distinction between the Sexes', Mitchell writes:

> It seems to me that in Freud's psychoanalytical schema, here as elsewhere, we have at least the beginnings of an analysis of the way in which a patriarchal society bequeaths its structures to each of us (with important variations according to the material conditions of class and race), gives us, that is, the cultural air we breathe, the ideas of the world in which we are born and which, unless patriarchy is demolished, we will pass on willy-nilly to our children and our children's children. (Mitchell 1975b: 49)

Mitchell moves away from any universalist reading of Freud's theory to a position which historicizes it as a theory appropriate to patriarchal capitalist societies.

As many feminists sympathetic to psychoanalysis have argued, Freud was, indeed, a product of his times. He was heavily influenced, for example, in his view of women by the nineteenth-century German philosopher, Arthur Schopenhauer, who described woman as driven by instinct rather than reason and biologically fitted for motherhood: 'she pays her debt to life not by action but by suffering, through the pangs of childbirth, subjugation to the man, to whom she should be a patient and cheerful companion' (Schopenhauer 1977: 28; original 1851). Whether we look at biology, medicine or philosophy in the German-speaking world in the nineteenth and early twentieth centuries, we find similar views of women. Most often they are grounded in anatomical studies. For example, the anatomist Theodor Ludwig von Bischoff (1807–82) published a study of women's skulls and brain sizes, 'Entwarf auf Grund von Hirn- und Schädelstudien eine Theorie über die Minderwertigkeit des weiblichen Gehirnes' (Outline of a Theory of the Inferiority of the Female Brain Based on the Study of Brains and Skulls), which he used as evidence for his conclusion that 'the differences between the sexes concerning both body and mind show without any doubt that the female sex is not suited to study and cultivation of the sciences, especially medicine' (quoted in Dohm 1982: 97).[2] In von Bischoff's view women were biologically destined for motherhood.

Although Freud shared many of the widespread prejudices about women in the period, his work marked a real step forward in its move away from biological determinism. For Freud both femininity and masculinity were psychic *constructs* which were acquired via the process of psycho-sexual development. Gender was not inborn, indeed Freud writes of infants as 'polymorphously perverse'. However, in the acquisition of 'normal' gendered subjectivity, one factor was decisive: the absence or presence of the penis. Femininity took the forms that it did, according to Freud, in response to the absence of the penis in women. Women and femininity were thus defined in terms of lack.

The idea that women are defined by lack rather than by difference in any positive sense, a lack which, in Freud, results in penis-envy, was decisive in early second-wave feminist rejections of psychoanalysis as a thoroughly patriarchal set of theories. Simone de Beauvoir (1972; original 1949) and Betty Friedan (1965; original 1963) both rejected psychoanalytic discourse as defining women as inferior to men. Difference as inequality was also the reading given to psychoanalysis by such classic texts as Kate Millett's *Sexual Politics* (1971), Shulamith Firestone's *The Dialectic of Sex: The Case for Feminist Revolution* (1972; original 1970) and Germaine Greer's *The Female Eunuch* (1970). These books reject psychoanalysis and call instead for theories of the social construction of femininity. Why then have so many feminists turned to psychoanalysis over the last three decades?

In 1970s Britain – the context in which Juliet Mitchell wrote *Psychoanalysis and Feminism* – socialist feminists were attempting to supplement Marxist theory of capitalist societies in ways which would account not only for class but also for patriarchal relations. A move towards psychoanalysis had already been made in Louis Althusser's influential essay 'Ideology and Ideological State Apparatuses (Notes Towards an Investigation)' (1971). Here Althusser drew on Lacan's theory of the structure of subjectivity laid down in his essay 'The Mirror Phase' to produce a general theory of ideology based on the misrecognition of the individual of her/himself as the unified, intentional Subject, the source of meaning. In this conceptualization, ideology is the ever-necessary condition of existence of the conscious subject and conversely 'the category of the subject is constitutive of all ideology' (Althusser 1971: 160). Following Althusser, Mitchell sought to use Freud and Lacan to produce a theorization of patriarchy which could fill the gaps in Marxist theory, enabling women to account for the sexual division of labour, gender and patriarchy. Subsequently many feminists who were interested in using psychoanalysis for feminism tended to move away from socialist feminism and the project of supplementing Marxism and to concentrate on psychoanalysis in its own terms.

Psychoanalysis is concerned first and foremost with the acquisition of what is assumed to be healthy, mature, gendered subjectivity. The basic psychoanalytic presupposition that gendered subjectivity is *acquired* rather than *inborn* accounts for much of the attraction of psychoanalytic theory for feminists. Freud developed a radical theory of the acquisition of gender which assumed that infants are initially ungendered. According the Freud, although infants are born with anatomically sexed bodies, they do not have already gendered psyches. Moreover, for Freud, subjectivity and identity are not only acquired via the processes of psycho-sexual development, they also remain precarious throughout life. In accounting for the transition of the individual from a pre-Oedipal state of polymorphous perversity to maturity, Freud posited the constitution of what he called the 'unconscious'. Those desires incompatible with the laws of sociality, that is, those desires that refuse to conform to the incest taboo and the conventions of mature heterosexuality, are rendered unconscious via repression. The unconscious is the site of meanings and desires, unsanctioned by the laws of society, and it is a constant threat to the apparent unity and sovereignty of the conscious subject.

Feminist theoretical and political writings have engaged with psycho-analysis in a number of ways.[3] The reading of psychoanalytical models of gender difference in each approach varies – sometimes dramatically. For much feminist psychoanalysis the point of departure is Jacques Lacan's rereading of Freud in the light of Saussurean linguistics. Privileging one particular emphasis in Freud's work which can be found in texts such as *The Interpretation of Dreams* (1976; original 1900) and *The Psychopathology of Everyday Life* (1975c; original 1901), Lacan developed Freud's theory of the acquisition of gendered subjectivity into a general theory of society and culture. According to Lacan both meaning and subjectivity are structured in relation to a primary signifier, the Phallus, which governs the symbolic order of society and culture. Control of the phallus is control of the laws and meanings of society. This position of control is the position of the Other. It is not a position open to either men or women. It could only ever be occupied by figures such as the all-knowing, self-present God of the Judeo-Christian tradition. Subjectivity is founded on the misrecognition by the individual of himself as Other. This structure of misrecognition is laid down in the mirror phase.

In the mirror phase the infant learns to misrecognize itself as a whole, unified and autonomous being. The pre-Oedipal experience of the body in fragments, that is the lack of a definite sense of unified, embodied self, separate from the world around it, defines the state of the pre-mirror-phase infant. This is compounded by the lack of control over the satisfaction of needs and desire which will become the motivating force behind language. Governed by a fragmented sense of self and unable to distinguish itself as a separate entity, the infant overcomes its fragmentation by identifying with an 'other', an external mirror image:

> We have only to understand the mirror phase *as an identification*, in the full sense that analysis gives to the term: namely the transformation that takes place in the subject when he assumes an image – whose predestination to this phase-

81

effect is sufficiently indicated by the use, in analytic theory, of the ancient term *imago*.

This jubilant assumption of his specular image by the child at the *infans* stage, still sunk in his motor incapacity and nursling dependence would seem to exhibit in an exemplary situation the symbolic matrix in which the *I* is precipitated in a primordial form, before it is objectified in the dialectic of identification with the other, and before language restores to it, in the universal, its function as subject. (Lacan 1977: 2; original 1949)

This process of misrecognition becomes the basis for all future identifications by the subject of itself as autonomous and sovereign once it has entered the symbolic order of language. In reality subjectivity is divided, based on misrecognition. It is the subject's lack of fullness, lack of self-presence and the power to control meaning that motivates language. The process of assuming subjectivity invests the individual with a temporary sense of control and of sovereignty which evokes a 'metaphysics of presence' (Derrida) in which s/he becomes the source of the meaning s/he speaks and language appears to be the expression of meaning fixed by the speaking subject. Yet, in Lacanian-based theories, the speaker is never the author of the language within which s/he takes up a position. Language pre-exists and produces subjectivity and meaning.

In Lacanian theory the symbolic order is necessarily patriarchal since the difference which makes meaning possible is guaranteed by a transcendental primary signifier, the Phallus. The Phallus has an ambiguous status in Lacan: at times it is symbolic, defining relations of lack shared by both women and men. At other times it can be read a representing the penis. As such, it offers men the possibility of imaginary identifications with the position of the Other, the position of absolute power from which meaning and the Law are defined. The primacy of the Phallus as the signifier of difference means that, for women, subjectivity is a masculine-defined subjectivity. Western thought is thus both logocentric, privileging the word, and phallocentric, privileging the phallus. In feminist appropriations of this theory these two aspects are seen as integrally related. Western culture is phallologocentric. Lack of power and control is the defining feature of subjectivity, but the form this lack takes differs for men and women. Post-Lacanian feminists have taken up the idea of lack developed by Lacan as a structuring principle underpinning the construction of gendered subjectivity in the patriarchal symbolic order. In Lacanian theory, gendered subjectivity is acquired via a process of psycho-sexual development that begins with the pre-Oedipal phase and progresses via the mirror phase the Oedipus and castration complexes, to the formation of the unconscious and the entry of the individual as a gendered subject into the symbolic order of language and the law. It is the acquisition of language in the symbolic order which enables the individual to disavow the lack of unity, power and control on which his or her subjectivity is based.

In both Freud and Lacan lack can be read as taking a gendered form which relates back to the absence or presence of the penis. The centrality of lack is related to the privileging of the penis in the Oedipal phase and in the constitution of gendered subjectivity. It is the fear of castration which precipitates the resolution of the Oedipus complex in boys. The patriarchal symbolic order, structured as it is around the primacy of the Phallus as the signifier of difference, allows men to misidentify with the position of the Other, that is the control of the Phallus and the satisfaction of desire, a position not available to women on account of their status as always already castrated. Women's position in the symbolic order is thus doubly determined by lack. Access to the Phallus is only available to women via motherhood and giving birth to a male child. Moreover, the only positions open to women are male-defined. Most feminist appropriations of psychoanalysis shift their emphasis away from the Oedipus and castration complexes to focus on the pre-Oedipal phase in which the child is said to be in a symbiotic relationship with the mother. It is in this phase that feminists attempt to find the basis for alternative theories of feminine difference which would allow it to be seen in positive terms.

FEMINIST OBJECT RELATIONS THEORY

A return to the pre-Oedipal phase of psycho-sexual development is central to American feminist appropriations of the object relations theory of Winnicott, Fairbairn and Guntrip.[4] Feminist object relations theory – developed in the work of Nancy Chodorow (1978), Dorothy Dinnerstein (1976), Jane Flax (1980), Jessica Benjamin (1988) and Carol Gilligan (1982) – identified distinctive aspects of femininity: 'the powerful and lasting effects of the submerged pre-Oedipus, women's fluid ego boundaries and relationally structured identities, the complicated negotiations and multiple repressions by which women reach adulthood, and their ambivalent but determining mother-daughter bond' (Hirsch 1992: 280). Perhaps the most influential feminist object relations theorist is Nancy Chodorow. Her rewriting of psychoanalysis privileges the pre-Oedipal relationship of the infant with the mother and examines the subsequent differential development of girls and boys. Her theory is outlined in a short chapter in Rosaldo and Lamphere's *Women, Culture and Society* (Chodorow 1974) and developed in detail in *The*

Reproduction of Mothering (1978). For Chodorow, 'the fact that women universally are largely responsible for early childcare' leads her to focus on the conscious and unconscious effects of early involvement with a mother figure for children of both sexes (Chodorow 1974: 43).

Assuming the identification of like with like, Chodorow argues that mothering involves a woman in a double identification: with her own mother and with her child. She repeats the history of her own relationship with her mother, a process which results in a stronger bond between mother and daughter than between mother and son. One important effect of this stronger mother–daughter bond is that girls experience a lesser degree of individuation than boys and thus develop more flexible ego boundaries which create the psychological preconditions for the reproduction of women's subordination to men. In the socialization of boys, mothers encourage them to differentiate themselves from their mother, enabling them to develop a masculine identity based on their father or father substitute. However, the boy's relation with his father is qualitatively different from the girl's relationship with her mother, since the father generally plays a lesser role in child care, working for long hours outside the home:

> As a result, a boy's male gender identification often becomes a 'positional' identification, with aspects of his father's clearly or not-so-clearly defined male role, rather than a more generalized 'personal' identification – a diffuse identification with his father's personality, values and behavioural traits – that could grow out of a real relationship to his father. (Chodorow 1974: 49)

This difference between 'real' personal and positional identification is crucial to Chodorow's account of the differential constitution of femininity and masculinity. In the difficult process of differentiation from his mother, the boy both represses his feminine dimensions and learns to devalue femininity.

In *The Reproduction of Mothering*, Chodorow develops her argument that the differential development of girls and boys affects the emotional capacity of women and men in adult life. Women develop an openness to a range of 'equally deep and primary relationships, especially with their children, and, more importantly, with other women' (Chodorow 1974: 53). Men on the contrary do not develop the capacity for extensive personal relations and 'their relationships with other men tend to be based not on particularistic connection or affective ties, but rather on abstract, universalistic role expectations' (p. 53). Chodorow sees these typical masculine traits as prerequisites for the reproduction of patriarchy.

In this theory women's primary responsibility for parenting lies at the root of gender difference:

Women's mothering produces psychological self-definition and capacities appropriate to mothering in women, and curtails and inhibits these capacities and this self-definition in men. The early experience of being cared for by a woman produces a fundamental structure of expectations in women and men concerning mothers' lack of separate interests from their infants and total concern for their infants' welfare. Daughters grow up identifying with these mothers, about whom they have such expectations. This set of expectations is generalized to the assumption that women naturally take care of children of all ages and the belief that women's 'maternal' qualities can and should be extended to the nonmothering work that they do. All these results of women's mothering have ensured that women will mother infants and will take continuing responsibility for children. (Chodorow 1978: 208)

Chodorow argues that the role that women play in mothering is 'the basis for the reproduction of women's location and responsibilities in the domestic sphere' (p. 208):

This mothering, and its generalization to women's structural location in the domestic sphere, links the contemporary social organization of gender and social organization of production and contributes to the reproduction of each. That women mother is a fundamental organizational feature of the sex-gender system. It is basic to the sexual division of labour and generates a psychology and ideology of male dominance as well as an ideology about women's capacities and nature. (p. 208)

The role which women play as mothers is also central to the reproduction of the patriarchal family:

The sexual and familial division of labor in which women mother creates a sexual division of psychic organization and orientation. It produces socially gendered women and men who enter into asymmetrical heterosexual relationships; it produces men who react to, fear, and act superior to women, and who put most of their energies into the nonfamilial work world and do not parent. Finally it produces women who turn their energies towards nurturing and caring for children – in turn reproducing the sexual and familial division of labour in which women mother. (p. 209)

Chodorow's theory places the acquisition of differential gendered subjectivity firmly within the realm of the social, opening up the possibility, at least in theory, of changing gender norms through the transformation of the social organization of family life. Men's greater personal involvement in child care could, for example, transform the psycho-sexual structures governing masculinity and femininity and create the preconditions for the abolition of the sexual division of labour. Moreover, Chodorow identifies contemporary society as crisis ridden: 'Aspects of this system are in crisis internally and conflict with economic tendencies' (p. 219). Yet whereas Chodorow argues that change is inevitable, change for the better is not. This requires active feminist struggle.

DIFFERENCE IN POST-LACANIAN FEMINISM

If women have no access to society and culture:
  – they are abandoned to a state of neither knowing each other nor loving each other, or themselves;
  – they have no way to mediate the operations of sublimation;
  – love remains impossible for them.
If love for two is to happen, it has to go through the many. However, since society is organized by and for men in our traditions, women are unable to work with plurals. Women have to constitute a social entity if love and cultural fecundity are to take place. This does not mean that it is entirely as men that women come into today's system of power, but rather that women need to establish new values that correspond to *their* creative capacities. Society, culture, discourse would thereby be recognised as *sexuate* and not as the monopoly on universal value of a single sex – one that has no awareness of the way the body and its morphology are imprinted upon imaginary and symbolic creations. (Irigaray 1993: 67–8; original 1984)

Lacanian theory posits a symbolic order which is patriarchal and which, from a feminist perspective, represses or marginalizes anything other than a male-defined feminine. In the Lacanian order women are essentially objects of exchange in what Luce Irigaray describes as a 'homosexual economy', in which men use women as objects of exchange to cement the relations between themselves and women have no active part in the process. (Irigaray 1985: 171–2; original 1977). They are placed both symbolically and socially in relation to men and denied access to what Luce Irigaray calls the maternal feminine, a feminine which would allow them to realize their difference from men in positive terms. In post-Lacanian feminist theory attempts to rethink the symbolic order in non-patriarchal terms focus on the body of the mother and the maternal feminine. However the focus of this work is radically different from Chodorow's theory of mother–child relations.

Under patriarchy the maternal feminine is repressed by the processes of psycho-sexual development which enable the individual to enter the symbolic order as gendered subject. It is further marginalized by the structures of the patriarchal symbolic order which govern the Law, culture and sociality. It is exiled from the symbolic order – an order which women can only inhabit via a patriarchally defined femininity. Post-Lacanian feminists have identified the unconscious as the site of the repressed feminine which has its roots in the pre-Oedipal relationship with the mother, before the feminine takes on its patriarchal definition as lack. Julia Kristeva calls this realm the semiotic, and in her theory it continues to play an integral part in the language of the symbolic order.[5] Luce Irigaray goes further, to suggest that although repressed, the maternal feminine continues to play a role in women's lives. Woman's own desire, 'a desire of which she is not aware, moreover, at least not explicitly ... [is] one whose force and continuity are capable of nurturing repeatedly and at length all the masquerades of femininity that are expected of her' (Irigaray 1985: 27; original 1977). As such the maternal feminine is the potential source for resistance and change.

JULIA KRISTEVA

Feminist appropriations of Lacanian theory have attempted to go beyond the dualistic model of difference, defined by lack, in which women are lesser men. Among the most influential feminist rereadings of Lacan is the work of Julia Kristeva. Her work is wide-ranging, addressing questions of philosophy, theology, linguistics, literature, art, politics, and above all psychoanalysis. In her early work, Kristeva focuses on language as the site for a new politicized theory of the subject. In *Desire in Language* (1982), she summarizes her project as 'to describe the signifying phenomenon, or signifying phenomena while analyzing, criticizing and dissolving "phenomenon", "meaning" and "signifier"' (p. vii). This work on language is part of a broader attempt to challenge the marginalization of the feminine in Western thought.

Kristeva rewrites aspects of Lacanian theory of the constitution of the individual as gendered subject in the symbolic order, reinstating the importance of the feminine, yet effectively detaching it from actual women. In her work, the Lacanian concepts of the Imaginary and the Symbolic become two distinct processes, the Semiotic and the Symbolic, both of which constitute signification. Here the body of the mother plays a central structuring role:

> The mother's body ... mediates the symbolic law organizing social relations and becomes the ordering principle of the semiotic *chora*. ... The semiotic *chora* is no more than the place where the subject is both generated and negated, the place where his unity succumbs before the process of charges and states that produce him. (Kristeva 1986b: 95)

This theory of the *subject in process* is one of the most influential aspects of Kristeva's work. Rather than seeing subjectivity as a fixed, humanist essence, Kristeva sees it as constituted in language and subject to the laws of the symbolic order. Language, with both its masculine (symbolic) and feminine (semiotic) dimensions, becomes a potential site for revolutionary change, an idea most fully developed in Kristeva's *Revolution in Poetic Language* (1984). The language of the symbolic order varies in the degree to which it is governed by symbolic and semiotic dimensions, and poetic language, in particular, is a strong site for the articulation of the semiotic.

In the course of the 1970s, Kristeva's work focused less on literary language and more on psychoanalytic approaches to femininity and mother-hood in the West. For example, her essay 'Stabat Mater' (1986c) looks at the demise of the cult of the Virgin Mary and its implications for understanding motherhood. The essay incorporates Kristeva's own experience of mother-hood and argues that neither traditional idealizations of the virgin mother nor feminist negations or rejections of motherhood are adequate. For Kristeva motherhood marks women's difference and she argues that in the Judeo-Christian tradition it 'is perceived as a conspicuous sign of the *jouissance* of the female (or maternal) body, a pleasure that must at all costs be repressed: the function of procreation must be kept strictly subordinated to the rule of the Father's name' (1986c: 138). Because women's access to the symbolic order is via the Father, it requires the repression of the maternal body. In the process the feminine becomes the unconscious of the symbolic order. The conclusion to be drawn from this is that women must find a third way which allows them access to the symbolic order without their embracing a masculine model of femininity.

Like other theorists whose work has been influenced by poststructuralism, Kristeva emphasizes both process and plurality and resists replacing existing dominant master discourses with alternative grand narratives, be they social-ist, feminist or otherwise. Her own writing plays a role that is analogous to the feminine in relation to the patriarchal symbolic order. It seeks to disrupt monolithic power structures. Thus, for example, in 'A New Type of Intellectual: The Dissident' (1986d) she develops a critique of the possibility of collective political action since, as she sees it, the politically active intellectual is caught up in the very logic of power that she or he seeks to undermine. To speak is to inhabit the kind of discourse permitted by the patriarchal Law of the symbolic order:

> A woman never participates as such in the consensual law of politics and society but, like a slave promoted to the rank of master, she gains admission to it only if she becomes man's homologous equal. A woman is trapped within

the frontiers of her body and even of her species, and consequently feels *exiled* both by the general clichés that make up a common consensus and by the very powers of generalisation intrinsic to language. This female exile in relation to the General and to Meaning is such that a woman is always singular, to the point where she comes to represent the singularity of the singular – the fragmentation, the drive, the unnameable. This is why philosophy has always placed her on the side of that singularity – that fragmentation prior to name or to meaning which one calls the Daemon – she is demonic, a witch. (Kristeva 1986d: 296)

Yet even if the feminine is different or other in relation to existing symbolic language and meaning, it can only be thought within the symbolic. The conclusion to be drawn from this is the need to transform the symbolic order with its patriarchal structuring of difference.

LUCE IRIGARAY

The transformation of the symbolic order is an idea taken up rather differently by Luce Irigaray, whose work is marked by a critique of Western philosophy, rationality and the legacy of the Enlightenment, all of which are seen as founded on the exclusion of the maternal feminine. Like Kristeva, Irigaray writes in the context of the psychoanalytic and poststructuralist questioning of the primacy of conscious rational subjectivity. The idea that the speaking subject is produced within the symbolic order of language effectively decentres the knowing subject of knowledge. Irigaray's critique of Western thought is informed by the postmodern questioning of the foundations of knowledge and its insistence that the conditions of knowledge always lie outside of the knowledge in question. Her diagnosis of the existing symbolic order as one in which reason, the subject and language are male leads her to argue that the West is in fact a *monosexual* culture in which women are seen as a lesser form of men. As she puts it in her influential text *This Sex Which is Not One* (1985; original 1977), women's difference is not represented by the patriarchal symbolic order, nor are women's interests served by the laws and language of this order:

The society we know, our own culture, is based on the exchange of women. Without the exchange of women, we are told, we would fall back into the anarchy (?) of the natural world, the randomness (?) of the animal kingdom. The passage into the social order, into the symbolic order, as such, is assured by the fact that men, or groups of men, circulate women among themselves, according to the rule known as the incest taboo. (Irigaray 1985: 170; original 1977)

In order to be heard within the symbolic, women have to 'speak like men'. The plural, nonpatriarchal feminine remains outside the symbolic order since, under patriarchy, there is only masculine representation:

> To claim that the feminine can be expressed in the form of a concept is to allow oneself to be caught up again in a system of 'masculine' representations, in which women are trapped in a system of meaning which serves the auto-affection of the (masculine) subject. (pp. 122–3)

According to Irigaray the Western tradition is founded on systems of thought in which the exclusion of the maternal feminine becomes the precondition for language and subjectivity. In *This Sex Which is Not One* she explains this position in relation to female sexuality. She argues that:

> Female sexuality has always been conceptualized on the basis of masculine parameters. Thus the opposition between 'masculine' clitoral activity and 'feminine' vaginal passivity, an opposition which Freud – and many others – saw as stages or alternatives in the development of a sexually 'normal' woman, seems rather too clearly required by the practice of male sexuality. . . .
>
> About woman and her pleasure, this view of the sexual relation has nothing to say. Her lot is that of 'lack', 'atrophy' (of the sexual organs), and 'penis envy', the penis being the only sexual organ of recognised value. Thus she attempts by every means available to appropriate that organ for herself: through her somewhat servile love of the father-husband capable of giving her one; through her desire for a penis-child, preferably a boy; through access to the cultural values still reserved 'by right' for males alone and therefore always masculine, and so on. Woman lives her desire only as the expectation that she may at last come to possess an equivalent of the male organ. (pp. 23–4)

In an argument not unlike those found in the North American radical feminism discussed in chapter 2 above, Irigaray posits the likely existence of a different female sexuality in ancient civilizations:

> As Freud admits, the beginnings of the sexual life of a girl child are so 'obscure', so 'faded with time,' that one would have to dig down very deep indeed to discover beneath the traces of this civilization, of this history, the vestiges of a more archaic civilization that might give some clue to women's sexuality. That extremely ancient civilization would undoubtedly have a different alphabet, a different language. . . . Woman's desire would not be expected to speak the

same language as man's, and woman's desire has doubtless been submerged by the logic that has dominated the West since the Greeks. (p. 25)

In the order of reason which has governed Western thought since the rise of Ancient Greek philosophy, feminine otherness is denied and reconstituted as a male-defined otherness. This results in the denial of subjectivity to potentially non-male-defined women. A maternal feminine subjectivity, were it to be realized, would enable women to step outside of patriarchal definitions of the feminine and become subjects in their own right. Whereas the unconscious in Freud and Lacan lays claim to fixed universal status, for Irigaray its actual form and content is a product of history. Thus, however patriarchal the symbolic order may be in Lacan, it is open to change. The question is how this change might be brought about. For Irigaray, the key to change is the development of a female imaginary. This can only be achieved under patriarchy in a fragmented way, as what she terms the excess that is realized in margins of the dominant culture. The move towards a female imaginary would also entail the transformation of the symbolic, since the relationship between the two is one of mutual shaping. This would enable women to assume subjectivity in their own right. Although, for Irigaray, the imaginary and the symbolic are both historical and changeable, this does not mean that, after thousands of years of repression and exclusion, change is easy.

In a move not unlike that of ecofeminists, Irigaray suggests that the symbolic order, men and masculinity are shaped by patriarchy in ways which are immensely problematic not just for women but also for the future of the planet. The apparently objective, gender-neutral discourses of science and philosophy – the discourses of a male subject – have led to the threat of global nuclear destruction. In *An Ethics of Sexual Difference* (1993; original 1984), Irigaray suggests that the patriarchal male subject is himself shaped by the loss of the maternal feminine which motivates a desire for mastery:

> Man's self-affect depends on the woman who has given him being and birth, who has born/e him, enveloped him, warmed him, fed him. Love of self would seemingly take the form of a long return to and through the other. A unique female other, who is forever lost and must be sought in many others, an infinite number of others. The distance for this return can be conquered by the transcendence of God. The (female) other who is sought and cherished may be assimilated to the unique god. The (female) other is mingled or confused with God or the gods. (Irigaray 1993: 60–1; original 1984)

Irigaray takes this theme further in *Thinking the Difference: For a Peaceful*

Revolution (1994; original 1989) when she suggests that the desire for god-like mastery and transcendence has dire consequences for the world:

> Huge amounts of capital are allocated to the development of death machines in order to ensure peace, we are told. This warlike method of organising society is not self-evident. It has its origin in patriarchy. It has a sex. But the age of technology has given weapons of war a power that exceeds the conflicts and risks taken among patriarchs. Women, children, all living things, including elemental matter, are drawn into the maelstrom. And death and destruction cannot be associated solely with war. They are part of the physical and mental aggression to which we are constantly subjected. What we need is an overall cultural transformation. Mankind [*le peuple des hommes*] wages war everywhere all the time with a perfectly clear conscience. Mankind is traditionally carnivorous, sometimes cannibalistic. So men must eat to kill, must increase their domination of nature in order to live or to survive, must seek on the most distant stars what no longer exists here, must defend by any means the small patch of land they are exploiting here or over there. Men always go further, exploit further, seize more, without really knowing where they are going. Men seek what they think they need without considering who they are and how their identity is defined by what they do.
>
> To overcome this ignorance, I think that mankind needs those who are persons in their own right to help them understand and find their limits. Only women can play this role. Women are not genuinely responsible subjects in the patriarchal community. That is why it may be possible for them to interpret this culture in which they have less involvement and fewer interests than do men, and of which they are not themselves products to the point where they have been blinded by it. Given their relative exclusion from society, women may, from their outside perspective, reflect back a more objective image of society than can men. (Irigaray 1994: 4–5; original 1989)

The destructive force of the patriarchal symbolic order makes all the more pressing Irigaray's project of creating a female imaginary and symbolic, specific to women, which might in its turn transform the male-defined symbolic order in the West, in which women figure only as lesser men. In this process, separatism becomes a strategy in the struggle for a non-patriarchal society in which sexual difference is both voiced and valued:

> Let women tacitly go on strike, avoid men long enough to learn to defend their desire notably by their speech, let them discover the love of other women protected from that imperious choice of men which puts them in a position of rival goods, let them forge a social status which demands recognition, let them earn their living in order to leave behind their condition of prostitute – these are certainly indispensable steps in their effort to escape their proletarianization on the trade market. But if their goal is to reverse the existing order – even if

that were possible – history would simply repeat itself and return to phallocrat-ism, where neither women's sex, their imaginary, nor their language can exist. (1994: 106; original 1989)

FEMININITY AS MASQUERADE

In *This Sex Which is Not One*, Luce Irigaray describes the male-to-male, homosexual economy in which women become mere objects of exchange as follows:

> Thus all economic organization is homosexual. That of desire as well, even the desire for woman. Women exist only as an occasion for mediation, trans-action, transition, transference, between man and his man, indeed between man and himself. (Irigaray 1985: 193)

In this economy of the same, relations between women, in particular lesbianism, become equivalent to male homosexuality based on masquerade motivated by penis envy:

> Freud makes this clear in his analyses of female homosexuality.
> A woman chooses homosexuality only by virtue of a 'masculinity complex'. ... Whether this complex is a 'direct and unchanged continuation of an infantile fixation' ... or a regression toward an earlier 'masculinity complex,' *it is only as a man that the female homosexual can desire a woman who reminds her of a man.* That is why women in homosexual relationships can play the roles of mother and child or husband and wife.
> The mother stands for phallic power; the child is always a little boy; the husband is a father-man. And the woman? She 'doesn't exist.' She adopts the disguise that she is told to put on. She acts out the role that is imposed on her. The only thing really required of her is that she keep intact the circulation of pretense by enveloping herself in femininity. Hence the fault, the infraction, the misconduct, the challenge that female homosexuality entails. The problem can be minimized if female homosexuality is regarded merely as an imitation of male behaviour. (Irigaray 1985: 194; original 1977).

The masquerade of 'acting like a man' is, for Irigaray, a serious distortion of the transformative role of relations between women. In her view, relations between women are the precondition for women's escape from the male-defined feminine which patriarchy imposes upon them.

The idea of femininity as masquerade has recently become a popular way of theorizing gender, in particular among feminist queer theorists.[6] Among

93

other influences, this work looks back to an essay by the psychoanalyst Joan Riviere published in the *International Journal of Psychoanalysis* in 1929. This essay, entitled 'Womanliness as a Masquerade', reflects social attitudes to gender in the period, including the assumption that intellectual pursuits are 'masculine'. It also reaffirms Freud's notion that masculinity in women is related to penis envy. Where it is interesting for present-day theory, however, is in the conclusions that it draws about femininity in general, namely that it *is* masquerade. Riviere argues that 'women who wish for masculinity may put on a mask of womanliness to avert anxiety and retribution feared from men' (1986: 35; original 1929). Her argument is based on case studies of women who are successful in areas defined at the time as masculine, especially intellectual pursuits. Riviere recounts in detail one particular case:

> Some time ago, in the course of an analysis of a woman of this kind, I came upon some interesting discoveries. She conformed in almost every particular to the description just given, her excellent relations with her husband included a very intimate affectionate attachment between them and full and frequent sexual enjoyment; she prided herself on her proficiency as a housewife. She had followed her profession with marked success all her life. She had a high degree of adaptation to reality and managed to sustain good and appropriate relations with almost everyone with whom she came in contact.
>
> Certain reactions in her life showed, however, that her stability was not as flawless as it appeared; one of these will illustrate my theme. She was an American woman engaged in work of a propagandist nature, which consisted principally in speaking and writing. All her life a certain degree of anxiety, sometimes very severe, was experienced after every public performance, such as speaking to an audience. In spite of her unquestionable success and ability, both intellectual and practical, and her capacity for managing an audience and dealing with discussions, etc., she would be excited and apprehensive all night after, with misgivings whether she had done anything inappropriate, and obsessed by a need for reassurance. This need for reassurance led her compulsively on any such occasion to seek some attention or complementary notice from a man or men at the close of the proceedings in which she had taken part or been the principal figure; and it soon became evident that the men chosen for the purpose were always unmistakable father-figures, although often not persons whose judgement on performance would in reality carry much weight. There were clearly two types of reassurance sought from these father-figures: first, direct reassurance of the nature of compliments about her performance; secondly, and more important, direct reassurance of the nature of sexual attentions from these men. To speak broadly, analysis of her behaviour after her performance showed that she was attempting to obtain sexual advances from the particular type of men by means of flirting and

coquetting with them in a more or less veiled manner. The extraordinary incongruity of this attitude with her highly impersonal and objective attitude during her intellectual performance, which it succeeded so rapidly in time, was a problem. (p. 36)

Analysis then showed that her behaviour 'was an unconscious attempt to ward off the anxiety which would ensue on account of the reprisals she anticipated from the father figures after her outstanding intellectual performance' (p. 37). Riviere concludes that:

> Womanliness therefore could be assumed and worn as a mask, both to hide the possession of masculinity and to avert the reprisals expected if she was found to possess it – much as a thief will turn out his pockets and ask to be searched to prove that he has not the stolen goods. The reader may now ask how I define womanliness or where I draw the line between genuine womanliness and the 'masquerade'. My suggestion is not, however, that there is any such difference; whether radical or superficial, they are the same thing. (p. 38)

The important point in Riviere's analysis for subsequent feminist theory is the suggestion that all womanliness is masquerade. Appropriations of this idea are discussed further in chapter 5.

Anti-Oedipus

A major critique of feminist appropriations of post-Freudian and post-Lacanian psychoanalysis has come from feminist queer theory which rejects what Judith Butler calls the 'heterosexual matrix' (the assumption of a heterosexual norm as the only possible 'normal' mode of sexuality) underpinning psychoanalysis. This has led both to attempts to rethink Lacanian psychoanalysis, as for example in Butler's exploration of the lesbian phallus, and to engagements with the work of Deleuze and Guattari.[7] Rosi Braidotti, for example, sees Deleuze (together with Foucault) as offering the conceptual tools with which to 'rethink feminist theory' along more politically productive lines (1991: 146). Elizabeth Grosz also draws on Deleuze and Guattari in her attempt to refigure lesbian desire. In her view their work is useful 'because they refuse to structure it with reference to a singular signified, the phallus, and because they enable desire to be understood not just as feeling or affect, but also as doing and making' (1995: 180). 'Deleuze's work', she argues, 'unsettles the presumptions of what it is to be a stable subject and thus problematizes any assumption that sex is in some way the center, the secret, or truth of the subject' (p. 214).

The main focus of Deleuze and Guattari's critiques of psychoanalysis is the normative nature of psychoanalytic theory and the related role of representation in Freud and Lacan:

> Psychoanalysis's great discovery was desiring production, productions of the unconscious. But with Oedipus, this discovery was hastily concealed by a new idealism: the unconscious as factory has been replaced by a classical theatre; the unities of production of the unconscious have been replaced by representation. (Deleuze 1968: 232, quoted in Braidotti 1991: 112)

In *Anti-Oedipus*, they argue for a move beyond the theory of desire and subjectivity found in Freud and Lacan, with its emphasis on the Oedipus complex, the Phallus as transcendent signifier, and desire as lack, to what they call 'schizo-analysis,' in which desire is the basis of all social production:

> Desire produces reality, or stated another way, desiring-production is one and the same thing as social production. It is not possible to attribute a special form of existence to desire, a mental or psychic reality that is presumably different from the material reality of social production. Desiring-machines are not fantasy-machines or dream-machines, which supposedly can be distinguished from technical and social machines. (Deleuze and Guattari 1977: 30)

The relationship between desire and the social is direct, unmediated by Freud's primary processes of condensation and displacement:

> The truth of the matter is that social production is purely and simply desiring production itself under determinant conditions. We maintain that the social field is immediately invested by desire, that it is the historically determined product of desire, and that libido has no need of any mediation or sublimation, any psychic operation, in order to invade and invest the productive forces and the relations of production. (Deleuze and Guattari 1977: 29)

In abandoning the Oedipal framework which structures desire in Freud and Lacan, Deleuze and Guattari embrace what they term the 'organless body'. Sexual difference no longer serves as the basis of subjectivity. This move does away both with the female body as defined by lack and the heterosexual matrix. However, it also entails the disappearance of the female body as specific in its own right. The focus on the body as desiring machine beyond sexual difference is a move which is seen as dangerous by feminist critics in a world where inequality between the sexes still reigns and women are defined in male terms. Irigaray, for example, asks in *This Sex which is Not One* whether Deleuze's desiring machine has not usurped the place of woman or the feminine:

> And don't we run the risk once more of taking back from woman those as yet unterritorialized spaces where her desire might come into being? Since women have long been assigned to the task of preserving 'body matter' and the 'organless', doesn't the 'organless body' come to occupy the place of their own schism? Of the evacuation of woman's desire in woman's body? (Irigaray 1985: 141; original 1977)

Deleuze sees women, whatever their numbers, as a minority which can challenge the system, and move it beyond binary oppositions. He calls this process 'becoming-woman', yet it, too, loses its gender specificity in Deleuze's theory, a move which is also difficult for feminists to endorse. Thus despite her endorsement of the usefulness of Deleuze and Guattari's theory as tools with which to rethink feminism, Rosi Braidotti articulates her reservation about their theory as a whole as follows:

> Deleuze's desiring machines amalgamate men and women into a new, supposedly gender-free sexuality; I shall want to argue, however, that this drive towards a post-gender subjectivity, this urge to transcend sexual difference to reach a state of multiple differentiation is not fully convincing. Although I see the consistency in Deleuze's argument – from his global rejection of binary opposition to the rejection of the man/woman dichotomy in favour of the continuum of interacting embodied subjectivities – I am puzzled by the consequences that this may have for women. Can feminists, at this point in their history of collective struggles aimed at redefining female subjectivity, actually afford to let go of their sex-specific forms of political agency? Is the bypassing of gender in favour of a dispersed polysexuality not a very masculine move? Its masculinity derives from the point that Deleuze explained so clearly: he argued that there is no 'becoming-man', that insofar as he is the empirical referent of a system of domination, man is doomed to the stasis of self-preservation, then indeed the only alternative left is the 'becoming-woman'. But when this 'becoming woman' is disembodied to the extent that it bears no connection to the struggles, the experience, the discursivity of real life women, what good is it for feminist practice? Deleuze's multiple sexuality assumes that women conform to a masculine model which claims to get rid of sexual difference. What results is the dissolution of the claim to specificity voiced by women. The gender-blindness of this notion of 'becoming-woman' as a form of 'becoming-minority' conceals the historical and traditional experience of women: namely of being deprived of the means of controlling and defining their own social and political and economic status, their sexual specificity, their desire and jouissance. A 'multiplicity' or polysexuality that does not take into account the fundamental asymmetry between the sexes is but a subtler form of

discrimination. It reinstates and reinforces women's subordinate position. (Braidotti 1991: 120–1)

CONCLUSION

How then might we summarize the psychoanalytic contribution to feminist debates on the politics of difference? The importance of psychoanalysis for feminist theories of difference undoubtedly lies in its rejection of biological determinism and its insistence on the unconscious dimensions of subjectivity. After the advent of psychoanalysis, it is arguably impossible to think of adequately theorizing either subjectivity or social forces such as sexism and racism without a theory of the unconscious. The usefulness of Freudian and Lacanian psychoanalytic models of the acquisition of gendered subjectivity, however, remains a contested area within feminism, as does their rewriting by feminist theorists ranging from Julia Kristeva and Luce Irigaray to Judith Butler and Elizabeth Grosz.

Like Kristeva and Irigaray, postmodern feminists working outside of France often bring together psychoanalytic and poststructuralist ideas to produce new forms of postmodern feminism. The topics covered range from attempts to theorize the body in non-essentialist ways to moves to dislodge the heterosexism of psychoanalysis. Thus, for example, Judith Butler criticizes the identification of the semiotic in Kristeva with the body of the mother, since, she argues, this gives this body an apparently pre-cultural meaning and status as the source of a necessarily marginalized and repressed feminine, the counterpart to the patriarchal symbolic order. As part of her critique of heterosexual matrix, she further argues that Kristeva's theory denies symbolic meaning to non-heterosexuals, rendering lesbianism unthinkable within the terms of the symbolic order.[8] Critics of these feminist appropriations of psychoanalysis would want to ask whether or not the whole post-Freudian and Lacanian patriarchal edifice is worth reclaiming and transforming. Others, influenced by Foucault's assessment of psychoanalysis in *The History of Sexuality, Volume One* (1981) might want to ask whether the institution of psychoanalysis, both as clinical practice and methods of social and cultural analysis, does not actually produce the forms of sexuality and gendered subjectivity which it claims to describe. Both the postmodern appropriations of psychoanalysis and the Foucauldian critique are discussed in the following chapter, which turns its attention to postmodern feminisms.

CHAPTER 5
The Production and Subversion of Gender: Postmodern Approaches

The body is the primary referent in visually grounded categorizations of people. Modern theories of sexual and racial difference have described and classified bodies according to anatomical, biological and phenotypic characteristics.[1] Nineteenth-century science, in particular, ascribed different intellectual, emotional, physical and sexual qualities to women and men and to different 'races' on the basis of their bodies. It drew on questionable techniques such as phrenology – a science concerned with classifying groups according to the shape of skulls and size of brain – to prove women's intellectual inferiority to men, to identify different races and to ground the supposed inferiority of non-white peoples. This type of science was also used to identify the 'criminal classes'.[2] Today much mainstream and common-sense thinking still assumes that the body is the obvious and transparent sign of a person's gender and race, guaranteeing the meanings and values attributed to them. Bodies are seen as the source of the sexually and racially specific characteristics of the individual and the search goes on for a homosexual gene. Moreover, the gender and racial characteristics popularly ascribed to different bodies still bear traces of nineteenth-century theories of sexual and racial difference which were used to justify social inequalities based on both male and white supremacy. In the case of gender, biologically and psychically based theories of female difference continue to serve as justifications for viewing women primarily in relation to motherhood, domesticity and related forms of paid work.

As we have seen in previous chapters, the female body has been central to a range of feminist approaches to difference. In radical feminist analysis it is the primary site both of women's difference from men, and of the exercise of patriarchal power over reproduction, motherhood, sexuality and women's labour power. For radical psychoanalytic theorists like Luce Irigaray, it is the basis for accessing women's different and repressed imaginary.[3] In socialist feminism, meanings of the body are seen as historically and socially produced in the interests of particular class, gender and racialized interests. However, it is in postmodern forms of feminism that the most developed attempts have been made to theorize the body in non-essentialist and historically specific ways.

Since the 1970s poststructuralist theories of meaning, subjectivity and power have radically challenged approaches to difference which see it as grounded in biology, human nature or in universal structures of the psyche. Often termed 'postmodern', this poststructuralist theory – which draws primarily on the work of Jacques Derrida and Michel Foucault – has challenged the foundational status of the body as the guarantee of both racial and gender difference.[4] The term 'postmodern' remains highly contentious. The range of theories usually described as postmodern includes, in particular, the work of Lyotard (1984) and Baudrillard (1981). Not all commentators would call Derrida or Foucault 'postmodern' and this is a term that Derrida himself has refused when it has been applied to his work on deconstruction. None the less a strong argument can be made that the different forms of poststructuralist theory share a postmodern impulse in their approaches to language, meaning, subjectivity and power. Above all they challenge ideas of fixed meaning, unified subjectivity and centred theories of power. Post-structuralist theory has been taken up by many within feminism as an effective tool for understanding subjectivity, gender and society and for devising strategies for change. However, poststructuralist theory remains controversial and continues to be fiercely attacked on various counts, particularly by radical feminists.[5] This chapter looks at poststructuralist feminism, its conceptions of difference and its implications for feminism as a broad-based political movement. It examines a number of key issues raised by poststructuralism and its feminist advocates and critics. These include gender, the body and subjectivity; identity, difference and the category 'woman'; the question of Truth; feminist narratives; pluralism and relativism; the feminine in Western thought; discourse, power and the body; gender as performance; and postmodern politics. The chapter looks at how post-structuralist approaches to gender have problematized the body as the foundation and guarantee of difference and the implications of this for feminism. It further examines those Foucauldian approaches to the body which theorize it as the effect of power. Poststructuralism and the question of race is discussed in more detail in chapter 7.

GENDER, THE BODY AND SUBJECTIVITY

Since the 1700s feminists in the West have struggled against the dominant meanings given to anatomical difference and their ideological role in restricting middle- and upper-class, white women to the family – the reality for working-class women and women of colour was mostly otherwise. Much of this struggle has been liberal in the sense that activists have argued that despite their biological difference women – given equal access to education – could be as rational, moral and socially active and useful as men. Writing in the 1790s of the effects on women of their limited education, Mary Wollstonecraft argued that such character traits as women displayed were the effects of socialization and education and not of biology:

> I shall not go back to the remote annals of antiquity to trace the history of woman, it is sufficient to allow that she has always been either a slave or a despot, and to remark that each of these situations equally retards the progress of reason. The grand source of female folly and vice has ever appeared to me to arise from narrowness of mind, and the very constitution of civil governments has put almost insuperable obstacles in the way to prevent the cultivation of female understanding. (Wollstonecraft 1975: 144; original 1792)

As was suggested in chapter 1, the classic liberal feminist strategy, when faced with questions of difference, is to accept women's anatomical difference from men but to argue that this does not define women's essential nature. The sexual dimensions of bodies, liberal feminists argue, should not matter when it comes to evaluating humankind. This position implicitly endorsed the long-established mind/body split in Western thought.

After 1968, inspired by the development of radical feminism, much second-wave feminism moved away from liberalism's privileging of women's equality on the basis of sameness to focus instead on women's difference from men. As was argued in chapter 2, radical feminism developed sharp analyses of the many forms of oppression to which women are subject in patriarchal societies. Whereas radical feminist speculations about the origins and continuing basis of patriarchy focus on men's power to control women's bodies – our sexuality, labour and procreative power – they argue that for women patriarchy produces colonized forms of female identity and subjectivity. Radical feminist writing – particularly writing with an ecofeminist tendency – often seeks to offer alternative positive images of women by championing many, of the qualities traditionally ascribed to women, valuing them over traditionally 'male' characteristics and reversing some of the binary oppositions underpinning conceptions of gender in Western societies. This writing has attempted to imagine what a true, non-patriarchally defined femaleness might be. In the process it has looked to women's bodies as a site of female difference and power grounded in women's sexuality and motherhood.

Poststructuralist theory has challenged all theories of sexual and gender difference which appeal to the fixed meanings of bodies. The basis for this challenge is the assumption that there is no such thing as natural or given meaning in the world. Language does not reflect reality but gives it meaning. Meaning is an effect of language and, as such, always historically and culturally specific. Moreover meaning can never be fixed once and for all. It is the effect of what Jacques Derrida calls *différance*, a process of difference and deferral which ensures that any fixing is a temporary retrospective effect. Derrida has further argued that meaning tends to be structured in terms of hierarchical binary oppositions, such as male/female, white/black, advanced/primitive and so on.[6] The fact that language is plural, that signifiers have no one fixed meaning, means that there are many competing definitions of gender difference. Following Foucault, these meanings are produced within a range of institutionally located discourses such as medicine, psychology, religion, fashion, advertising, literature, the media and the arts. Thus, from poststructuralist perspectives, the meanings ascribed to bodies are culturally produced, plural and ever changing. Moreover, these competing meanings are part of broader relations of power and have implications for both women and men. They affect femininity and masculinity as forms of lived and embodied subjectivity and women and men's positions in society. The meanings of different bodies at particular moments in history are thus sites of struggle in which men's and women's interests are at stake. These meanings are constituted within a wide range of often competing and conflicting discourses and are effects of both power and resistance. To insist, for example, that the meanings of 'woman' are neither singular nor stable and are effects of power, including class and racial power, is to suggest that what it means to be a woman varies. This is not, however, to suggest that particular, socially and culturally produced forms of gendered subjectivity do not contain elements which may be shared by women across classes, races and cultures. Nor is it to suggest that particular forms of embodied, gendered subjectivity are somehow inauthentic and not lived as real. Ideas of true femininity and masculinity are replaced by competing discursive constructions of gender. There is no authentic female subjectivity, to be found somewhere beyond discourse or patriarchal ideology, as some early feminists suggested.

The fundamental poststructuralist idea that discourses produce meaning and subjectivity, rather than reflecting them, makes language and subjectivity ongoing sites of political struggle. This struggle involves both the defining and contesting of difference in discourses which have different degrees of power to shape social relations. In poststructuralist approaches which draw on the work of Foucault, discourse is more than linguistic meanings. It is material in the sense that it is located in institutions and practices which define difference and shape the material world, including bodies. For example, dominant nineteenth-century discourses of femininity, which, among other things, denied middle-class women access to higher education, the professions and public life, also prescribed the form that girls' education should take. This had material implications for their physical, intellectual and emotional development, shaping bodies, minds and emotions in particular ways which were thought to be conducive to women's apparently natural roles as wives and mothers. They also defined female modesty in ways which precluded any useful knowledge of the female body and female sexuality. These processes formed the subjectivity of girls and women as embodied subjects in ways which promoted physical, mental and emotional problems.

By the end of the nineteenth century, ideas about healthy women's bodies and minds had changed sufficiently for popular conduct books to launch fierce attacks on the rigorous restriction of girls' minds and bodies. Instead of denying girls and women knowledge of their bodies, sexuality and reproduction, instruction in women's biology and the mechanisms of sexual intercourse were recommended and tight corsets rejected, though still in the interests of healthy motherhood:

[Girls] must know that the corset, in their growing girlhood, prevents their proper development, and in their maturer years restricts them so that lungs, heart, and liver and abdominal organs can do but half their work, and that very poorly. They should be taught that allowing their clothes to hang from their hips is harmful in the extreme, and induces a multitude of ills that unfit them for maternity. . . . One physician has said: 'Woman by her injurious style of dress is doing as much to destroy the race as is man by alcoholism.' Another physician, Dr. Ellis, says, 'The practice of tight lacing has done more within the last century towards the physical deterioration of civilized man, than has war, pestilence and famine combined.' (Drake 1901: 42–3)

This marked a discursive shift – motivated in part by the rise of eugenics – in the politics of women's bodies. Whereas tight corsets had previously signified the desirable norm for women, shaping their bodies accordingly, they are now blamed for a range of female ills, including the so-called degeneration of the race.

Poststructuralist theory suggests that not only meaning, but also individual subjectivity is produced within discourse. Discourses define what it means to be a woman or man and the available range of gender-appropriate and transgressive behaviour. We learn who we are and how to think and behave through discursive practices. Moreover, subjectivity is embodied, and discursive practices shape our bodies, as well as our minds and emotions, in socially gendered ways. In poststructuralism, the individual is never a fully coherent intentional subject as in the liberal tradition. The individual is the site for competing and often contradictory modes of subjectivity which together constitute a particular person. Modes of subjectivity are constituted within discursive practices and lived by the individual as if she or he were a fully coherent intentional subject. The key question here – posed by many feminist critics of postmodernism – is whether this means that we are mere passive effects of discourse, bereft of agency. Poststructuralist feminists would answer in the negative, arguing that it is only by assuming forms of subjectivity, which include the dimension of agency, that we can think, communicate and act in the world.

IDENTITY, DIFFERENCE AND THE CATEGORY 'WOMAN'

Poststructuralist analysis – particularly that which draws on the work of Jacques Derrida – assumes that identity in Western cultures is not something given, it is rather a precarious and temporary effect of difference. The relations of difference involved are historically and socially specific, and they change. For example, men define themselves in relation to women. In this process women become the Other, that is, what men are not. Whiteness is defined in a relationship of difference from conceptions of blackness. Modern Europe defines itself in relation to its colonized and postcolonial Others. Difference in this model is always a relationship and – more often than not – a hierarchical one. The idea that identity is both temporary and precarious, without a firm grounding in natural gender difference, for example, in 'being a woman', has proved controversial within feminism, especially among those writers and activists who see identity as the precondition for effective political action.[7]

The social and cultural status and meaning of woman as a biological category has been at the centre of the debate about the usefulness of poststructuralist theory to feminism – a debate which has been underway since at least the late 1970s. In Britain in the late 1970s, for example, the short-lived but influential journal *M/F* (1978) aroused considerable hostility among feminists for what was seen as its anti-humanist dissolution of the concept 'woman'. How, it was asked, could women organize together and develop new positive identities if there were no essence of womanhood grounded in the shared experience of 'being a woman' on the basis of which women could come together in the spirit of sisterhood? While sisterhood based on shared experience as a woman in a patriarchal society was an important idea in early second-wave feminism, it was soon undermined by the very different experiences of women from different classes and racialized groups or lesbian and bisexual women. These different forms of shared experience became the basis for identity politics. Poststructuralism offered a way of theorizing and explaining both the strengths and limits of an idea of sisterhood that was unproblematically grounded in 'being a woman'. It also complexified ideas of female subjectivity and identity by suggesting that they were internally fractured and often contradictory.

One important focus of feminist poststructuralist analysis has been to deconstruct the binary oppositions on which traditional ideas of difference rest. The process of deconstruction reveals how binary oppositions are not expressions of a natural order, but rather discursively produced under specific historical conditions. The meanings of 'woman' and 'female' are thus cultural and they change. Moreover the binary oppositions which produce these meanings involve hierarchical relations of power and serve particular interests. Often new and resistant identities are formed in reaction to the ways in which hegemonic groups define other groups and individuals. For example, the heterosexist mainstream has long defined homosexuals as 'queer'. Queer in this context is the opposite of 'normal'. As we saw in chapter 3, this signifier, which was for a long time only a term of abuse, has been reappropriated not only by homosexual men but also by lesbians, trans-sexuals, transvestites and some heterosexuals as a form of identity which puts into question the very concept of the normal, suggesting that there is no such thing. From the perspective of queer theory, all sexual practice and all forms of sexual and gender identity are social and cultural. It is patriarchy and heterosexism which privilege some practices and identities over others, defining them as normal or natural.

Concepts of sisterhood in the 1970s had their roots in the radical feminist identification of the global and trans-historical status of patriarchy as a set of material and ideological practices oppressive to women as a class. As we saw in chapter 2, from a radical feminist perspective patriarchal oppression is the primary form of oppression. On the basis of this oppression women everywhere can organize in sisterhood. The assumptions about who 'women' are in early radical feminist writing have, of course, been challenged from within the women's movement by groups of women – working-class, lesbian and of colour – who do not identify with the implicit ideas of woman or women's shared oppression which have underpinned much white, middle-class, feminist polemic. These critiques led directly to what became known as identity politics. In forms of feminism founded on identity politics, women come together on the basis of a shared identity which is often grounded in the idea of an authentic core self:

> Identity, thus understood, supposes that a clear dividing line can be made between I and not-I, he and she; between depth and surface, or vertical and horizontal identity; between us here and them over there. The further one moves from the core the less likely one is thought to be capable of fulfilling one's role as the real self, the real Black, Indian or Asian, the real woman. The search for an identity is, therefore, usually a search for that lost, pure, true, real, genuine, original, authentic self, often situated within a process of elimination of all that is considered other, superfluous, fake, corrupted or Westernized. (Minh-ha 1990: 371)

Yet identity politics can and did allow for a greater degree of complexity than a grounding in ideas of an authentic self might suggest. Identity can be seen as both social and cultural, produced in part in response to oppressive social relations of class, race and sexuality. Writing of lesbian identity politics, for example, Sheila Jeffreys describes how it is possible to recognize difference without denying a shared, if located identity:

> Within Women's Liberation, and lesbian feminism in general, considerable work has been done by Black and ethnic minority women to assert their own different identities without radically destabilising the idea that there is such a thing as a lesbian. This work has been done by Black lesbians, Jewish lesbians, Chicana lesbians, Asian and Indigenous lesbians all of whom have been asserting a lesbian identity. This common identity does probably arise from western urban culture and would not necessarily transfer outside of that arena. Indigenous lesbians in Australia, for instance, have questioned the relevance of a word based on a Greek island for their identity and have pointed out that woman-loving in traditional indigenous culture does not allow room for an urban lesbian identity. (Jeffreys 1996: 368)

Poststructuralist approaches to difference question the foundations of both global and trans-historical accounts of patriarchy and of essentialist forms of identity politics. In the former, women often appear as an obvious and unproblematic category. In the latter, identity comes from belonging to a specific group of women, rather than a category of women as such. Poststructuralism suggests that ideas of shared identity are not the obvious outcome of being of colour, lesbian or working-class but discursively produced in relation to hegemonic discourses which privilege whiteness, heterosexuality and the middle and upper classes. Moreover, they are open to change. New forms of identity are both personally and politically important in resisting sexist, racist and heterosexist definitions of individuals and for imagining a different future. However, the basis for a shared politics in poststructuralist approaches tends to be shared forms of social oppression rather than shared identities.

The idea that we cannot assume in advance what the meaning of the categories 'woman' and 'women' mean has become the site of serious opposition to poststructuralist feminism. Nancy Hartsock, for example, argues that:

> Somehow it seems highly suspicious that it is at the precise moment when so many groups have been engaged in 'nationalisms' which involve redefinitions of the marginalized Others that suspicions emerge about the nature of the 'subject', about the possibilities for a general theory which can describe the world, about historical 'progress'. Why is it that just at the moment when so many of us who have been silenced begin to demand the right to name ourselves, to act as subjects rather than objects of history, that just then the concept of subjecthood becomes problematic? Just when we are forming our own theories about the world, uncertainty emerges about whether the world can be theorized. Just when we are talking about the changes we want, ideas of progress and the possibility of systematically and rationally organizing human society become dubious and suspect? (Hartsock 1990: 163–4)

These objections to poststructuralism and postmodernism rest on the assumption that to question the Western Enlightenment category of the subject is to undermine the possibility of subjecthood. They are shared by many feminist writers who advocate the importance of identity politics and they highlight a fundamental question in poststructuralism about the relationship between a deconstructive approach to subjectivity and the issue of agency. While it is the case that some versions of poststructuralism show little interest in the question of lived subjectivity or agency, this has not been the case in many feminist appropriations of Foucault, Derrida, Deleuze, Irigaray and Kristeva. Here agency is seen as discursively produced in the social interactions between culturally produced, contradictory subjects. Subjecthood is necessary to communication and action in the world and social change requires visions of how societies could be different which are often produced by marginalized groups. Subjectivity and agency are not, however, fixed prior to language and the discursive practices in which individuals assume subjectivity. This is not to say, as some critics have argued, that the material world ceases to exist and is replaced by discourse. It is rather to insist that the meanings of the material world are produced within discourse.

107

THE QUESTION OF TRUTH

All poststructuralist analysis – whether Derridean or Foucauldian in orientation – shares a scepticism towards modern notions of Truth. In this sense poststructuralist theory is postmodern. It questions the major project of modern Enlightenment philosophy and science which is to map the world accurately and to produce true knowledge. Twentieth-century science has long since moved beyond the boundaries of this modern project, recognizing the relative status of different scientific theories. In the arts and human sciences, however, in particular in the realm of politics, modern ideas of truth still play an important role.

Ideas of truth and science have been central in many Enlightenment theories of liberation and progress. Whereas liberal humanism has long subscribed to a narrative of progress based on education and legislation within a parliamentary democracy, the other major modern narrative of progress; Marxism, subscribes to the Enlightenment project of development and progress based on class struggle, which should eventually result in a more just and equal society.

Unlike Marxism, which juxtaposes historical materialism and ideology and asserts that historical materialism can give us access to truth about the world, poststructuralist theory suggests that there is no single truth. In place of Truth we find a range of competing discourses which make truth claims. For example, the natural and social sciences and religion make claims to the truth of their versions of what gender difference means. The competing discourses which constitute the discursive field are equivalent neither in their explanatory power nor in their effects. Nor do their truth claims enjoy equal status. They are hierarchized by the relations of power which inhere within discursive fields, privileging some versions and voices over others. Who and what is privileged is an ongoing site of political struggle.

FEMINIST NARRATIVES AND METANARRATIVES

Since the eighteenth century the Western Enlightenment tradition which includes liberal social movements such as liberal feminism has subscribed to a liberal humanist metanarrative of progress and development. Liberalism urges the rights of the individual to realize him/herself to the full. Humanism posits a sovereign, rational subject with free will and sees reason as the source of human progress. Liberal humanism is a metanarrative that proposes universal human rights and assumes that Western societies are the most

108

developed and humane societies. As such they allegedly offer the most desirable ways of life. According to this theory, progress and development towards a more humane society are the outcomes of rational action, founded on education and the rule of law. As Avtar Brah points out, liberal humanism is a narrative which was even used to justify colonialism; she quotes, for example, John Stuart Mill's description of the form that 'the ideal rule of a free people over a barbarous or semi-barbarous' people should take (Brah 1996: 222). It is a metanarrative increasingly coming under attack in the face of postcolonial critiques, global ecological crises and the massive discrepancies in wealth, health and standards of living between the Third and the First worlds. The liberal agenda of freedom and equality for all tends to assume that it is possible to define what is universally good and true. In practice this has often meant the privileging of a set of Western norms and standards irrespective of their implicit Eurocentricity. On the other hand, conceptions of universal human rights have been and remain central to liberation struggles throughout the world.

One of the key features of postmodern social theory is its challenge to what Jean François Lyotard has called 'grand narratives' of emancipation. Poststructuralist feminists have taken account of this challenge in several ways. First they insist on the cultural and historical specificity of the meanings given to general concepts and precepts such as universal human rights. They argue that while such goals are politically desirable, the actual form they take may exclude and oppress. In campaigning for human rights, it is important not to speak on behalf of others in ways which silence them and obscure real material differences. Indeed the possibility of speaking for others in ways that do not do violence to them has been questioned by postcolonial writers, for example, Gayatri Spivak (1988), whose arguments are discussed in chapter 8. It is, however, equally important not to deny others access to metanarratives of emancipation simply because their origin is Western and they have been used in the past to justify colonialism. Important here is how discourses of human rights are appropriated by oppressed groups. Western feminists, in particular, need to be aware of the implications of measuring the needs of women in other societies simply according to Western norms. Indeed Third World feminist critiques of Western feminism – for example Chandra Mohanty's influential essay 'Under Western Eyes' – argue that Western feminism tends to view Third World women as victims of forms of patriarchy based on less rational and enlightened cultural norms:

> Clearly Western feminist discourse and political practice is neither singular nor homogenous in its goals, interests or analyses. However it is possible to trace a coherence of effects resulting from the implicit assumption of 'the West' (in all

its complexities and contradictions) as the primary referent in theory and praxis. . . . I am trying to uncover how ethnocentric universalism is produced in certain analyses. As a matter of fact, my argument holds for any discourse that sets up its own authorial subjects as the implicit referent, i.e., the yardstick by which to encode and represent cultural Others. (Mohanty 1991: 52, 55)

Mohanty shows how the effects of this strategy in practice are to produce an undifferentiated Third World subject who is a passive victim of patriarchy and tradition, placed outside of history and without agency. These critiques are explored in more detail in chapter 8.

Many feminist critics of postmodern theory claim that the Western Enlightenment discourse of emancipation with its ideas of representation is essential to the feminist project. They argue, among other things, that criticism of the Enlightenment emancipatory project is a luxury available only to those who no longer need it. Thus postmodernism is seen to express 'the claims and needs' of white, privileged Western men who have had their Enlightenment and can afford to be critical (Di Stefano 1990: 75). The assertion by critics of postmodern theory that feminism necessarily stands on Enlightenment ground with women as its constituency is not without political consequences. It begs the question as to whether Enlightenment metanarratives have a monopoly interest in progressive social change. It is also blind to the historically specific class and ethnic interests that structure many feminist Enlightenment narratives. Both poststructuralists and post-modernists argue that no narrative can be truly universal and totalizing. All narratives are necessarily partial, founded on selection and exclusion. As Gayatri Spivak notes: 'We cannot but narrate,' but 'when a narrative is constructed, something is left out. When an end is defined, other ends are rejected, and one might not know what those ends are' (1990: 18–9). Thus the invoking of Western feminist theories – for example, emancipatory liberal feminism or Marxist feminism – as general theories of historical progress often leads to a denial of the specificity of black and Third World women's interests.

PLURALISM AND RELATIVISM

If poststructuralism has been used to question the universalist aspirations of Western Enlightenment discourses of emancipation, where does this leave feminism? It is an often repeated criticism of postmodern thinking that its insistence on the partiality of metanarratives and their truth claims can only lead to pluralism, relativism and ultimately to individualist politics. Critics argue that feminist politics is impossible from within postmodern perspectives because 'feminism itself depend[s] on a relatively unified notion of the social subject "woman", a notion that postmodernism would attack' (Di Stefano 1990: 77). Without the category 'woman', it is argued, we descend into a 'pluralism . . . [that] reduces us to being an other among others; it is not a recognition, but a reduction of difference to absolute indifference, equivalence, interchangeability (p. 77). To avoid relativism, critics argue, women need a shared category 'woman' and a general theory of oppression and liberation.

This challenge to postmodern feminism has been answered in different ways as feminists have attempted to rethink the basis of political action. Diane Elam, for example, in her book *Feminism and Deconstruction*, calls for a feminism based on an 'ethical activism' and a 'groundless solidarity':

> Groundless solidarity is the possibility of a community which is not grounded in the truth of a presocial identity. Solidarity forms the basis, although not the foundation, for political action and ethical responsibility. That is to say, groundless solidarity is a stability but not an absolute one; it can be the object of conflict and need not mean consensus. . . . There is a sense in which groundless solidarity could be said to constitute a moral community, but only in a very limited and restricted sense. This notion of community could not be equated with organic totality, or have a natural foundation any more than it would lay claim to absolute solidarity. The community of groundless solidarity could cross natural borders, just as it might be the meeting place for any number of different ethnicities, religious affiliations, and sexualities, for instance. Groundless solidarity, then, could be understood as a political coalition brought together on the basis of shared ethical commitments, but it would make no claim to inclusiveness. (Elam 1994: 109)

Politically disabling relativism is, thus, not the only alternative to general theories which make universalist truth claims. Poststructuralism and postmodernism can offer partial and located theory and practice. In this context, 'partial' refers to the incomplete and interested nature of both theory and practice. Located theory is grounded by the specificity of the phenomenon or practice which it seeks to explain. Feminist poststructuralist analysis is concerned neither with the abandonment of theory nor of subjectivity. It does not argue for relativism, but rather that theory and practice are necessarily always partial, historically specific and interested. Pluralism – postmodern or otherwise – allows for the representation of many competing and sometimes conflicting voices, histories and interests, for example, black feminist as well as white feminist perspectives. Yet pluralism in societies governed by class, racism, sexism and heterosexism is always structured by

111

relations of power. An adequate feminism requires that the structural relations of inequality between different groups of women and their interests be recognized and addressed. These structural relations may take the form of class, racism, ethnocentrism or heterosexism. Speaking of race, for example, bell hooks argues that 'Postmodern theory that is not seeking simply to appropriate the experience of "Otherness" to enhance the discourse or to be radically chic should not separate the "politics of difference" from the politics of racism' (1991: 26). Difference in this context is structured via the power relations of racism which impose negative meanings on people who are non-white and deny them, as a group, both a voice and equal access to material wealth and social power, circumscribing the degree to which they can realize their differences in positive ways. The exclusion of people of colour from the histories and cultural traditions of Western societies does not mean that they do not figure at all. Rather they become objects in a Western narrative of progress which excludes the history of racist brutality and resistance realized in slavery and colonialism.

THE FEMININE IN WESTERN PHILOSOPHY

> Moreover, woman is always associated with passivity in philosophy. When-ever it is a question of woman, when one examines kinship structures, when a family model is brought into play. In fact as soon as the question of ontology raises its head, as soon as one asks oneself 'what is it?,' as soon as there is intended meaning. Intention: desire, authority – examine them and you are led right back . . . to the father. It is even possible not to notice that there is no place whatsoever for woman in the calculations.
>
> Ultimately the world of 'being' can function while precluding the mother. No need for a mother, as long as there is some motherliness: and it is the father, then, who acts the part, who is the mother. Either woman is passive; or she does not exist. What is left of her is unthinkable, unthought. Which certainly means that she is not thought, that she does not enter into the oppositions, that she does not make a couple with the father (who makes a couple with the son).
> (Cixous 1987: 64)

One of the most important feminist critiques of institutionally validated traditions of knowledge in the modern West has been the highlighting of their androcentrism. 'Man', his history and his culture have been at the centre of modern quests for knowledge in all disciplines. The absence of women as sites and sources of knowledge and culture, and the de-legitimation of forms of knowledge associated with women in the wake of the scientific revolution, became central issues in second-wave feminism. As was argued in chapter 1, many modern theories and studies of sexual and gender difference have taken man as the norm and sought to establish the ways in which women differ from men. Psychoanalysis is a classic example of this approach, but it has long been true, too, of more conventional sciences and social sciences. Until second-wave feminism, for example, very little social scientific research took women or girls as its focus. Although feminists have set out to remedy this state of affairs, it is still a widespread norm. For example, most medical studies of 'general' illness take men as their objects. Androcentrism was also a characteristic of the arts and humanities. History, literature and art history were all preoccupied with men's contribution to society and culture. The rationale for this tended to be the assumption that women's natural primary orientation towards domesticity and reproduction meant that they were either absent from or of insignificant importance in these spheres. Their domain was that of the family and child-rearing.

Yet despite the absence of women from traditions of knowledge in the West, most markedly from philosophy, the 'feminine' has long played a distinct role in male-defined thought. Poststructuralist feminists in particular have pointed to the recent proliferation of discourses of the feminine within mainstream thought which they see as part of the current 'crisis' of the (implicitly male) subject of Western philosophy.[8] As we saw in chapter 4, much postmodern psychoanalytic feminism that draws on Lacanian theory sees the emergence of discourses on the feminine in recent philosophical theory as a symptom of the crisis of the masculine subject. Among the proliferation of discourses of the feminine are those which challenge women's status as silenced 'other'. This challenge is visible not only in the context of a crisis in traditional philosophy but also in a broad-based, diverse feminist movement. Thus, in a range of discourses from North American radical feminism to French feminist psychoanalytic theory, the feminine is ascribed a new and politically creative role: 'the symbolic absence of the feminine is the source of its strength as a counter strategy by which to destabilize the symbolic' (Braidotti 1991: 101). As Rosi Braidotti argues in her book *Patterns of Dissonance*, 'One of the main issues for women in contemporary philosophy is the need to speak about the bodily roots of the thinking process, of all human intellect, and to reconnect theoretical discourse to its libidinal and consequently unconscious foundations' (1991: 8). She continues this line of thought by asking: 'How are women to overcome the objectified state in which they have been fixed by the male gaze? How are women to elaborate a truth which is not removed from the body, reclaiming the body for themselves? How are women to develop and transmit a critique which respects and bears the trace of the intensive, libidinal force that sustains it?' (p. 8). At issue here is the embodied nature of subjectivity and knowledge.

In her analysis of the relations between femininity, women, feminism and philosophical modernity, Rosi Braidotti points to the need 'to analyse philosophy's "marketing of the other" as well as its "becoming woman" in terms of their relation to the theoretical, political and affective transformations brought about in and by the women's movement' (1991: 9). Braidotti has in mind, for example, the ways in which 'woman' and the 'feminine' figure in the work of philosophers such as Derrida and Deleuze. In Derrida's *Spurs* the feminine plays the role of the structurally excluded Other that threatens the illusionary unity of Western philosophy:

> There is no such thing as the essence of woman because woman averts, she is averted of herself. Out of the depths, endless and unfathomable, she engulfs and distorts all vestige of essentiality of identity, of property. And the philosophical discourse, blinded, founders on these shoals and is hurled down these depthless depths to its ruin. There is no such thing as the truth of woman, but it is because that non-truth is 'truth'. Woman is but one name for the non-truth of truth. (Derrida 1979: 50–1)

The metaphorical status of woman in this text as 'one name for the non-truth of truth' symbolises the force of *différance* which undermines all apparent unity and identity.

As was suggested in the previous chapter, for Deleuze women are a force for change which can potentially subvert the traditional structures of philosophy. Deleuze writes that 'Women, regardless of their number, are a minority, definable as a state or a sub-set; but they only create by rendering possible a becoming, which is not their property, which they still have to enter, including those who are not women' (Deleuze 1978, quoted in Braidotti 1991: 108). Here women as a group which includes 'those who are not women' marks a radical departure from any idea of woman grounded in the body. It is a move towards a post-gender world also signalled in Donna Haraway's image of the cyborg which is discussed later in this chapter. Commenting on Deleuze's notion of the feminine, Rosi Braidotti explains:

> In other words, the process of subversion that Deleuze advocates does not aim at a mere reversal of the balance of power, but rather at overcoming the dialectic of identity/otherness which governs classical philosophical thought. Women have a special role to play in this process insofar as they have been the referents for a certain vision of the 'feminine' as simulacrum, or structural 'other' of the classical system of representation. Although women are not the only minority concerned by and involved in criticizing dialectical dualism, they are nonetheless crucial. Thus, Deleuze recognises that the feminine is one of the constant elements of this system, not as a necessary symbolic absence

114

(Lacan) or as an alternative strategy (Derrida); rather it acts as one of the preconditions for conceptuality. (Braidotti 1991: 109)

As we saw in chapter 4, it has been French feminist theorists such as Kristeva, Cixous and Irigaray who have gone the furthest in theorizing the challenge that the feminine offers to Western traditions of thought. Yet even here, what has emerged often has an ambivalent relationship with the sphere of actual women. For Braidotti, as for many feminists influenced by post-structuralist theory, women cannot afford to abandon attention to the embodied nature of the feminine in favour of an idea of 'postgender' in a world where gender difference is material and often the basis for inequality.

In her collection of essays *Nomadic Subjects* (1994), Braidotti sets out to 'redefine the transmobile materialist theory of feminist subjectivity that is committed to working within the parameters of the postmodern predicament, without romantizing it but also without nostalgia for an allegedly more wholesome past' (1994: 4). Drawing on Deleuze, she invokes what she calls the 'political fiction' of the nomadic subject: 'as Deleuze put it, the point of being an intellectual nomad is about crossing boundaries, about the act of going, regardless of destination' (Braidotti 1994: 22–3):

> The starting point, for my scheme of feminist nomadism, is that feminist theory is not only a movement of critical opposition of the false universality of the subject, it is also the positive affirmation of women's desire to affirm and enact different forms of subjectivity. This project involves both the critique of existing definitions and representations of women and also the creation of new images of female subjectivity. The starting point for this project (both critical and creative) is the need to have real life women in positions of discursive subjectivity. The key terms here are embodiment and the bodily roots of subjectivity and the desire to reconnect theory to practice. (Braidotti 1994: 158)

DISCOURSE, POWER AND THE BODY: FOUCAULDIAN PERSPECTIVES

To expose the foundational categories of sex, gender, and desire as effects of a specific formation of power requires a form of critical inquiry that Foucault, reformulating Nietzsche, designates as 'genealogy'. A genealogical critique refuses to search for the origins of gender, the inner truth of female desire, a genuine or authentic sexual identity that repression has kept from view; rather, genealogy investigates the political stakes in designating as an *origin* and *cause* those identity categories that are in fact the *effects* of institutions, practices, discourse with multiple and diffuse points of origin. The task of this inquiry is to center on – and decenter – such defining institutions: phallogocentrism and compulsory heterosexuality. (Butler 1990: viii–ix)

Apart from psychoanalysis and deconstruction, the other central area in which feminists have appropriated and developed poststructuralist theory has been in their engagement with the work of Foucault. Part of the project of this postmodern feminism is to question the foundations of modern theories of sexual difference, racial difference, and heterosexism. It further sets out to show how foundationalist categories such as the body, nature and the normal are discursively produced and are effects of power. Poststructuralism, in its Foucauldian forms, also suggests that embodied subjectivity is an effect of discourses that produce multiple and often contradictory modes of subjectivity. This move away from rationalist views of subjectivity as sovereign intentional consciousness allows for the theorization of women's contradictory subjectivity and their investments in discourses of gender that can be read as oppressive.

Several key feminist concerns figure centrally in Foucault's work: the body as a site of power central to the constitution of subjectivity, the dispersed, discursive nature of power and power's link with knowledge. These ideas are explored in Foucault's historical studies of the penal system, *Discipline and Punish* (1979) and of sexuality. In *The History of Sexuality, Volume One*, Foucault sets out a distinctive approach to power that poststructuralist feminists have appropriated. His model of power is developed in the context of a consideration of how sexuality has functioned to shape and regulate bodies and subjectivities over the last three centuries. His aim in *The History of Sexuality* is to rethink what he calls the 'repressive hypothesis': the theory that since the seventeenth century sexuality has been repressed, 'driven out, denied and reduced to silence' (1981: 4). Foucault argues that the repressive hypothesis is part of a widely accepted, indeed hegemonic juridico-discursive understanding of how power works in society. In this model, power is centred and functions by repression. Juridico-discursive models of power – for example Marxism, psychoanalysis or some forms of radical feminism – assume that power is a negative, limiting relation guaranteed by institutions that uphold a central law, for example, the state in capitalist societies, the law of the phallus in psychoanalysis or patriarchal law in radical feminism. This centred power works uniformly at all levels and throughout society. In the area of sexuality, for example, it works via binary oppositions such as licit/illicit and permitted/forbidden. On the basis of these oppositions, it censors, excludes and denies. While acknowledging that repression has played a role in the deployment of sexuality over the last 300 years, Foucault decentres this role, suggesting that it is merely part of much broader and more complex strategy of power.

> I do not maintain that the prohibition of sex is a ruse; but it is a ruse to make prohibition into the basic constituent element from which one would be able to write the history of what has been said concerning sex starting from the modern epoch. All these negative elements – defenses, censorships, denials – which the repressive hypothesis groups together in one great central mechanism destined to say no, are doubtless only component parts that have a local and tactical role to play in a transformation into discourse, a technology of power, and a will to knowledge that are far from being reducible to the former. (1981: 12)

Feminists have taken up this approach as a more productive and useful way of analysing patriarchy. In the case of sexuality Foucault outlines the proliferation of discourses linked to sexuality which developed in the late eighteenth and nineteenth centuries. These included discourses of population (control of fertility and eugenics), psychology, psychiatry, biology, medicine, ethics and pedagogy (1981: 33). Each of these discourses produced subject positions and embodied forms of subjectivity which governed the behaviour of individuals in the interests of broader strategies of power. They emerge from what Foucault terms localized centres of power and form networks which together constitute an overall strategy. Foucault contests the notion that there is any such thing as sex outside of the range of discourses that constitute sexuality. Postmodern feminists, in particular Judith Butler, have made similar arguments, suggesting that there can be no concept of sex outside of gender, there is only gender. This is discussed further below.

For Foucault, power inheres in all types of relation (familial, sexual, economic and so on). Often we are not even aware of it. He gives the example of the role of confession in the production of sexual subjects. Beginning with the Catholic confessional, this mode of discourse was taken up within a wide range of other discourses, culminating in psychoanalysis at the turn of the last century. It remains central to contemporary popular culture from women's magazines to talk shows. The forms of subjectivity produced within the confessional mode of discourse are, Foucault argues, effects of a form of power which has become so naturalized that we no longer recognize it as such:

> The obligation to confess is now relayed through so many different points, is so deeply ingrained in us that we no longer perceive it as the effect of a power that constrains us; on the contrary, it seems to us that truth, lodged in our most secret nature, 'demands' only to surface; that if it fails to do so, this is because a constraint holds it in place, the violence of power weighs it down, and it can

117

finally be articulated only at the price of a kind of liberation. Confession frees, but power reduces one to silence, truth does not belong to the order of power, but shares an original affinity with freedom: the traditional themes in philosophy, which a 'political history of truth' would have to overturn by showing that truth is not by nature free – nor error servile – but that its production is thoroughly imbued with relations of power. (1981: 60)

Foucault accounts for the hegemony of the juridico-discursive model of power in terms of the possibility that it seems to offer of stepping outside of it. Thus, for example, in this model of power, confession appears to be liberatory. Similarly, to defy censorship appears as an act of freedom which eludes power. Yet, for Foucault, this is an important illusion that allows for the success of a much more complex set of power relations: 'We are dealing not nearly so much with a negative mechanism of exclusion as with the operation of a subtle network of discourses, special knowledges, pleasures and powers' (1981: 72). Against the juridico-discursive theory of power, Foucault sets a decentred model that does not assume in advance any unity of domination or centralization in, for example, the state:

> The analysis, made in terms of power, must not assume that the sovereignty of the state, the form of the law, or the overall unity of a domination are given at the outset, rather, these are only the terminal forms power takes. It seems to me that power must be understood in the first instance as the multiplicity of force relations immanent in the sphere in which they operate and which constitute their own organization as the process which, through ceaseless struggles and confrontations, transforms, strengthens, or reverses them; as the support which these force relations find in one another; and lastly, as the strategies in which they take effect, whose general design or institutional crystallization is embodied in the state apparatus, in the formulation of the law, in the various social hegemonies. (1981: 92–3)

Foucault's view of power is for feminists one of the most controversial aspects of his work.[9] His insistence that there is no escaping power, that it is always already present and that it produces the forms of resistance with which one attempts to counter it is rejected by feminists anxious to hold on to the idea that it is possible to reach a position beyond power. Other feminists argue that Foucault offers no basis for criteria by which to choose between good and bad forms of power. Nancy Fraser, for example, argues that:

> [Foucault] adopts a concept of power that permits him no condemnation of any objectionable features of modern societies. But at the same time, and on the other hand, his rhetoric betrays the conviction that modern societies are utterly without redeeming features. Clearly what Foucault needs, and needs

desperately, are normative criteria for distinguishing acceptable from unacceptable forms of power. (Fraser 1989: 33)

For Foucault decisions about good and bad are political questions which can only be answered in context. He himself insists that he has never 'presumed that "power" was something that could explain everything' (1991: 148).

Against the juridico-discursive model of power as merely repressive, Foucault suggests that we need an 'analytics of power'. He proposes certain guiding principles which might be used in order to identify the nature and workings of power in any area of social and cultural analysis. These include the following propositions:

1 'Power is not something that is acquired, seized, or shared', it is a relationship. (1981: 94)
2 Relations of power inhere in all other types of relationship (economic relations, sexual relations, knowledge relations).
3 Power is not only restrictive and repressive, it is also productive.
4 Power comes from below and from a number of different sources. It is not uniform in the forms that it takes.
5 'Power relations are both intentional and nonsubjective'. (p. 94)
6 'There is no power that is exercised without a series of aims and objectives'. (p. 95)
7 'Where there is power, there is resistance, and yet, or rather consequently, this resistance is never in a position of exteriority in relation to power'. (p. 95)
8 Although arising in local centres, 'No "local centres", no "pattern of transformation" could function if, through a series of sequences, it did not eventually enter into an overall strategy' (p. 99). This is manifest in apparatuses and institutions.

From a feminist perspective, Foucault's analytics of power has both strengths and limitations. It is an approach which enables feminists to theorize both the repressive and productive dimensions of power relations, including relations of power that are patriarchal but none the less offer women forms of subjectivity and pleasure that are experienced as pleasurable. It does not assume a uniformity in the ways in which patriarchal power relations work and it allows for resistance, even as it suggests broader strategies of power which manifest themselves in institutions. However, it denies feminists the security and guarantees of centred models of power which see it as something that can be escaped.

In Foucault's work, discourses produce subjects within relations of power that potentially or actually involve resistance. The subject positions and modes of embodied subjectivity constituted for the individual within particular discourses allow for different degrees and types of agency both compliant and resistant. The discursive field, which produces meanings and subjectivities, is not homogenous. It includes discourses and discursive practices which may be contradictory and conflicting and which create the space for new forms of knowledge and practice. While there is no place beyond discourses and the power relations that govern them, resistance and change are possible from within. In the *History of Sexuality, Volume One* (1981), Foucault gives the example of the homosexual who is the creation of a set of discourses that endow him with a subjectivity which facilitates the production of a resistant reverse discourse:

> As defined by the ancient civil or canonical codes, sodomy was a category of forbidden acts; their perpetrator was nothing more than the juridical subject of them. The nineteenth-century homosexual became a personage, a past, a case history, and a childhood, in addition to being a type of life, a life form, and a morphology, with an indiscreet anatomy and possibly a mysterious physiology. . . . (p. 43)
>
> . . . There is no question that the appearance in nineteenth-century psychiatry, jurisprudence, and literature of a whole series of discourses on the species and subspecies of homosexuality, inversion, pederasty, and 'psychic hermaphrodism' made possible a strong advance of social controls into this area of 'perversity'; but it also made possible the formation of a 'reverse' discourse: homosexuality began to speak on its own behalf, to demand that its legitimacy or 'naturality' be acknowledged, often in the same vocabulary, using the same categories by which it was medically disqualified. (p. 101)

This strategy of turning hegemonic discourses back on themselves can be found, for example, in the mobilization of sexology in the interest of human rights by lesbians and homosexual men at the turn of the nineteenth century, a strategy found in Radclyffe Hall's classic lesbian novel, *The Well of Loneliness*, which was discussed in chapter 3.

FEMINIST APPROPRIATIONS OF POSTSTRUCTURALISM

A range of poststructuralist feminist theorists, influenced to different degrees by Foucault, Deleuze, Lacan and Irigaray, have sought to theorize the body and its relation to difference and gendered subjectivity. Key examples of this development can be found in the work of Jane Gallop, Elizabeth Grosz and Judith Butler. Gallop (1988), for example, challenges the culture–biology opposition as a restatement of traditionally oppressive binary oppositions in which women are placed outside of culture. She argues that it is not biology itself but rather the ideological use made of biology that is oppressive. Like Irigaray, Gallop uses psychoanalysis to develop a different understanding of corporeality in which the female body is a site of resistance to patriarchy, but one which is refused representation by the patriarchal symbolic order. Elizabeth Grosz (1994, 1995) is critical of what she identifies as the tendency in much postmodern writing to analyse the representation of bodies without due attention to their materiality. The exclusion of the materiality of bodies is, she argues, the unacknowledged condition for the dominance of reason. Drawing on a range of twentieth-century philosophers, in particular Foucault, Deleuze and Irigaray, she argues that there are 'two broad kinds of approach to theorizing the body ... in twentieth-century radical thought. One is derived from Nietzsche, Kafka, Foucault and Deleuze, which I will call "inscriptive"; the other is more prevalent in psychology, especially psychoanalysis and phenomenology'. She refers 'to this second approach as the "lived body"' (1995: 33). In drawing this distinction, Grosz works with ideas of the body as 'a surface on which social law, morality, and values are inscribed' versus 'the lived experience of the body, the body's internal or psychic inscription' (p. 33). In an attempt to disrupt the binary oppositions which she sees as defining the body – inside/outside, subject/object, active/passive, fantasy/reality, surface/depth – Grosz variously uses the image of the body as a hinge or threshold, located between psychic interiority and sociopolitical exteriority, and the image of a Möbius strip.[10] This latter image is motivated by the wish to avoid 'both dualism and monism,' to produce 'a model which insists on (at least) two surfaces which cannot be collapsed into one another and which do not always harmoniously blend with and support each other; a model where the join, the interaction of the two surfaces is always a question of power' (Grosz 1994: 189). Grosz concludes that 'sexual differences, like those of class and race, *are* bodily differences' and that 'the body must be reconceived, not in opposition to culture but as its preeminent object' (1995: 32). Moreover, a new language is needed to articulate women's specific difference.

It is, however, in the work of Judith Butler (1990, 1993) that new approaches to embodiment emerge most strongly. Butler is critical of philosophy's tendency to 'miss the body or, worse, write against it' (1993: ix). Using Foucault and psychoanalysis, she attempts to theorize the materiality of the body and the ways in which 'bodies are materialised as sexed' in the light of a critique of heterosexism. She wishes to go beyond the conventional limits of constructionist theories to consider 'how such constraints not only produce the domain of intelligible bodies, but produce as well a domain of unthinkable, abject, unlivable bodies' (1993: xi).

Starting from the premise 'that bodies only appear, only endure, only live within the productive constraints of certain highly gendered regulatory schemas' (1993: xi), Butler suggests a way of theorizing these schemas via the concept of performativity. In other words, gendered subjectivity is acquired through the repeated performance by the individual of discourses of gender. Moreover, Butler argues that 'there is no gender identity behind the expressions of gender. . . . Identity is performatively constituted by the very 'expressions' that are said to be its results' (1990: 24–5). This 'performativity must be understood not as a singular or deliberate "act", but, rather, as the reiterative and citational practice by which discourse produces the effects that it names' (1993: 2). Drawing on Foucault, Butler suggests that such an approach would involve:

(1) the recasting of the matter of bodies as the effect of a dynamic of power, such that the matter of bodies will be indissociable from the regulatory norms that govern their materialization and the signification of those material effects;

(2) the understanding of performativity not as the act by which a subject brings into being what she/he names, but, rather, as that reiterative power of discourse to produce the phenomena that it regulates and constrains;

(3) the construal of 'sex' no longer as a bodily given on which the construct of gender is artificially imposed, but as cultural norm which governs the material-ization of bodies;

(4) a rethinking of the process by which a bodily norm is assumed, appro-priated, taken on as not, strictly speaking, undergone *by a subject*, but rather that the subject, the speaking 'I', is formed by virtue of having gone through such a process of 'assuming' a sex;

(5) a linking of this process of 'assuming' a sex with the question of *identifica-tion*, and with the discursive means by which the heterosexual imperative enables certain sexed identifications and forecloses and/or disavows other identifications. (Butler 1993: 2–3)

Here Butler reiterates several Foucauldian principles: that the body is an effect of power, that embodied subjectivity is discursively produced and that there is no sex outside of culture. Butler's appropriation of Foucauldian theory thus involves a decentred notion of the subject and of agency:

the agency denoted by the performativity of 'sex' will be directly counter to any notion of a voluntarist subject who exists quite apart from the regulatory norms which she/he opposes. The paradox of subjectivation (*assujetissement*) is precisely that the subject who would resist such norms is itself enabled, if not produced, by such norms. Although this constitutive constraint does not foreclose the possibility of agency, it does locate agency as a reiterative or rearticulatory practice, immanent to power, and not a relation of external opposition to power. (1993: 15)

Here Butler, following Foucault, locates resistance and the possibilities of transforming the status quo within the discursive field which produces both existing power relations and forms of subjectivity. There is no possibility within this model of either fully autonomous subjectivity or a space beyond power from which to act. Agency can, however, transform aspects of material discursive practices and the power relations inherent in them.

In bringing Foucault to bear on feminist and queer theory, Judith Butler challenges those distinctions between sex and gender which see sex as the biological basis on which gender is inscribed. For Butler, sex is as much a matter of culture as is gender, and the very distinction between the two is 'the effect of the apparatus of cultural construction designated by gender':

> It would make no sense, then, to define gender as the cultural interpretation of sex, if sex itself is a gendered category. Gender ought not to be conceived merely as the cultural inscription of meaning on a pregiven sex (a juridical conception); gender must also designate the very apparatus of production whereby the sexes themselves are established. As a result, gender is not to culture as sex is to nature; gender is also the discursive/cultural means by which 'sexed nature' or 'a natural sex' is produced and established as 'predis-cursive,' prior to culture, a politically neutral surface *on which* culture acts. (Butler 1990: 7)

Butler's focus on gender as performance and citation has, however, provoked strong criticism from radical feminists. Radical lesbian feminist Sheila Jeffreys, for example, interprets much recent postmodern feminism as part of what she terms a 'return to gender' exemplified in the 'lesbianandgay' theory of Judith Butler, Diana Fuss and others.[11] She argues that these postmodern theorists have invented 'a harmless version of gender as an idea which lesbians and gay men can endlessly play with and be revolutionary at the same time' (Jeffreys 1996: 359). For Jeffreys this marks a dangerous depoliticization. She argues that feminists of the 1970s and 1980s were 'engaged in the task of eliminating gender and phallocentric sexuality' (p. 362). This involved moving beyond the power relations of patriarchy. Not only does postmodernism declare this project impossible, it reinstates a version of gender which Jeffreys sees as 'depoliticised, sanitised and some-thing difficult to associate with sexual violence, economic inequality [and] women dying from backstreet abortions' (p. 359). In lesbian culture, Jeffreys

suggests, the postmodern return to gender is evident in the 1980s rehabilita-
tion of 'role playing and lipstick lesbianism' which Jeffreys sees as far from
subversive, as helping 'to shore up the facade of femininity' (p. 366). Rather
than constituting a political challenge to heterosexist patriarchy, Jeffreys sees
ideas of performative gender, celebrated by feminist queer theory, as a form
of liberal individualism:

> Post-modernist lesbian and gay theory performs the useful function of permit-
> ting those who simply wish to employ the tools and trappings of sexism and
> racism to feel not only justified but even revolutionary. Lesbian role-playing,
> sadomasochism, male gay masculinity, drag, Madonna's mimicry, her use of
> black men and black iconography, Mapplethorpe's racist sexual stereotyping,
> can be milked for all the pleasure and profit that they offer in a male
> supremacist culture in which inequality of power is seen as all that sex is or
> could be. The enjoyment of the status quo is then called 'parody' so that it can
> be retrieved by intellectuals who might otherwise feel anxious about the
> excitement they experience. For those post-modern lesbianandgay theorists
> who have no interest in taking their pleasures in these ways, the ideas of radical
> uncertainty, of the utopian or essentialist nature of any project for social
> change, provide a theoretical support for a gentlemanly liberalism and indi-
> vidualism. (p. 374)

This reading of queer theory draws attention to the dangers inherent in
postmodern approaches to difference that do not pay due attention to the
hierarchical relations of power which produce it.

FEMINIST CRITIQUES OF POSTSTRUCTURALISM AND POSTMODERNISM

> Post-modernism is intent on all these things, in particular in disengagement
> from the self (so that we will enjoy abuse of the body and not object to sado-
> masochism in all its forms); in a denial of our shared experience (so that we will
> not experience the joy of solidarity, of sisterhood, of community – all of which
> are enhanced by diversity); in disengagement from political practice (so that
> we will become fragmented communities, committed to nothing but violence
> and the same old abusive uses of power, crossdressed or not); to the fragmenta-
> tion of society (so that we will not assume any commonality with women from
> other countries or cultures or other times; again we will lose our history); to
> the silencing of all peoples because of the erection of artificial centres (so that
> we in the southern hemisphere, on the rim of the Pacific or anywhere not
> deemed the centre, will never be able to assume others know anything about

us at all; or those of us called epileptic, schizophrenic, or whatever newly invented label, will feel the same). (Hawthorne 1996: 496)

The radical feminist critique of gender as discourse and performance is part of a wider set of objections to postmodern feminism. Indeed poststructuralist and postmodern forms of feminism, as they have developed over the last twenty years, have provoked repeated attacks from many quarters, liberal, Marxist and radical feminist.[12] Whereas radical feminists frequently object to the reliance of postmodern feminists on male theorists, particularly Lacan, Derrida and Foucault, all feminist critics of poststructuralism are worried by the postmodern critique of metanarratives and poststructuralist theories of subjectivity. This is perhaps unsurprising given that liberalism, Marxism and radical feminism all have their own metanarratives and implicit theories of subjectivity which assume a particular type of human essence. Critics also object to what they see as the over-privileging of language, sometimes called the 'linguistic turn' in postmodernism, at the expense of material power relations of oppression: 'Postmodern theory elevated language to a pre-eminent place in the political, the word became reality, the cultural critic became the political activist by wielding a pen and the housewife who gets beaten up by her husband because she leaves one cobweb in a corner becomes strangely invisible' (Jeffreys 1996: 360). Two key factors disappear from view in this critique. One is the explicitly partial and located nature of postmodern feminist interventions. Whereas radical feminist theory tends to relate cultural practices directly to the reproduction of global patriarchal power making direct links between practices constituting gender and the violence of patriarchal power, postmodern interventions focus on specific areas of concern and do not assume that they are necessarily part of a spectrum of oppression, though they may well be. The second is a tendency in postmodern feminism either to privilege the cultural at the expense of the social or to collapse the social and the cultural. When signifying practices are understood only in terms of language, rather than as part of a broader Foucauldian concept of discourse that is material and embodied both in institutions and in individual subjects, social power relations disappear from view. Approaches that use discourse as it is developed in Foucault's later work, however, would approach social structures as forms of power relations which inhere in institutions and discursive fields, rather like Althusser's concept of ideological state apparatuses, but crucially without Althusser's centring of power in relation to the state and the reproduction of the relations of production. In a fully Foucauldian approach, discourse is much more than language; it involves disciplinary mechanisms which take a material form in both social and cultural institutions. Jeffreys thus fails to do

125

justice to the complexity and materiality of feminist approaches that use Foucauldian notions of discourse.

Foucauldian models of discourse and power offer poststructuralist feminists the tools with which to produce analyses that start from detailed examinations of the many localized forms which gender power relations take in a particular area of discursive practice. These then need to be located within broader strategies of power. As Foucault himself explained in an interview with Duccio Trombadori:

> The problems I pose are always concerned with local and particular issues. But I wonder: how could one do otherwise, for example, in the case of madness and psychiatric institutions? If we want to pose problems in a concise, accurate way, shouldn't we look for them in their most particular and concrete forms?
> . . .
> . . . Locating problems is indispensable for theoretical and political reasons. But that does not mean that there are not, however, general problems. After all what is more general in a society than the way in which it defines its relation to madness. Or the way in which society is recognized as 'rationality' personified. And why does society confer power on 'reason' and on its own 'reason'? Why is this rationality made to count as 'reason' in general, and why in the name of 'reason' can the power of some men be established over others? (Foucault 1991: 150–3)[13]

These questions, directed as they are in this example to reason and madness, could throw considerable light on the position of women. Yet Foucault's view of power also remains controversial among feminists who are sceptical towards the postmodern project because, in its critique of the juridico-discursive model, it denies women a place exterior to power from which to ground transformative political action. This lack of grounding is seen to be incompatible with feminism since feminists are said to need a position outside of power from which to speak and act in order to effect change. Poststructuralist feminists argue that the theory that all discursive practices and all forms of subjectivity constitute and are constituted by relations of power is only disabling if power is seen as always necessarily repressive. It is precisely such singular notions of power as repression that Foucault attempted to question in his historical studies.

As we have seen, the Foucauldian assumption that subjectivity is an effect of discourse is another source of controversy among feminists who want to maintain a unified concept of woman and women's experience. For Foucauldian feminists, subjectivity is realized in the material practices of everyday life that are also discursive practices. As Foucault argued in his case studies of psychiatry, the prison and sexuality, forms of subjectivity –

conscious, unconscious, rational and emotional – are produced through socially located discourses. The move away from any fixed qualities of women or femininity, which unite all women and ground politics, disturbs many feminists who are sceptical towards postmodernism.

POSTMODERN POLITICS: THE IMAGE OF THE CYBORG

In her influential essay 'A Manifesto for Cyborgs: Science, Technology and Socialist Feminism in the 1980s' (1990; original 1985), Donna Haraway outlines some key features of a possible postmodern feminist politics. The essay uses the image of the cyborg in a number of ways which relate to a broad range of feminist projects encompassing the need to tackle the nuclear and environmental threats, to utilize new technologies in progressive ways and to transform the inequalities of class, gender, race and sexuality. Haraway uses the cyborg image to undermine ideas of true identity based in nature, psychoanalysis and the heterosexual nuclear family. She invokes this image to suggest the possibility of a 'postgender' world, no longer structured by the family and the public/private divide. In this postgender world the sexed character of bodies would be erased and we would no longer hanker after some mythical originary wholeness but accept and enjoy our multiplicity. Yet the idea of a postgender world remains immensely problematic for feminists since, up until now, the unsexed body has in practice meant the male body. Haraway questions unproblematized ideas of 'women's experience', found, for example, in radical feminism, and seeks to problematize and rethink the binary opposition between nature and culture. She counterpoises multiple and fragmented identities to essentialist ideas of woman. None of this, however, necessarily implies abandoning, as does Haraway, non-essentialist, embodied, sexual difference, a move which is arguably both idealist and politically dangerous in the current political context.

Outside of feminism, cyborgs, for Haraway, signify both the destructive militaristic world of the Star Wars project and the science fiction narratives in which Man controls both nature and the machine: 'From one perspective, a cyborg world is about the final imposition of a grid of control on the planet, about the final abstraction, embodied in a Star Wars apocalypse waged in the name of defence, about the final appropriation of women's bodies in a masculinist orgy of war' (Haraway 1990: 196; original 1985). She argues that in late twentieth-century America, science has breached the boundary between human and animal and that we need to think about the possibilities of this in productive ways. Like many radical feminists and ecofeminists she argues for new ways of seeing humankind's relation to both nature and the

127

animal world and technology. Yet her answer differs radically from ecofeminism with its rejection of technology and its vision of living in harmony with the natural world. Haraway's is a perspective that dissolves fixed boundaries: 'Nature and culture are reworked; the one can no longer be the resource for appropriation or incorporation by the other. The relationships for forming wholes from parts, including those of polarity and hierarchical domination, are at issue in the cyborg world' (1990: 192; original 1985). She argues that we do not have to accept the Star Wars scenario: 'From another perspective, a cyborg world might be about lived social and bodily realities in which people are not afraid of their joint kinship with animals and machines, not afraid of permanently partial identities and contradictory standpoints' (p. 196).

For Haraway, as for other feminists influenced by poststructuralism, recognition of and respect for difference are crucial. She argues forcefully, for example, against singular ideas of feminism founded on essentialist notions of woman:

> It has become difficult to name one's feminism by a single adjective – or even to insist in every circumstance upon the noun. Consciousness of exclusion through naming is acute. Identities seem contradictory, partial and strategic. With the hard-won recognition of their social and historical constitution, gender, race and class cannot provide the basis for belief in 'essential unity'. There is nothing about being 'female' that naturally binds women. There is not even such a state as 'being' female, itself a highly complex category constructed in contested sexual scientific discourses and other social practices. Gender, race or class consciousness is an achievement forced on us by the terrible historical experience of the contradictory social realities of patriarchy, colonialism, racism and capitalism. Who counts as 'us' in my own rhetoric? Which identities are available to ground such a potent political myth called 'us,' and what could motivate enlistment in this collectivity? Painful fragmentation among feminists (not to mention among women) along every possible fault line has made the concept of woman elusive, an excuse for the matrix of women's domination of each other. For me – and for many who share a similar historical location in white, professional, middle-class, female, radical, North American, mid-adult bodies – the source of a crisis in political identity are legion. The recent history for much of the U.S. Left and the U.S. feminism has been a response to this kind of crisis by endlessly splitting and searches for a new essential unity. But there has also been a growing recognition of another response through coalition – affinity not identity. (Haraway 1990: 197; original 1985).

Feminist advocates of poststructuralist theory argue that its questioning of universals and the possibility of objectivity, and its focus on the very criteria by which claims to knowledge are legitimized, provide for theory which can avoid generalizing from the experiences of Western, white, heterosexual, middle-class women. By questioning all essences and relativizing truth claims, postmodern feminisms create a space for political perspectives and interests that have hitherto been marginalized. They also help guard against creating alternative generalizing theories. As Brah explains, 'in practice, proliferating discourses of the "postmodern" encompass various contradictory tendencies, including some that nurture a "flight from politics". Nonetheless, they do all foreground heterogeneity, pluralism, difference and power. And this *re-valorisation of the "multi"* can be made to work in the service of effecting politics which fosters solidarity without erasing difference' (Brah 1996: 227).

While many postmodern feminists acknowledge that there may at times be strategic needs for identity politics, defined by shared forms of oppression and political objectives, they argue that it is important to recognize the nature and limitations of essentialist foundations within identity politics. They propose a theory of identity which sees it as discursively produced, necessary but always contingent and strategic. Commenting on the relevance of postmodern theory to black identity politics, bell hooks suggests, for example, that, while the poststructuralist critique of subjectivity causes problems for black identity politics, it can also be liberating and enabling:

> Criticisms of directions in postmodern thinking should not obscure insights it may offer that open up our understanding of African-American experience. The critique of essentialism encouraged by postmodern thought is useful for African-Americans concerned with reformulating outmoded notions of identity. We have too long had imposed upon us from both the outside and the inside a narrow constricting notion of blackness. Postmodern critiques of essentialism which challenge notions of universality and static overdetermined identity within mass culture and mass consciousness can open up new possibilities for the construction of self and the assertion of agency. (hooks 1991: 28)

A positive and politically useful reading of poststructuralist theory would see subjectivity and identity as socially constructed and contradictory rather than essential and unified. Avtar Brah makes a similar point in her discussion of diaspora and identity:

> Our struggles over meaning are also struggles over different modes of being: different identities (Minh-ha 1989[b]). Questions of identity are intimately connected with those of experience, subjectivity and social relations. Identities are inscribed through experiences, subjectivity and social relations. Subjectivity – the site of processes of making sense of our relation to the world –

129

is the modality in which the precarious and contradictory nature of the subject-in-process is signified or *experienced* as identity. Identities are marked by the multiplicity of subject positions that constitute the subject. Hence identity is neither fixed nor singular; rather it is a constantly changing relational multiplicity. But during the course of this flux identities do assume specific patterns, as in a kaleidoscope, against particular sets of personal, social and historical circumstances. Indeed, identity may be understood *as that very process by which multiplicity, contradiction, and instability of subjectivity is signified as having coherence, continuity, stability: as having a core a continually changing core but the sense of a core nonetheless – that at any given moment is enunciated as the 'I'.* (Brah 1996: 123–4)

Feminist critics of poststructuralism often assume that to question met-anarratives, truth and subjectivity is to undermine the possibility of knowledge and political action in the world. Yet poststructuralism can also be read as rendering both subjects and knowledges provisional and differ-entiated according to the social and discursive location of the 'knowing' subject. Poststructuralist feminists would ask, for example, of Enlightenment narratives of emancipation: 'the emancipation of whom and from what?'. While Enlightenment narratives tend to make universalist claims, speaking, for example, of freedom and human rights for all, the ways in which they are realized in practice are often partial and exclusionary. This requires constant vigilance. Postmodern feminists tend to privilege consciously limited and located narratives and struggles which feed into the broader strategies of power. While postmodern feminists reject essentializing theories, they con-tinue to use theory strategically in the interests of understanding and transforming oppressive social relations. In their work theories have no external guarantee in 'truth' or 'reality', but rather a strategic status. In using theories postmodern feminists look to their material effectivity in the struggle for change. They argue that feminists do not need a single metanarrative in order to develop and use theories in politically effective ways. As post-modernists, we can use categories such as 'gender', 'race' and 'class' in social and cultural analysis but on the assumption that their meaning is plural, historically and socially specific. The effects of using such categories will depend both on how they are defined and on the social context in which they are used.

CHAPTER 6
Class

Leaning against the mop, she looked back at the expanse of floor she had just cleaned and shook her head in resignation at the muddy footmarks that followed her across the wet grey tiles. 'Dey doan care how hard a haffe work,' she thought bitterly, reaching into the pocket of her striped blue overall for the cigarettes she always kept there. She would have to do that hall again and again. That was how it always was in winter. Lighting the tip of the cigarette, she inhaled deeply, leaning back against the wall. The smoke relaxed her and she thought idly of telling them to wipe their feet before coming in, dismissing the thought almost instantly. Some of those white boys . . . you just couldn't talk to them.

'One day,' she vowed to herself, 'one day a gwine tell dem what to do wid dem jab.' She could imagine that, a smile lightening her face as she saw the anger and disbelief she would cause. It lasted as long as the cigarette, a dream, nothing else. She would never dare to tell them anything. Where else could she work? (Riley 1987: 1)

The anger of working class women toward middle class women is justified by lifelong class oppression, and the class system will not be changed until *both* middle class and working class women see how oppressive it is and unite to change it. (Bunch 1987: 101)

The conceptions of difference discussed in previous chapters, although varying radically, all take the body as their referent. Class as a signifier of difference is of a different order. This is not to say that class does not mark bodies. Indeed the materiality of class in terms of health, wealth, leisure and lifestyle clearly shapes them. Of all the categories used to distinguish difference – gender, sexual orientation, race, ethnicity, religion, culture – class has, in recent years, become perhaps the least fashionable. This shift away from considerations of class can be understood in a number of ways. It is due in part to the increasing postmodern scepticism towards general theories of history and society. In the case of Marxism, which has generated the most important theories of class over the last 150 years, doubts about its viability as a social theory have been reinforced by the collapse of socialist systems around the world – systems which claimed to be working towards truly classless societies. In the forefront of this process was the demise of the Soviet Union and its satellite states. This has been accompanied by much more detailed revelations about the negative effects of communist systems in other major countries like China where the Great Leap Forward and the Cultural Revolution can no longer serve, as they did in the late 1960s and 1970s, as icons for a young and idealistic Western youth.[1] However much Western socialists today might want to distinguish their positions from those of the former socialist bloc, socialism is now widely proclaimed as an experiment that failed. Yet the failures of socialism to date mean neither that class has ceased to matter nor that it is an inevitable structuring feature of societies; nor do they mean that Marxist theory has no further explanatory power.

A second and more long-term reason for the shift of emphasis away from considerations of class is the demise of popular forms of working-class identification which were long promoted by the labour movement and other working-class organizations and cultural institutions. In Britain this was a gradual effect of postwar policies such as secondary education and health care for all and the development of a wide-ranging welfare state. It was also an effect of the expansion of the media and with it ideologies of a classless society.

In pre-Second World War Britain, society was more rigidly segregated in class terms, both socially and culturally, than it has become in the postwar period where social mobility has increased. This segregation produced oppositional forms of class struggle in a wide range of areas. The pre- and interwar labour movement, in addition to its work on the wages front, had strong educational and cultural dimensions.[2] The restriction of most working-class children to an elementary education motivated a range of influential and successful adult education organizations, as well as campaigns for secondary education for all. Moreover, there were various cultural organizations – linked to the trade unions and political parties – which focused on questions of capitalism, class and culture.[3] The forms of positive identification promoted by the labour movement were primarily addressed to men. Women barely figured in left-wing political discourse other than in their role as domestic helpmate. The strength and appeal of positive, socialist constructions of working-class identity up to 1945 lay in the history and collective memory of class oppression and the struggle for change. Further sources of positive working-class identities were relatively stable working-class communities and their social institutions such as working men's clubs, chapels and the Co-operative Women's Guilds.

A third factor which throws light on the decline of Marxist theories of class is the development of postmodernity itself. Marxism, and the theories of class derived from it, is a quintessentially modern metanarrative of progress in which societies develop through a series of modes of production which should lead eventually to an egalitarian communist world order. Like other general theories which claim universal validity, Marxism has been relativized by the postmodern questioning of truth and progress and an increasing concern to theorize difference. It has been further reinforced by the tendency within postmodern culture to view differences in tolerant and sometimes even celebratory ways and to take insufficient account of the material social relations of inequality which produce them. The emphasis in recent feminist theory on voicing difference, for example, and on seeing social relations from a position open to and empathetic with the positions of others, sometimes shows tendencies to forget the *structural* relations of inequality which privilege white Western, middle-class, heterosexual women.

Theories of culture in the West before the 1945 – from Marx to Matthew Arnold and T. S. Eliot – tended to assert that bourgeois culture was superior to popular and working-class culture. In Britain all classes subscribed to this view. Indeed left-wing socialist cultural politics was marked by its critiques of popular culture, which was seen as a corrupting influence on working-class consciousness.[4] In the years after 1945, this increasingly became less and less the case. With the development of the postmodern market place came a tendency to play around with commodified signifiers of class, a move manifest in the undermining of high/low cultural distinctions and more especially in the blurring of class codes in popular culture and fashion. This has been accompanied by a tendency in the postmodern affluent West to challenge traditional class-based assumptions about value. For example, the massive spread of international, indeed global, capitalist corporations together with new technologies has brought with it forms of apparently classless popular culture and easy access to 'high' cultural forms. The market-driven commodification of all types of culture and the postmodern tendency to transgress the high/low cultural divide helped to change attitudes. For example, today millions of young people throughout the world – irrespective of class or cultural background – share in globalized forms of youth culture and consumption symbolized by the ubiquity of Coca-Cola and fashions which have their roots in black American ghetto culture. Yet this postmodern play, too, leaves the structural inequalities which produce class difference intact.

In Britain in the 1970s and 1980s, Marxist and socialist feminisms played a pioneering role in the development of feminist theory. Inspired by second-wave radical feminist texts from the USA, women in Britain, often from the New Left, set out to develop a Marxist feminism which might account for both patriarchy and capitalism and the connections between the two.[5] In the course of the 1980s, in response to criticism by black women, other women of colour, lesbian women and other marginalized groups, socialist feminists developed positions which no longer privileged class over a concern with race, gender and sexual orientation. Instead they sought to theorize the specificity of and interrelation between different types of oppression. The British socialist feminist journal, *Feminist Review*, founded in 1979, mirrored these developments and continues to argue for a materialist approach to feminist issues. In the United States where, as Sandra Harding has put it, 'marxian approaches lay beyond the pale of reasonable discussion' (1997: 383), socialist feminism gave rise to what became known as feminist standpoint theory. Standpoint theory, which is discussed in more detail below, had its roots in Marxism, but gradually developed in response to poststructuralism and the growing debate about difference into a position which aims to take account of a range of different and interrelated forms of oppression.

THEORIZING CLASS

How, then, do socialist feminists theorize class in postmodernity? Like most important categories, class is a contested term and its precise meaning depends on the discursive context in which it occurs. Moreover, it is a term which has multiple dimensions and levels. These span its narrow economic definition in classical Marxism to conceptions of class which are primarily social and cultural, as for example, its use to characterize the lifestyle, values and attitudes of particular groups within society. If the labour movement produced positive forms of working-class identity, the postwar period has seen the increasing hegemony of descriptive uses of class, in which it becomes detached from questions of structural difference and of identity and self-perception. For example, the definitions of class found in the censuses and surveys of social trends are based on job, income, lifestyle, taste, etc.[6] These constructions of class tend to be male-focused, and married women, in particular, become subsumed within their husband's class. Yet even in this broader usage, class is linked to questions of wealth, education and preferred cultural pursuits which are themselves connected to an individual's position within the labour market and access to wealth.

As Raymond Williams points out in *Keywords*, the history of the term 'class' is complex. Class has, of course, long been used as a general term of classification and in the educational context. In addition to this, Williams (1976: 59) identifies three significant further uses:

1   an objective social or economic category;
2   rank, i.e. relative social position determined by birth or social mobility;
3   a formation (which Williams defines as a perceived economic relationship and social, political and cultural organization).

The main distinction in play in these different uses is between those restricted to social and economic position and those which imply particular forms of culture and social organization. A further distinction is that between uses which imply value judgements – for example, inferior culture – and those that do not. These different usages are found in socialist feminism where, for example, particularly in the United States, feminists write about the oppressive interpersonal relations between middle- and working-class women, as well as about class as an economic category.

The development of Marxist theory from the 1840s onwards was a key factor in the rise of the term 'class' as a central signifier in theories of social difference. Writing in the *Communist Manifesto* of 1848 Marx and Engels argued that:

> The history of all hitherto existing society is the history of class struggles. Freeman and slave, patrician and plebeian, lord and serf, guildmaster and journeyman, in a word, oppressor and oppressed, stood in constant opposition to one another, carried on an uninterrupted, now hidden, now open fight, a fight that each time ended, either in a revolutionary re-constitution of society at large, or in the common ruin of the contending classes. . . .
>
> Our epoch, the epoch of the bourgeoisie, possesses, however, this distinctive feature: it has simplified the class antagonisms. Society as a whole is more and more splitting up into two great hostile camps, into two great classes, directly facing each other: Bourgeoisie and Proletariat. (Marx and Engels 1969: 40–1; original 1848)

In Marxist analysis, the capitalist mode of production is founded on a fundamental class antagonism between capital and labour. Class is first and foremost an economic category and class position is determined by whether or not an individual has access to control of the means of production. The capitalist class owns the means of production: the capital to set up and run

135

factories and employ labour to produce both goods and surplus value. The proletariat has only its labour power, that is, its ability to work.[7] In the day-to-day running of capitalist economies, the capitalist pays labour as little as possible and labour organizations fight to improve wages and conditions. In modern capitalist states, which do not rely on indentured or slave labour, the relations between capital and labour appear in the form of contracts between individuals – worker and employer – freely entered into. These relations of production are secured by ideology which is embedded in social and cultural practices. Thus class as an economic category also has crucial ideological dimensions.

Marx's own uses of the term class in different contexts involve both class as an economic category and class as a social and cultural formation. Writing, for example, of the French peasantry in the *Eighteenth Brumaire of Louis Bonaparte*, Marx argued that:

> Insofar as millions of families live under economic conditions of existence that separate their mode of life, their interests and their culture from those of other classes and put them in a hostile opposition to the latter, they form a class. (Marx 1975: 124; original 1852)

Here class is conceived of as an objective economic category with social and cultural effects. Marx goes on to argue that:

> Insofar as there is merely a local interconnection among these small-holding peasants, and the identity of their interests begets no community, no national bond and no political organization among them, they do not form a class. (p. 124)

In play here is the crucial Marxist political distinction between a class *in itself* – a group that shares a particular economic status and the social and cultural factors derived from this – and a class *for itself*, class as a self-conscious social and political movement and identity. In Marx's second definition the peasantry is not yet a class for itself and it would have to become one for revolutionary social change to occur. This distinction was taken up in relation to women as a group in feminist appropriations of Marxism, for example in feminist standpoint theory.

In Marxist theory, economic class position affects consciousness. As Marx himself put it in his early formulation in the *German Ideology*:

> We set out from real active men, and on the basis of their real life-process we demonstrate the development of the ideological reflexes and echoes of this

life-process. The phantoms formed in the human brain are also, necessarily, sublimates of their material life-process, which is empirically verifiable and bound to material premises. Morality, religion, metaphysics, all the rest of ideology and their corresponding forms of consciousness, thus no longer retain the semblance of independence. They have no history, no development; but men developing their material production and their material intercourse, alter, along with their real existence, their thinking and the products of their thinking. Life is not determined by consciousness, but consciousness by life. (1970: 47; original 1845)

The idea of life determining women's consciousness became important in socialist feminism, which, like other forms of feminism, privileged women's experience. The early Marxist model of ideology as 'phantoms' which are 'sublimates of [man's] material life process', was taken up by some second-wave socialist feminists in the 1970s and applied to patriarchy. They argued that under patriarchy women lived ideologies which, though related to their material position, offered a false image of it, promoting false consciousness.[8]

In early feminist standpoint theory in the United States, feminists appropriated the Marxist idea of the proletariat as a potentially revolutionary class for itself and extended it to women. Thus, just as for Marxists a grasp of historical materialism by the working class could facilitate an understanding of working-class exploitation within the labour process, so socialist feminism could enable women to understand the structural relations producing patriarchal forms of oppression. Nancy Hartsock, one of the pioneers of feminist standpoint theory, wrote in 1983 that 'the concept of a standpoint rests on the fact that there are some perspectives on society from which, however well intentioned one may be, the real relations of humans with each other and with the natural world are not visible' (1983a: 117). Women's position in society, she suggests, enables them, with the help of feminist theory, to gain 'a particular and privileged vantage point on male supremacy' (1983b: 284).

Much more influential in the development of second-wave socialist feminism in Britain was the theory of ideology sketched by Louis Althusser in his essay 'Ideology and Ideological State Apparatuses (Notes Towards an Investigation)' (1971) which became central to much Marxist feminism of the 1970s and 1980s. This approach to ideology, which sees it both as a condition of existence for human societies and as a set of material practices, is discussed in detail below.

In addition to feminist writing which treats class as structural, socialist feminism has also produced analyses of oppressive class behaviour. Indeed a striking feature of much US writing on class is its emphasis on its social as

137

opposed to structural dimensions. Class is seen to involve the oppressive assumption of social and cultural superiority by middle- and upper-class women:

> When class became an issue in the development of a lesbian feminist move-ment in D.C., I was apprehensive. Theoretically, I knew that class divisions existed and ought to be abolished, but I did not connect that to my behavior or to what was happening to women in the movement. Of course, I did not imagine that I was a class supremacist. Only after months of struggle (or should I say, fights, hostility, withdrawal, trauma) did I begin to understand that much of my behavior stemmed from being middle class and was oppressive to working class women.
>
> I finally recognized that class in our society is not only an economic system that determines everyone's place, but also patterns of behavior that go with and reflect one's status. When middle class women carry these attitudes and ways of behaving into the movement, it oppresses working class women. Class divisions and behavior come from male-dominated society, and it is absurd for us to perpetuate them. If middle class women remain tied to male class values and behavior, we cripple our growth and hinder the development of a movement that can free all women. Class struggle is not a question of guilt; it is a question of change, for our movement's survival.
>
> Classist behavior is rooted in one basic idea: class supremacy – that individuals of the upper and middle classes are superior to those of the lower classes. Middle class people are taught to think that we are better, and we act out that 'superiority' and self-righteousness daily in a thousand ways. Class supremacy, male supremacy, white supremacy – it's all the same game. If you're on top of someone, the society tells you that you are better. It gives you access to its privileges and security, and it works both to keep you on top and to keep you thinking that you deserve to be there. It tells you over and over that the middle class way is the right way and teaches you how to keep that way on top – to control people and situations for your benefit. No one in our movement would say that she believes that she is better than her working class sisters, yet her behavior says it over and over again. (Bunch 1987: 97–8)

SOCIALISM AND FEMINISM: LESSONS FROM THE FIRST WAVE

> The social democratic women's movement proves its equal importance as part of the revolutionary struggle for liberation by its clear separation in theory and practice from the fight for women's rights and bourgeois reformism. (Zetkin 1976: 56)

Socialist feminism of the first wave, extensive though it was, could not serve as a positive model of political organizing for women of the second wave.

When first-wave feminism put women's emancipation firmly on the polit-ical agenda in the years between 1880 and the First World War, the socialist movement could not help but respond. Nowhere was this response more clearly articulated than in Germany, the source of the highly influential text *Woman in the Past, Present and Future* (1971; original 1878) by August Bebel (subsequently retitled *Women and Socialism*), and home to internationally well-known women activists who wrote on the woman question, in partic-ular, Clara Zetkin.[9] First-wave feminism in Germany saw the development of parallel bourgeois and proletarian women's movements. Like other socialist feminists, Zetkin maintained a critical distance from all wings of bourgeois feminism and argued strongly that it was a class-based movement which did not serve the interests of the majority of women. She urged the importance of Marx's work for understanding the position of women and the economic and social changes necessary for their emancipation:

> Marx's works also make clear that the proletariat is the only revolutionary class, able to create, with a socialist society, the necessary social preconditions for the complete solution of the woman question, and this is something that it must do. Apart from the fact that the bourgeois struggle for women's rights neither will nor can fight for the social liberation of the working class woman, it is also incapable of resolving the difficult new conflicts which must arise from the social and legal equality of the sexes in the capitalist order. These conflicts will only disappear when the exploitation of people by people and the contra-dictions which they produce are overcome. (Zetkin 1977: 59)

The development of a proletarian women's movement in Germany was the result both of the Prussian Combination Act which forbade women access to political organizations and a recognition by activists that women had differ-ent needs and interests which must be addressed if they were to be won over to socialism.[10] Thus, for example, Ottilie Baader reported to the First International Congress of Socialist Women in 1909:

> If they [the women comrades] wanted to bring socialism to the mass of proletarian women, they had to take into account these women's political backwardness, their emotional peculiarities, their twofold burden at home and in the factory, in short, all the special features of their existence, actions, feelings and thoughts. Accordingly, they had in part to adopt different ways and means in their work, and seek other points of contact, than the male comrades did in their educational and organizational work among the male proletariat. (quoted in Thönnessen 1976: 30)

Proletarian women activists, like their male colleagues, rejected the notion that gender should be addressed separately from class. They argued that class society was the basis for women's oppression which required a fight directed at capitalism and not at men. Following arguments found in both Bebel's *Women and Socialism* and Frederick Engels' *Origin of the Family, Private Property and the State* (1972; original 1884), the key to women's oppression was seen to be the link between private property and monogamy which emerged in the course of history. Both writers drew on *Ancient Society* (1877) by the American anthropologist L. H. Morgan in their accounts of the origins of women's oppression. Engels argued that the development of private property with the emergence of class societies led to women's enslavement within the family and loss of social power. The answer was to reverse this situation by involving women in the productive process. Full emancipation would come when the process of production was fully socialized under communism. Engels' theory was taken up and sympathetically discussed at some length by socialist feminists of the 1970s and helped to shape the wages for housework campaigns.[11] His position was based on the assumption that the freeing of women from financial dependence on men would lead to other necessary changes in patriarchal social organization, a principle which was put into operation in the postwar period by the newly established socialist state in Germany, the German Democratic Republic, which is discussed below.

Bebel's and Engels' positions were popularized by first-wave socialist feminists. In her influential pamphlet *The Question of Women Workers and Women at the Present Time*, published in 1889, Zetkin argued that women had been oppressed since the demise of matriarchal law. This state of affairs had been rendered seemingly natural by morality and religion, whereas, in reality, it was a product of the relations of production in any period. Thus women had both an economic and reproductive role in the pre-capitalist family and lived a life equivalent to that of a domestic slave. Under capitalism this economic function was transferred to the factory, a process which both destroyed the basis of family life and created the conditions for women's emancipation. The first step in this path to liberation was an end to that economic dependence on men which had legitimated sexual exploitation. Thus Zetkin fought hard against the moves by men in the German Social Democratic Party to restrict women's access to work. This widespread tendency within many national labour movements was motivated by the view that access to work made women into competitors with men for jobs in which they were often seen as responsible for the lowering of wages. It was further strengthened by the desire of many working-class families to achieve a position similar to those middle-class families in which the wife and mother could afford to stay at home and care full-time for her husband and children.

WOMEN AND SOCIALISM IN EASTERN EUROPE: THE CASE OF THE GDR

In the GDR, where Marxism-Leninism provided officially sanctioned ways of understanding social relations, the emancipation of women was seen as an economic question linked to women's participation in the workforce under socialist relations of production. After the founding of the GDR, legislation was introduced to provide the material support necessary to enable women to work outside the home. This was above all an economic necessity given the shortage of labour power. An ideological campaign was also launched to persuade women to take up paid work. In 1968 further legislation sought to encourage positive discrimination towards women in education, training and promotion. In contrast to West Germany, many of the long-standing demands of German feminism, which were taken up in the Federal Republic by second-wave feminism, were met in the GDR by the East German state. These included, for example, contraception, abortion, equal pay and state nursery care. Yet in spite of such provisions and even the positive discrimination legislation of 1968, women remained concentrated in jobs with less economic and social power than men and continued to bear primary responsibility for home and children. Other issues on the Western feminist agenda, however, such as interpersonal and sexual relations between women and men, lesbianism, the sexual division of labour, and social norms of femininity and masculinity remained unexplored in the GDR until a new wave of women's fictional writing in the 1970s and 1980s began to question them.[12] Yet, even then, 'feminism' and 'patriarchy' remained terms from which most East German women chose to distance themselves, identifying them with a radical feminism which they saw as irrelevant to GDR society.

CLASS IN SECOND-WAVE FEMINISM

Where then does class analysis figure in contemporary feminism? As was suggested in the first two chapters of this book, classical liberal feminism, concerned as it is with the freedom and rights of women as abstract individuals, tends to show relatively little interest in questions of class. Where class is addressed, this is through discourses of equal opportunity and freedom of choice. Early second-wave radical feminism appropriated the term class from Marxism and applied it to all women as a group irrespective of the many differences between them. This identification of women as a class which

141

suffers universal patriarchal oppression served as the basis for a theory of classless, global sisterhood but failed to pay attention to the materially different social positions of, among others, middle- and working-class women and white women and women of colour. The goals and objectives which a largely middle-class movement defined in its early years did not take sufficient account of class inequality. This became obvious, for example, when working-class women and women of colour scrutinized the assumptions behind feminism's demands. More recent radical feminist writing often acknowledges the importance of class; however, the theory and practice underpinning it still tends to render the precise effects of class on the constitution of differences between women secondary or invisible. Moreover, class is often seen as an effect of male-dominated society, an analysis which privileges patriarchy over other forms of power:

> Understanding class behavior among women is a useful way to begin to understand class as a political mechanism for maintaining not only capitalism but also patriarchy and white supremacy. . . .
>
> Class distinctions are an outgrowth of male domination and as such, not only divide women along economic lines but also serve to destroy vestiges of women's previous matriarchal strength. For example, women in peasant agricultural, and lower class cultures are often called 'dominant' because they retain some of that matriarchal strength. Male-supremacist societies must try to eliminate this female strength. A primary means of doing this in the United States and in other countries is through the domination and promotion of middle class values, including an image of the female as a passive, weak, frivolous sex object, and eager consumer. Thus, the class system not only puts some women in a position of power over others but also weakens us all. Analyzing how patriarchy, white supremacy, and capitalism reinforce one another is crucial to the future of feminism. (Bunch 1987: 94–5; original 1974)

MARXIST FEMINISM

It is in the socialist feminist tradition that class has been most important. In the postwar West, the development of socialist feminism took a very different path from the way in which the woman question was addressed in socialist Eastern Europe. Until the advent of second-wave feminism there was little obvious presence of socialist feminism on the Left. This changed radically in the 1970s when women influenced by both the New Left and the advent of second-wave feminism in the United States made a concerted attempt to develop a Marxist feminism which could account for both capitalism and patriarchy. Unlike turn-of-the-century socialist feminists, women of the second wave refused to defer questions of women's liberation until after a socialist revolution. While they endorsed the importance of understanding the ways in which existing patriarchal relations are grounded in the capitalist mode of production, they refused to reduce patriarchy to capitalism.

Much of early second-wave work on gender in the early 1970s, particularly in Britain, was focused on the relationship between capitalism and patriarchy. Attempts were made to extend the parameters of Marxism to address women's oppression, but also to complement the absences and blind spots within Marxism where gender was concerned. Attempts to apply Marxism to the position of women led to analyses of women's economic position within capitalist economies. Marxist feminists asked how patriarchal gender relations helped to maintain and reproduce the social relations of capitalism. This perspective was applied to a wide range of different areas and issues. For example, in the 1970s, Marxist feminists in Britain did considerable work on women's position in the labour market. They argued, for example, that capitalism has an interest in maintaining gender identities and relations which guarantee a low-paid expendable female workforce in manufacturing and service industries, a largely feminized and low-paid public sector, and an unpaid workforce to care for children, the elderly and disabled in their own homes. They further argued that this benefits men since it gives them privileged access to better paid jobs, public life and leisure outside work. The gender-segregated, low-paid female workforce served as a reserve army of labour for capitalism:

> It is through a consideration of patriarchal and capitalist relations inseparably structuring the sexual division of labour that we must consider women as a reserve. Economically, for capital they are a reserve like any other; from the point of view of women's subordination, the *specific* characteristics of female labour are, as we shall see, *defined by* women's position as a reserve. Thus the *particular* articulation of women's subordination through their position as a reserve is only a general economic benefit to capital. Our interest in female labour as a reserve does not then quite place it within the terms in which Marx defines 'reserve army of labour'. Married women at least do not become a reserve because they are thrown out of social production, but *become available* for social production with advances in commodity production and hence consumption. (Bland et al. 1978: 62)

Marxist feminism also raised the question of extending the Marxist notion of productive labour to include the hidden area of unpaid domestic labour which was essential for the reproduction of the workforce. One solution to

143

this problem of unpaid, hidden labour was seen to lie in wages for housework – a socialist feminist campaign in several Western countries in the 1970s:

> Wages for housework demands us to look at women's work and at women's lack of money. The facts are familiar to many of us: a 1970 survey by Chase Manhattan Bank showed that the wives of Wall Street employees work 99.6 hours a week in the home, performing services that would cost $257.53 on the open market. (Poorer women presumably spend even more time on housework, with fewer babysitters and appliances, more mending and budget food preparation.) Without money of our own, women are often trapped. Unpaid work is 'worthless' – as experience in finding a paid job, in 'economic terms' (no one includes it in the GNP) and for self-value in a money oriented society. Economic dependence has kept many women in intolerable marriages. (Lovelock 1995: 77; original 1978)

In their broader analyses, Marxist feminists stressed that patriarchy predated capitalism and that an extended perspective was needed to understand its structures and persistence. Both August Bebel and Frederick Engels in the 1870s and 1880s had suggested that patriarchy originated with the development of private property. However the forms of economic analysis and solutions that this perspective suggested did not seem adequate to second-wave Marxist feminists. It was the areas of sexuality and human reproduction – privileged by radical feminism – which demanded a much more adequate theorization and here ideology was seen to play a crucial role. In their search for a more adequate theory of ideology and subjectivity, British Marxist feminists of the 1970s looked to the work of the French structuralist Marxist, Louis Althusser, in particular his essay 'Ideology and Ideological State Apparatuses' (Notes Towards an Investigation)' (1971), and attempted to extend the type of analysis found in this essay to patriarchy.

Althusser's essay, which falls into two main parts, is concerned with what he calls ideological state apparatuses and the role they play in the reproduction of capitalist relations of production. These apparatuses include the family, which Althusser suggests, together with education, is the most important ideological apparatus under capitalism. It plays a central role in the reproduction of a willing workforce and the other social strata that make up society. Unlike the police, the army and the courts – the Repressive State Apparatuses – the Ideological State Apparatuses 'function massively and predominantly *by ideology*, but they also function secondarily by repression, even if ultimately, but only ultimately, this is very attenuated and concealed, even symbolic' (Althusser 1971: 138). They operate by interpellating individuals as subjects within specific ideologies. These subjects internalize particular meanings and values as obvious and true. Marxist feminists extended Althusser's arguments about Ideological State Apparatuses to suggest that the reproduction of society took not only class but gendered forms which were also produced by these apparatuses.

In the second part of his essay, entitled 'On Ideology,' Althusser theorized what he termed 'ideology in general' which is the precondition of both subjectivity and human sociality. At the centre of this theory is the category of the 'subject' which 'is constitutive of all ideology insofar as all ideology has the function (which defines it) of 'constituting' concrete individuals as subjects' (p. 160). In this theory Althusser draws on Lacan's theory of the constitution of the imaginary subject in the mirror phase, a process based on a structure of misrecognition. This use of Lacan signalled what was seen as an important way forward for Marxist feminism in the 1970s: the move into psychoanalysis as a way of complementing Marxism. It was this perspective which informed Juliet Mitchell's important book *Psychoanalysis and Feminism* (1975a). Yet Marxist feminism also brought an economic perspective to bear on a range of other central feminist issues, which affect ideology and subjectivity, such as pornography, advertising and the sex industry.[13] In each case Marxist feminists argued the need for the practice in question to be seen as a capitalist industry as well as a key site for the exploitation of women's bodies and the patriarchal construction of sexuality.

British Marxist feminism of the 1970s was motivated by the wish to develop Marxist theory to a point where it might adequately theorize gender as well as class. Yet to remain Marxist ultimately meant to privilege economic relations over other forms of power at least in the last instance. The feminist refusal to prioritize class over gender remained a problem in the eyes of orthodox Marxists and led in part to the development of what soon became redefined as socialist feminism, a term which was taken not to imply the necessary privileging of class relations over gender, sexuality or race.

Like radical and liberal second-wave feminisms, Marxist feminism, too, had failed in its early years to take account of race. By 1980, black feminists were making their voices clearly heard in their critiques of Marxist feminism for its blindness to questions of race:

It is not just our herstory before we came to Britain that has been ignored by white feminists, our experiences and struggles here have also been ignored. These struggles and experiences, because they have been structured by racism, have been different to those of white women. (Carby 1982: 219)

These critiques were extended by black and Third World feminists to include the absence of questions of imperialism and colonialism. Critiques of the limits of Marxist feminism also came from lesbian feminists who argued for the necessary inclusion of the effects of heterosexism in any adequate feminist analysis.[14] In the USA feminist standpoint theory was also subject to critiques of its failure to address differences other than those produced by class.

The political challenges to socialist feminists to take differences seriously and develop theories which might help people to understand the mechanisms by which they are constituted in hierarchical and oppressive ways have been strengthened in the realm of theory by the increasing impact within feminist circles of poststructuralism. Since the latter half of the 1980s, socialist feminism has taken a stand on the importance of different types of oppression in any analysis of patriarchal societies, in particular class and race. It has taken as its founding principle the non-hierarchization of different form of oppression and their integral relation to one another. In the process many socialist feminists have looked to poststructuralist theory, in particular that developed by Foucault.

DEVELOPMENTS IN SOCIALIST FEMINISM

How then is difference conceptualized in recent socialist feminist analysis? The first point to be made is that, for socialist feminism, difference is material. Drawing variously on Althusser's definition of ideologies as material practices located in state apparatuses and Foucault's theory of the materiality of discourses, socialist feminism suggests that gender is constituted in material practices that are governed by power relations of class, race and heterosexism as well as patriarchy. Ideologies of gender are thus much more than ideas. They are realized in the practices of everyday life and they are not only material but are also historically and socially specific. Moreover, economic interests will always play a part in constructions of gender, whether this be the need to maintain an unpaid domestic labour force or the modes of femininity and masculinity propagated by the sex industry. We cannot, however, know in advance of any analysis what the role of the economic will be.

Socialist feminism insists on a vision of a different future which requires the transformation of the whole of the social order. Much activist socialist feminism is still rooted in the institutions of the broader labour movement. Feminists work in the trade union movement, the Labour Party and on the picket lines. This involvement at a grass roots level often cuts across classes. Thus, in the Miners' Strike in Britain in 1985, working-class women from various mining communities around the country formed support groups engaging in public politics as never before (see figure 6.1). Support for the miners also came from feminist groups of all sorts. In socialist feminist

6.1 Miners' strike: Women demonstrating in London, 11 August 1974. Photograph: Jenny Matthews/Format

analysis, exploitative class, race and gender interests will persist until capitalism as a social system is transformed. Class, race, and location affect all areas of life, from the sexual division of labour to sexuality, motherhood and family life. Ideology as a set of material practices, linked to class, race and gender interests, is fundamental to the reproduction of patriarchal, racist, heterosexist capitalism. Socialist feminism insists on the recognition that relations of difference are for the most part relations of inequality and exploitation, however innocuous they may appear in the postmodern market place. It rests on an ethics which does not support pure forms of cultural relativism, even as it seeks to avoid the pitfalls of Eurocentrism and to understand the structuring effects of imperialism in both its colonial and postcolonial forms.

THE DEVELOPMENT OF FEMINIST STANDPOINT THEORY IN THE UNITED STATES

In 1983, the publication of Nancy Hartsock's *Money, Sex and Power* changed the landscape of feminist theory. . . . The central concern of the book, and the

147

source of its lasting influence, is Hartsock's epistemological and methodological argument. Her goal is to define the nature of the truth claims that
feminists advance and to provide a methodological grounding that will
validate those claims. The method she defines is the feminist standpoint.
Borrowing heavily from Marx, yet adapting her insights to her specifically
feminist ends, Hartsock claims that it is women's unique standpoint in society
that provides the justification for the truth claims of feminism while also
providing it with a method with which to analyze reality. (Hekman 1997:
341)

The key assumptions of feminist standpoint theory are that knowledge is
always situated – it is the product of a particular set of material relations – and
that it is produced from a range of different standpoints. Moreover the forms
of knowledge produced from different material positions are not all equally
valid. Some positions allow better access to the real conditions governing
society. Nancy Hartsock, for example, argues that 'the concept of a standpoint rests on the fact that there are some perspectives on society from which,
however well intentioned one may be, the real relations of humans with each
other and with the natural world are not visible' (Hartsock 1983a: 117). Thus
whereas the ruling group in society represents its own partial perspective as
true, oppressed groups can achieve a more accurate view of society. Just as,
within Marxism, historical materialism offers the means of a true analysis of
society, so feminism can enable women to see the material relations governing their lives in a truer light which can form the basis for change. In 'The
Feminist Standpoint' (1983b), Hartsock argues that a feminist version of
historical materialism 'might enable us to lay bare the laws of tendency which
constitute the structure of patriarchy over time' (p. 283). It was precisely
women's structural position within patriarchal societies that provided the
basis for a better understanding of social relations. 'Women's lives', Hartsock
suggests, made 'available a particular and privileged vantage point on male
supremacy' (1983b: 284).

Feminist standpoint theory initially confined itself to questions of gender.
However, in response to the increasing political pressure in the 1980s to
address multiple forms of oppression, and the impact of poststructuralism,
standpoint theorists began to diversify standpoint theory. Donna Haraway's
essay 'Situated Knowledges: The Science Question in Feminism and the
Privilege of Partial Perspective' (1991b; original 1988) was particularly
influential here. Haraway emphasizes standpoint theory's debt to Marxism,
recounting how 'Marxist starting points offered a way to get to our own
versions of standpoint theories, insistent embodiment, a rich tradition of
critiquing hegemony without disempowering positivisms and relativisms
and a way to get to nuanced theories of mediation' (1991b: 186; original

148

1988). Moving beyond Marxism in the direction of poststructuralism, she argues against global metanarratives:

> We also don't want to theorize the world, much less act within it, in terms of Global Systems, but we do need an earthwide network of connections, including the ability partially to translate knowledges among very different – and power-differentiated – communities. We need the power of modern critical theories of how meanings and bodies get made, not in order to deny meanings and bodies, but in order to build meanings and bodies that have a chance for life. (Haraway 1991b: 187; original 1988)

While critical of global narratives, Haraway does not endorse a relativism that abandons all truth claims. She suggests that the natural, social and human sciences have always striven to explain the world and their explanations have proved reductionist when they have privileged one point of view:

> Science has been about a search for translation, convertibility, mobility of meanings, and universality – which I call reductionism only when one language (guess whose?) must be enforced as the standard for all the translations and conversions. What money does in the exchange orders of capitalism, reductionism does in the powerful mental orders of global sciences. There is, finally, only one equation. That is the deadly fantasy that feminists and others have identified in some versions of objectivity, those in the service of hierarchical and positivist orderings of what can count as knowledge. That is one of the reasons the debates about objectivity matter, metaphorically and otherwise. Immortality and omnipotence are not our goals. But we could use some enforceable, reliable accounts of things not reducible to power moves and agonistic, high-status games of rhetoric or to scientistic, positivist arrogance. (1991b: 187–8; original 1988)

Like many of the postmodern feminist theorists discussed in chapter 5, Haraway insists on the importance of the body, suggesting that the denial of the embodied nature of knowledge leads to the (white, male, middle-class) 'conquering gaze from nowhere':

> I would like to proceed by placing metaphorical reliance on a much maligned sensory system in feminist discourse: vision. Vision can be good for avoiding binary oppositions. I would like to insist on the embodied nature of all vision and so reclaim the sensory system that has been used to signify a leap out of the marked body and into a conquering gaze from nowhere. This is the gaze that mythically inscribes all marked bodies, that makes the unmarked category claim the power to see and not be seen, to represent while escaping representation. This gaze signifies the unmarked positions of Man and White, one of the many nasty tones of the word 'objectivity' to feminist ears in scientific and

technological, late-industrial, militarized, racist, and male-dominant societies, that is, here, in the belly of the monster, in the United States in the late 1980s. I would like a doctrine of embodied objectivity that accommodates paradoxical and critical feminist science projects: Feminist objectivity means quite simply *situated knowledges*. . . . (1991b: 188; original 1988)

Whereas reductionist Western narratives of objectivity rely on the mind/ body split, Haraway suggests that 'feminist objectivity is about limited location and situated knowledge, not about transcendence and splitting of subject and object. It allows us to become answerable for what we learn how to see' (1991b: 190; original 1988). This is the basis for Haraway's redefinition of science. For Haraway the feminist standpoint theorists' goal is 'an epistemology and politics of engaged, accountable positioning' which she equates with 'better accounts of the world, that is, "science"':

> Above all rational knowledge does not pretend to disengagement: to be from everywhere and so nowhere, to be free from interpretation, from being represented, to be fully self-contained or fully formalizable. Rational knowledge is a process of ongoing critical interpretation among 'fields' of interpreters and decoders. Rational knowledge is power-sensitive conversation. (1991b: 196; original 1988)

Haraway further suggests that oppressed groups do not automatically possess the ability to see social relations more clearly: ' "Subjugated" standpoints are preferred because they seem to promise more adequate, sustained, objective, transforming accounts of the world. But *how* to see from below is a problem requiring at least as much skill with bodies and language, with the mediations of vision, as the "highest" technoscientific visualizations' (1991b: 191; original 1988). As in the Marxism which gave rise to standpoint theory, how to see from below remains a political problem.

CONCLUSIONS

Second-wave socialist feminism has its roots in Marxism. Going beyond traditional Marxism, it sought from its inception to bring together class and gender. Like liberal and radical feminists, socialist feminists learned in the 1980s from critiques of their work by women of colour and lesbian women that any claims to explain patriarchy were undermined by the collapsing of differences between women. Whereas socialist feminists have always insisted on the importance of class, they failed initially to take account of questions of race, colonialism and sexual orientation. More recent work has sought to put this right.

Even in the postmodern West, class differences remain tied to questions of access to wealth, power and the ability to shape the nature of the society in which we live. Differences in wealth, which have increased in the Western world over the last two decades, affect access to education, type of work, material quality of life, health, lifestyle and access to the institutions which control the distribution of wealth and other forms of social power. They also affect cultural codes of femininity and even the female body itself.

Class continues to matter for feminism to the degree that the movement seeks fundamental changes in the position of all women. As socialist feminists have long argued, this implies fundamental changes in the social order as a whole. Yet this change necessarily has implications for the privileges enjoyed by middle- and upper-class women. The insistence on the importance of class to feminist analysis, and grass roots involvement with organizations representing working-class interests, has enabled socialist feminists to maintain links with a wider constituency of women. At base socialist feminism remains a social and intellectual politics committed to a new social order.

CHAPTER 7
Race, Racism and the Problem of Whiteness

Racism, the belief in the inherent superiority of one race over all others and thereby the right to dominance. Sexism, the belief in the inherent superiority of one sex over the other and thereby the right to dominance. (Lorde 1984: 115)

The reason racism is a feminist issue is easily explained by the inherent definition of feminism. Feminism is the political theory and practice to free *all* women: women of color, working-class women, poor women, physically challenged women, lesbians, old women, as well as white economically privileged heterosexual women. Anything less than this is not feminism, but merely female self-aggrandizement. (Smith 1983b: 61)

By and large within the women's movement today, white women focus upon their oppression as women and ignore differences of race, sexual preference, class and age. There is a pretense to a homogeneity of experience covered by the word *sisterhood* that does not in fact exist. (Lorde 1984: 116)

Gender is rarely the only significant biologically grounded signifier of social and cultural difference. In racist societies, where whiteness is hegemonic, skin colour and phenotype are inescapable markers of difference. However much an individual might want to escape racial categorization and be seen merely as an individual, s/he finds her/himself confined by white societies' implicit and explicit definitions of whiteness and racial otherness. These definitions are not merely the property of prejudiced individuals, they are structural, inhering in the discourses and institutional practices of the societies concerned.

The major emancipatory discourses which developed in the Western world in the wake of the Enlightenment – liberal humanism, Marxism and feminism – were, at the same time, universalist in their aspirations and Eurocentric in their assumptions and practices. They assumed that white Western cultures and societies were the most advanced while at the same time assimilating racist stereotypes of people who were not white. They further failed to recognize the significance of structural racism to their projects.

Skin colour and phenotype are among the most important signifiers of difference in contemporary Western societies. In racialized thinking these physical characteristics of individual bodies serve as the guarantee for racial classification. Race is often assumed to be natural, yet race, as we think of it today, is very much a product of modernity. The classification of people into supposedly distinct races began in earnest in the eighteenth century with the development of the natural sciences.[1] The categories which writers in the modern period used to construct ideas of racial difference have never been purely descriptive. They included an evaluative dimension which linked character to body and privileged the category of Caucasian bodies over all other types.[2] The meanings attributed to nineteenth-century racial categories included value judgements about beauty, intellect, morality, emotionality, sexuality and other physical capacities. These judgements about the meaning of racial difference – whether implicitly or explicitly racist – were used to justify practices such as colonialism, slavery and segregation and they have become part of an often-unquestioned set of assumptions which still permeates Western cultures today. They surface in common-sense thinking, popular and 'high' culture and help to structure the everyday practices of institutions ranging from education and policing to social welfare and medicine.[3]

Racist ideas and imagery take two main forms. There are those that define difference in purely negative terms and those that, in fixing the nature of Others, celebrate their difference from a white Western norm. This latter celebration most often takes the form of 'primitivism'. In primitivist discourses, the white world's Others are seen as closer to nature, more authentic and less contaminated by modern industrial society. Like many discourses on women, primitivism variously sees non-Western, non-white Others as more spiritual, more intuitive, more physical, more sensual and more sexual. The obverse of this is that they are defined as less rational and less sophisticated than their white Western counterparts.[4]

Like the nineteenth-century constructions of difference from which they derive, contemporary racist images of non-white people – both negative and celebratory – vary between different groups and they are often gender-specific. In Britain, for example, popular racist stereotypes of people from South-east Asia and the Indian subcontinent are not the same as those of people of African descent. Western racism has tended to define people from the East as exotic, sensual, irrational and sometimes violent. Irrationality and violence are stereotypes regularly applied, for example, to Saddam Hussain's Iraq and to Muslim fundamentalist regimes. People of African descent are more often characterized as lazy, less intelligent, hypersexual, physically strong, likely to excel in sport and endowed with natural rhythm. These racist definitions of people who are classified as non-white are produced via sets of binary oppositions. The unspoken counterparts to the qualities attributed to people of colour – for example rationality, enterprise and suppression of emotion – are assumed to be quintessentially white. The persistence of these racist stereotypes has meant that women and men of colour continue to face ingrained, centuries-old prejudices that construct their Otherness in negative and exotic ways. They are denied those qualities seen as white except, perhaps, in the case of 'exceptional' individuals.

UNMARKED WHITENESS

Classical racism consistently placed white people at the top of its scales of racial difference, seeing them as the most advanced of the different races. In the late twentieth-century Western world this assumption lives on both in the ideologies of the radical Right and in the normative status usually given to whiteness by mainstream society.[5] Whereas right-wing extremism privileges whiteness as a racial category, this is rarely the case outside of these circles. In mainstream discourses of race, whiteness functions as an unmarked neutral category, a norm which is equivalent to being human. Rather than being a racially marked category, whiteness signifies an absence of colour. Discourses of race are silent about the status of whiteness as a socially and historically changing construct and its role in the perpetuation of racist assumptions. One consequence of this failure to recognize the racialized nature of whiteness is that race and racism come to be seen as the problem and responsibility of people of colour. Audre Lorde powerfully voices this issue:

> Whenever the need for some pretense of communication arises, those who profit from our oppression call upon us to share our knowledge with them. In other words, it is the responsibility of the oppressed to teach the oppressors their mistakes. I am responsible for educating teachers who dismiss my children's culture in school. Black and Third World people are expected to educate white people as to our humanity. (Lorde 1984: 114–15)

Viewed from a white perspective, the invisibility of whiteness as a

154

racialized category in the Western world often makes it difficult for those white people who benefit from racism to realize their part in maintaining the status quo. This has been the case with the women's movement. As second-wave feminism developed, the emphasis placed on patriarchy, shared oppression and sisterhood tended to render questions of race invisible. It took vocal protests by black women and other women of colour to begin to open the eyes of white women to their complacency where race was concerned.

There have tended to be three common responses by white feminists to the question of racism. The first is a liberal refusal to see racialized difference. This finds expression in assurances such as: 'I am not prejudiced. Colour doesn't matter to me. We are all the same'. Implicit in this response is the assumption that racism is an individual rather than a structural phenomenon that pervades all social institutions and practices. As bell hooks points out in relation to the American experience, the predominance of individualized, personal explanations of racism and sexism leads to a failure to perceive the causal structural relations producing racism and sexism.

> American women of all races are socialized to think of racism solely in the context of race hatred. Specifically in the case of black and white people, the term racism is usually seen as synonymous with discrimination or prejudice against black people by white people. For most women, the first knowledge of racism as institutionalized oppression is engendered either by direct personal experience or through information gleaned from conversations, books, television, or movies. Consequently the American woman's understanding of racism as a political tool of colonialism and imperialism is severely limited. To experience the pain of race hatred or to witness that pain is not to understand its origin, evolution, or impact on world history. (hooks 1986: 119; original 1982)

The reduction of racism to individual prejudice involves a refusal on the part of white women to recognize that black women have structurally different social positions, overdetermined not only by gender and class, but also by racism.

A second common response to racism among white women is a disabling sense of guilt which often leads to inaction. In order to move beyond guilt white women need to address their own racial privilege. They need to recognize their role in perpetuating racist social relations, either actively or passively via the failure to take racism seriously and challenge its effects:

> For as long as any difference between us means one of us must be inferior, then the recognition of any difference must be fraught with guilt. To allow women of Color to step out of stereotypes is too guilt provoking, for it threatens the

complacency of those women who view oppression only in terms of sex.
(Lorde 1984: 118)

A third response is to recognize racism as a problem that affects women of
colour but to see it as a 'black' problem rather than one that should be
fundamental to the lives of white women. This position is often justified by
statements such as 'Of course I abhore racism but I have no right to speak for
women of colour'. Missing in this analysis is the recognition that racism is
grounded in a binary *relation* of difference in which whiteness is the dominant
term. Racism functions by privileging whiteness. To fail to question this
privilege is to leave intact the binary oppositions on which racist discourse is
founded. The idea that racism is a 'black' problem marks a position from
which women fail to see that the meanings of whiteness, too, are not
naturally given but rather discursively produced within hierarchical power
relations.

A fourth response to racism which remains much less widespread is the
conscious recognition of racism as a structuring force in both the material
practices shaping societies and the production of individual subjectivities,
whether white or of colour. From this position racism is understood to have
both individual and structural dimensions which are often invisible from the
privileged position of whiteness and as such require conscious problemat-
ization by white women.

The history of white women's failure to confront racism is a long one. In
her history of black women and feminism, *Ain't I a Woman* (1986; original
1982), bell hooks points out how white women have often been complicit in
black women's dual oppression by racism and sexism. In North America, this
began on the slave plantations where black women were sexually exploited
and forced to breed new generations of slaves:

> The enslaved black woman could not look to any group of men, white or
> black, to protect her against sexual exploitation. Often in desperation, slave
> women attempted to enlist the aid of white mistresses, but these attempts
> usually failed. Some mistresses responded to the distress of female slaves by
> persecuting and tormenting them. Others encouraged the use of black women
> as sex objects because it allowed them respite from unwanted sexual advances.
> In rare cases, white mistresses who were reluctant to see sons marry and leave
> home purchased black maids to be sexual playmates for them. Those white
> women who deplored the sexual exploitation of slave women were usually
> reluctant to involve themselves with a slave's plight for fear of jeopardizing
> their own position in the domestic household. Most white women regarded
> black women who were the objects of their husband's sexual assaults with
> hostility and rage. Having been taught by religious teachings that women were

156

inherently sexual temptresses, mistresses often believed that the enslaved black woman was the culprit and their husbands the innocent victims. (hooks 1986: 36; original 1982)

In the context of slave plantations, it was often in the interests of white women to perpetuate rather than resist the exploitation of black women. The question of white women's interests has remained central in determining whether or not white women in general, and white feminists in particular, have addressed racism as a serious political issue. Questions of interest remain central today in so far as the end of racism would also mean an end to the benefits that white women enjoy as a result of white privilege. This is a point made clearly by the current backlash against affirmative action in the United States.

THEORIZING WHITENESS

The initial structure of modern discourse in the West 'secretes' the idea of white supremacy. I shall call this 'secretion' – the underside of modern discourse – a particular logical consequence of the quest for truth and knowledge in the modern West. To put it crudely, my argument is that the authority of science, undergirded by a modern philosophical discourse guided by Greek ocular metaphors and Cartesian notions, promotes and encourages the activities of observing, comparing, measuring, and ordering the physical characteristics of the human bodies. Given the renewed appreciation and appropriation of classical antiquity, these activities are regulated by classical aesthetic and cultural norms. The creative fusion of scientific investigation, Cartesian epistemology, and classical ideals produced forms of rationality, scientificity and objectivity which, though efficacious in the quest for truth and knowledge, prohibited the intelligibility and legitimacy of the idea of black equality in beauty, culture, and intellectual capacity. (West 1982: 48)

The last few years have finally seen 'whiteness' emerge as a theoretical and political problem, ripe for analysis, deconstruction and transformation.[6] The emergence of whiteness as a largely invisible norm has a long history which is also the history of the development of modernity via the scientific search for knowledge and the colonial project of subduing, Christianizing and 'civilizing' other cultures. The establishment of the hegemony of whiteness as the signifier of civilization and development served to deflect attention from the economic and political interests which motivated colonial expansion. Within the colonial powers themselves, it served as a unifying factor in the face of massive class inequality, a feature which continues to surface in contemporary Britain in the tabloid press's appeals to Britain's imperial past.

157

Many assumptions about whiteness and colonized Others prevalent in the era of empire persist into the present and surface repeatedly in both individual and institutional racist practices.

Constructions of whiteness are rarely uniform other than in their claims – implicit or explicit – to superiority over the non-white. Recently work has begun on analysing the cultural construction of whiteness in a range of cultural practices such as religion, literature, fine art, beauty contests and the cinema.[7] This work demonstrates the need both for historical specificity in understanding whiteness and an awareness of the long history of many contemporary assumptions about whiteness and their roots in scientific racism and colonialism. Ideas of whiteness formed, for example, through religious iconography, painting, sculpture, and media images involve norms of beauty and judgements about intellect and character that implicitly function by distinguishing a white norm from Others who are different. Norms of whiteness are also gendered, implying different characteristics in women and men. Sometimes they are class specific and involve other forms of hierarchy linked to nationality. Their unity derives from their supposed difference from the non-white.

The dominant meanings attached to whiteness in Western societies can be found throughout the spectrum of 'high' and popular cultural texts and practices. For individual white people, however, they remain implicit until confronted by difference. As Ruth Frankenberg's study of a group of white American women suggests, understandings of race and racism depend both on the range of discourses to which particular white women have access and the immediate social environments in which they live (Frankenberg 1993). Other crucial determinants of white attitudes are the degree to which white women come into contact with women of colour and the nature of such contacts.

REDEFINING DIFFERENCE: BLACK FEMINISM AND FEMINISMS OF COLOUR

> The people who practice Racism – everyone who is white in the US – are victims of their own white ideology and are impoverished by it. But we who are oppressed by Racism internalize its deadly pollen along with the air we breathe. Make no mistake about it, the fruits of this weed are dysfunctional lifestyles which mutilate our physical bodies, stunt our intellects and make emotional wrecks of us. (Anzaldúa 1990b: xix)

The recent emphasis on difference in feminist theory and politics has, in part, been a response to black and Third World women's critiques of white

158

Western feminism. The emphasis on sisterhood in the 1970s, and on the shared global oppression of women, belied the failure of a largely white and middle-class movement to recognize racism and colonialism as fundamental forms of oppression in the lives of women of colour. As the above quotation from Gloria Anzaldúa suggests, this oppression affects not only the material social position of women and men of colour but also their physical, intellectual and emotional lives. It is a crucial element shaping subjectivity and agency. Not only have white feminist cultural theory and politics tended, for the most part, to ignore the effects of racism on women of colour, they have also largely ignored the very existence of women of colour, failing to value their culture and learn from their varied histories of struggle against patriarchy, racism and colonialism.

If, at the beginning of second-wave feminism, white women's history and cultural achievements were marginalized or hidden from history and required an extensive work of recovery, this was even more the case for women of colour. As the African-American critic Barbara Smith argued in 1977: 'Black women's existence, experience, and culture and the brutally complex systems of oppression which shape these are in the "real world" of white and/or male consciousness beneath consideration, invisible, unknown' (Smith 1986: 168; original 1977). Largely excluded both from analyses of how patriarchy functions and from the development of new feminist historical and cultural canons, black feminists and other feminists of colour set out to recover their lost histories and their cultural production. They also sought to develop modes of analysis that contest the marginalization or absence of questions of racism in much white feminist theory and analysis, offering alternative approaches to the question of difference.

The term 'black feminism' is used in a range of different ways. Whereas in the United States 'black feminism' is most often used to refer to the work and politics of feminists of African descent, in Britain it has been used as an explicitly political category to forge alliances between all women who are subject to racism. This has at times included women of African, Afro-Caribbean and South Asian descent, and even white minorities such as Irish women:[8]

> [B]eing 'black' in Britain is about a state of 'becoming' (racialized); a process of consciousness, when colour become the defining factor about who you are. Located through your 'otherness' a 'conscious coalition' emerges: a self-consciously constructed space where identity is not inscribed by a natural identification but a political kinship (Sandoval 1991). Now living submerged in whiteness, physical difference becomes a defining issue, a signifier, a mark of whether or not you belong. Thus to be black in Britain is to share a common structural location; a racial location. (Mirza 1997b: 3)

In the United States of America – the source of most black feminist theory and scholarship – other groups of minority women have fought for recognition of their ethnic specificity, for example as Asian American, Native American, Hispanic American or Chicana women. They are usually included within the more general term 'women of colour', a term which can also include African-American women. In this chapter 'black feminism' is used to refer to work by women of African descent and 'women of colour' is used as a broader inclusive term for women who are not defined as white.

KEY ISSUES IN BLACK FEMINISM

The Centrality of Racism

There have always been Black women activists – some known, like Sojourner, Harriet Tubman, Frances E. W. Harper, Ida B. Wells Barnett, and Mary Church Terrell, and thousands upon thousands unknown – who had a shared awareness of how their sexual identity combined with their racial identity to make their whole life situation and the focus of their political struggles unique. Contemporary Black feminism is the outgrowth of countless generations of personal sacrifice, militancy, and work by our mothers and sisters.

A Black feminist presence has evolved most obviously in connection with the second wave of the American women's movement beginning in the late 1960s. Black, other Third World, and working women have been involved in the feminist movement from its start, but both outside reactionary forces and racism and elitism within the movement itself have served to obscure our participation. In 1973 Black feminists, primarily located in New York, felt the necessity of forming a separate Black feminist group. This became the National Black Feminist Organization (NBFO).

Black feminist politics also have an obvious connection to movements for Black liberation, particularly those of the 1960s and 1970s. Many of us were active in those movements (civil rights, Black nationalism, the Black Panthers), and all of our lives were greatly affected and changed by their ideology, their goals, and the tactics used to achieve their goals. It was our experience and disillusionment within these liberation movements, as well as experience on the periphery of the white male left, that led to the need to develop a politics that was antiracist, unlike those of white women, and antisexist, unlike those of Black and white men. (Combahee River Collective 1983: 210)

Feminism, as liberation struggle, must exist apart from and as part of the larger struggle to eradicate domination in all its forms. We must understand that patriarchal domination shares an ideological foundation with racism and other forms of group oppression, that there is no hope that it can be eradicated while these systems remain intact. This knowledge should consistently inform the direction of feminist theory. (hooks 1989: 22)

Perhaps the most important principle in black feminism is the refusal to see racism and sexism as discreet and separate forms of oppression. Black feminists insist on seeing the two as interrelated.

Racism not only classifies certain groups of women as *different* on the basis of phenotype and skin colour, but also as *inferior*. Skin colour and phenotype matter because racist discourse and practices make them matter. White supremacist practice has systematically defined people of colour as different in negative ways. Black feminism is a response both to these racist definitions of blackness and to the devaluating of women of colour on the basis of their difference. Black feminism is thus a challenge to exclusion from a predominantly white women's movement and the refusal of white feminists to acknowledge the centrality of racism and recognize how it creates material differences in black women's lives (see figures 7.1 and 7.2).

For most black women and many women of colour, race remains the primary form of oppression, compounded by class and gender. While the gender issues which the white women's movement has taken up are relevant to women of colour, often they are differently affected by them. Campaigns in the 1970s and 1980s for the rights to free abortion and contraception, for example, failed to take account of the different racially motivated treatment of black women and women of colour where these issues were concerned. For black women and women of colour, the right to choose has often meant the right not to have abortions, injections of Depo-Provera or sterilization.[9]

Yet if black feminism is first and foremost a response to racist definition and exclusion, it is also much more than this. It involves an investigation of the historical and contemporary experience and culture of black women and the celebration of black women's difference. Various strands have emerged in the wealth of black feminist work published over the last few decades. These include moves to recover black women's history, literature, art, music and other cultural forms and to construct black female traditions. They further include attempts to identify the specificity of black female subjectivity and experience and to develop a black feminist aesthetics.

Reclaiming History

The histories of black people and other people of colour, both in the West and in their encounters with the West, are histories of oppression and resistance. Tied in with the histories of colonialism, slavery and segregation,

7.1 Demonstration against US intervention in Grenada, 5 November 1983. Photograph: Jenny Matthews/Format

they are histories in which racist ideas and practices play a central role. Yet they are also histories of resistance to racism in all its forms. Crucial in these other histories are positive narratives of historical agency and self-definition in the face of racist stereotypes and Eurocentric narratives of history.

7.2 Barking Hospital striking cleaners march to Pritchard's (private cleaning contractors). Photograph: Brenda Prince/Format

Whereas histories of oppression throw important light on the present as well as the past, histories of resistance provide alternative traditions in which to ground positive ideas of difference and new forms of subjectivity.

The history of oppression and its present-day legacies in the United States is the central theme of bell hooks's account of the relationship between feminism and racism, *Ain't I a Woman* (1986; original 1982). hooks gives many examples of the intermeshing of sexism and racism in the lives of black women from the slave plantations to the present day. At the centre of her project is the belief that this history is crucial for an understanding of black women's position today. She argues that black women continue to suffer a double oppression: sexism and racism. Her work is, in part, a critical unmasking of racial stereotypes of difference which have persisted into the present. She argues that racist discourses and practices refuse to relinquish ideas and stereotypes which have their roots in classical racism and slavery. She suggests, for example, that attitudes towards black women formed under slavery – in particular ideas of black female sexuality – persist into the present day and are widespread in contemporary media representations. These include the assumption that black woman are sexually loose and available, an assumption which has deep roots in Western ideas of African women. In the United States of America this stereotype was reinforced on the plantations, where black women were sexually abused and exploited. Then, as now, this led to the tendency to see black women as responsible for the sexual assaults upon them. hooks further argues that positive images of black women in American culture are restricted to 'long suffering, religious, maternal' figures who are self-sacrificing and self-denying (hooks 1986: 66; original 1982).

Black feminist concern with history extends to literature, music and the arts. In the feminist cultural politics of the 1970s and 1980s, the absence of black women from the rewritings of literary and other forms of cultural history and the construction of alternative artistic and literary traditions, confirmed black feminists' suspicions of white racism. White feminist work on women's culture took little account of black women's achievements. Black feminists played little part in redefining canons. At best they found themselves offered token spaces in white-controlled anthologies. Writing in 1977, Barbara Smith argued that the absence of black feminist perspectives was essentially a political question. The development of black feminism, she suggested, suffered from the lack of a political movement able to:

> give power or support to those who want to examine Black women's experience through studying our history, literature and culture. There is no political presence that demands a minimal level of consciousness and respect from those who write and talk about our lives. Finally there is not a developed body of Black feminist political theory whose assumptions could be used in the study of Black women's art. (Smith 1986: 170; original 1977)

Smith stresses the political importance of history, literature and culture, as well as black feminist political theory. If the history of oppression is important to understanding the current position of black women, the history of agency, resistance and creativity is no less important. Much work has been done within black feminism to recover the history of black foremothers. These include women who resisted slavery, political activists, and writers, musicians and artists. This work recovers a radically different history from that found in most white-dominated institutions and helps articulate positive notions of difference and tradition.[10] At issue is a different history of black women and black women's creativity which can be found in a wide range of areas from history and anthropology to fiction. A major objective of this work is the creation of positive traditions and histories which do not see black women only in terms of their victimization by racist white societies. It includes the uncovering of lost histories of black women's participation in literature and the arts, and the rescuing of other cultural forms such as oral traditions from the margins of what is considered valuable by dominant cultural institutions and their gatekeepers. This work of recovery is funda-mental to present-day feelings of worth and value. It offers the basis from which black culture can demand recognition and respect. It helps to counteract the widespread and deeply ingrained stereotypes of black people which either depict them as victims, or only celebrate particular aspects of black culture and creativity – in particular physical prowess in sport and dance and musical achievement – which allow for a continued denial on the part of white society of black people's intellectual and other artistic achiev-ements.

Re-theorizing Difference

During the years of Black Reconstruction, 1867–77, black women struggled to change negative images of black women perpetuated by whites. Trying to dispel the myth that all black women were sexually loose, they emulated the conduct and mannerisms of white women. But as manumitted black women and men struggled to change stereotypical images of black female sexuality, white society resisted. Everywhere black women went, on public streets, in shops or at their places of work, they were accosted and subject to obscene comments and even physical abuse at the hands of white men and women. (hooks 1986: 55; original 1982)

For black women and other women of colour, the social marking of difference is part of everyday life. It can take many forms, from the negative stereotyping of everyday racial abuse to a romantic, often primitivist, cele-bration of black and Asian female difference which reaffirms deep-rooted racist stereotypes. Yet in both cases racism defines, contains and controls. One of the key issues for black feminism has been the assertion of the right to redefine the meanings of difference. This has meant contesting long-established assumptions and stereotypes and asserting new meanings. In the face of mainstream white scholarship which has consistently defined black women as different – often in racist ways – and excluded them, a key focus of black feminism has been to identify and challenge the negative images of black women's difference that have persisted since slavery.[11] Another has been to reconceive this difference, locating it in an historically separate experience which has produced different positive cultural traditions.

Some black feminists, influenced by the broader Afrocentric movement within black thought, have taken ideas of difference further, locating black women's difference beyond their immediate environment in their African roots. Here questions of authenticity and belonging are important. Particular constructions of Africanness ground positive articulations of difference and identity. That the Africa in question has little to do with the historical and social reality of the multifarious countries and cultures which make up contemporary Africa is of little importance. Whereas white Western narratives of the development of European civilization work by constructing a history which links Egypt, Greece and Rome with Renaissance and post-Renaissance Western Europe, suppressing what does not fit this narrative, Afrocentric history reverses Eurocentric history, rewriting the meaning of ancient Egypt, as the source of black rather than white civilizations, and privileging those aspects of African history and culture which testify to the complexity of African civilizations:[12]

> We take up our story in Africa, six thousand years after the Ancient Egyptians first began to establish Africa's creativity and genius in the world, and shortly before the Europeans first set foot on African soil for the purpose of plunder. By this time, our African ancestors had established a variety of cultures and societies, using whatever means of production were available to them. We were living as nomads, as hunters and gatherers, as members of settled farming communities and as residents of flourishing trading towns and cities. We were living in feudal societies, paying taxes to local chiefs and rulers; in slave societies, where power, class and privilege were already strictly established; and in communal societies, where resources and decision-making were shared, often on a matriarchal basis. Above all we were living in societies which we ourselves had determined.
>
> With the exception of Ancient Egypt, which is more often than not portrayed in books and films as a civilisation in which full-blooded, black African people played no part, we rarely hear talk of the Africa which existed before the Europeans arrived. Yet African societies matched, and in some cases excelled those in Europe. (Bryan et al. 1985: 3)

The ground-breaking British black feminist text, *The Heart of the Race*, for example, from which this quotation comes, attempts to create a history that links black women in Britain today with an African heritage stretching back through slavery to Ancient Egypt:

> Our culture shapes and determines our identity. To convey our sense of self, as Black women, we must first generate a positive understanding of the long cultural tradition which has fashioned our way of life here in Britain. . . .
>
> The unique feature of our culture is that its roots and base is Africa. To acknowledge its origins is also to identify the unchanging seam which is common to all Black cultures in the diaspora. Our African origin is the cornerstone of our lifestyle and our perception of the world, the internal dynamic which has enabled us continuously to resist new assaults on our way of life. (Bryan et al. 1985: 183)

In writing this history the use of 'we' creates a sense of unity that, while powerful, tends to mask cultural and historical difference. The aim is to create a positive history that stresses black achievement and resistance to racism and imperialism, and which asserts the importance of self-determination.

Afrocentric approaches to black women locate their culture within a tradition with identifiable African features which Patricia Hill Collins suggests in her book *Black Feminist Thought* (1990) give rise to a shared world view:

> Every culture has a worldview that it uses to order and evaluate its own experiences (Sobel 1979). For African-Americans this worldview originates in the Afrocentric ideas of classical African civilizations, ideas sustained by cultures and institutions of diverse West African ethnic groups (Diop 1974). By retaining significant elements of West African culture, communities of enslaved Africans offered their members alternative explanations for slavery than those advanced by slaveowners (Herskovits 1941; Gutman 1976; Webber 1978; Sobel 1979). Confining African-Americans to all-black areas in the rural South and the northern urban ghettos fostered the continuation of certain dimensions of this Afrocentric worldview (Smitherman 1977; Sobel 1979; Sudarkasa 1981; Asante 1987). While essential to the survival of African-Americans, the knowledge produced in Black communities was hidden from and suppressed by the dominant group and thus remained extant but subjugated. . . .
>
> Within African-American extended families and communities, Black women fashioned an independent standpoint about the meaning of Black womanhood. These self-definitions enabled Black women to use African-derived conceptions of self and community to resist negative evaluations of Black womanhood advanced by dominant groups. In all, Black women's

167

grounding in traditional African-American culture fostered the development of a distinctive Afrocentric women's culture. (Collins 1990: 10–11)

In its strongest forms, Afrocentrism works as what Foucault calls a reverse discourse.[13] It reverses the meanings and values commonly found in Eurocentric history, re-fixes the meaning of blackness and offers apparently authentic forms of black subjectivity. Patricia Hill Collins takes a more differentiated approach to Afrocentrism, advocating a meshing of theory and lived experience which can acknowledge and respect differences without fixing them outside history or contemporary social relations:

> Individual African-American women have long displayed various types of consciousness regarding our shared angle of vision. By aggregating and articulating these individual expressions of consciousness, a collective, focused group consciousness becomes possible. Black women's ability to forge these individual, unarticulated, yet potentially powerful expressions of everyday consciousness into an articulated, self-defined, collective standpoint is the key to Black women's survival. ... For Black women the struggle involves embracing a consciousness that is simultaneously Afrocentric and feminist. (1990: 26)

IDENTITY POLITICS

Black feminism in general and Afrocentric feminism in particular have, at times, taken the form of identity politics. Very much a feature of feminism in the United States in the 1980s, identity politics focuses on the oppressions of specific groups of women: black, Hispanic, Native American, lesbian and many others. One important feature of identity politics is the sense of solidarity and positive identity that it offers to marginalized groups, forming a basis from which to develop strategies for contesting specific forms of oppression. The identities imposed on marginalized groups and minorities by dominant white, heterosexist cultures are identities against which new senses of self and group are defined. These new identities are also shaped by resistance to specific forms of group oppression.

Perhaps the major problem with identity politics is the tendency to define identity in particular fixed ways which ultimately work to exclude many of those women that the group in question wants to reach and represent. An example of this, discussed in chapter 3, was the narrow definition of lesbian feminism in the 1970s which eventually provoked a reaction from lesbians who did not wish to conform to the dress codes and sexual mores prescribed by the movement. In a strong criticism of identity politics in the black feminist context, Heidi Safia Mirza suggests that:

Identity politics, a political ideology that consumed the 1980s, was based on the premise that the more marginal the group the more complete the knowledge. In a literal appropriation of standpoint theory, the claim to authenticity through oppressive subjecthood produced a simplistic hierarchy of oppression. The outcome was the cliché-ridden discourse which embodied the holy trinity of 'race, class and gender' (Appiah and Gates 1995), within which black women, being the victims of 'triple oppression', were the keepers of the holy grail.

The solution within this conceptualization of oppression was to change personal behaviour rather than wider structures. In a time when what should be done was replaced by who we are (Bourne 1987: 1), the freedom to have was replaced by the freedom to be (Melucci 1989: 177). Identity politics offered no radical way forward in the critical project of revealing how we come to be located in the racialized and sexualized space where we reside. (Mirza 1997b: 9)

Although this may well be recognized by many women as an accurate description of some aspects of the nature and implications of identity politics as they developed in the 1980s, they undoubtedly played a more positive role for many women than this account would suggest. Coming together on the basis of specific oppressions, for example as black lesbians, was crucial in contesting the marginality and invisibility of particular groups of women, voicing their presence and needs and analysing the power relations structuring the oppressions to which they were subject. bell hooks, for example, although critical of the restrictive impulse of identity politics, suggests, writing of African-American women, that:

Contemporary African-American resistance struggle must be rooted in a process of decolonization that continually opposes re-inscribing notions of 'authentic' black identity. This critique should not be made synonymous with a dismissal of the struggle of oppressed and exploited peoples to make ourselves subjects. Nor should it deny that in certain circumstances this experience affords us a privileged critical location from which to speak, this is not a reinscription of modernist master narratives of authority which privilege some voices by denying voice to others. Part of our struggle for radical black subjectivity is the quest to find ways to construct self and identity that are oppositional and liberatory (hooks 1991: 29).

POSTMODERN BLACKNESS

Appeals to a common black women's experience and a black female identity can be problematic and exclusive when they do not pay due attention to differences between black women. Among other things, these differences encompass history, class, sexuality, region and religion. What is often shared across these differences is the experience of racism. Identity politics was one answer to the question of differences between women, yet feminists anxious to avoid fixing the meanings of difference in advance have increasingly turned to postmodern theories of subjectivity, meaning and power. These are seen to offer ways of theorizing subjectivity and identity as discursively produced, multiple and changeable. In the introduction to a volume of essays entitled *Black British Feminism*, Heidi Safia Mirza writes of postmodernism:

> Postmodern theory has allowed the celebration of difference, the recognition of otherness, the presence of multiple and changeable subjectivities. Black women, previously negated and rendered invisible by the inherent universalizing tendency of modernity, finally have a voice. We appear to have 'arrived'. Here we are, afforded the status of *Black British Feminism*.
> Postmodernity has opened up the possibility of a new 'feminism of difference'. Such a feminism now allows black women the legitimation to do what we have been doing for long time, in our own way; we have now been afforded an intellectual space to valourize our agency; redefine our place on the margins. (Mirza 1997b: 19)

The endorsement of postmodern theory is tempered, even in Mirza's case, by an awareness of the discrepancy between postmodern theory and actual social practices which continue to reproduce exclusive racist and sexist social relations. In her essay 'Postmodern Blackness', bell hooks points out that 'Very few African-American intellectuals have talked or written about postmodernism' (1991: 23). She explains this absence in terms of the exclusive style of much postmodern writing, which has been written by white male academics, its refusal to see the relevance of work by black women and its obliviousness to the reality of racist oppression. She argues that even those postmodern discourses which claim to create the space for the articulation of difference and otherness are often exclusionary:

> Postmodern discourses are often exclusionary even as they call attention to, appropriate even, the experience of 'difference' and 'Otherness' to provide oppositional political meaning, legitimacy, and immediacy when they are accused of lacking concrete relevance. . . .
> Critical of most writing on postmodernism, I perhaps am more conscious of the way in which the focus on 'Otherness and difference' that is often alluded to in these works seems to have little concrete impact as an analysis or standpoint that might change the nature and direction of postmodernist theory. (hooks 1991: 23, 24)

Despite her reservations, hooks does, however, acknowledge the potentially liberatory power of postmodern notions of blackness which do not limit it to essentialist versions of subjectivity and identity:

> Employing a critique of essentialism allows African-Americans to acknowl-
> edge the way in which class mobility has altered collective black experience so
> that racism does not necessarily have the same impact on our lives. Such a
> critique allows us to affirm multiple black identities, varied black experience.
> It also challenges colonial imperialist paradigms of black identity which
> represent blackness one-dimensionally in ways that reinforce and sustain white
> supremacy. This discourse created the idea of the 'primitive' and promoted the
> notion of an 'authentic' experience, seeing as 'natural' those expressions of
> black life which conform to a pre-existing pattern or stereotype. Abandoning
> essentialist notions would be a serious challenge to racism. Contemporary
> African-American resistance struggle must be rooted in a process of decoloni-
> sation that continually opposes re-inscribing notions of 'authentic' black
> identity. (hooks 1991: 28)

Just how far it is possible to be a black female or male postmodern subject in racist societies is a real question. Writing of the American context, Glenn Jordan has suggested that both the history and current material reality of racism rule out the possibility of any truly postmodern black subjectivity restricting it to the nihilism of the ghetto and the lure of consumption.[14] While the black middle class in the US is expanding, the often unemployed working class faces a desperate future which Cornel West describes as follows:

> The exodus of stable industrial jobs from urban centers to cheap labour
> markets here and abroad, housing policies that have created 'chocolate cities
> and vanilla suburbs' (to use the popular musical artist George Clinton's
> memorable phrase), white fear of black crime, and the urban influx of poor
> Spanish-speaking and Asian immigrants – have all helped erode the tax base of
> American cities just as the federal government has cut its support and
> programs. The result is unemployment, hunger, homelessness, and sickness for
> millions.
> And pervasive spiritual impoverishment grows. The collapse of meaning in
> life – the eclipse of hope and absence of love of self and others, the breakdown
> of family and neighbourhood bonds – leads to the social deracination and
> cultural denudement of urban dwellers, especially children. We have created
> rootless, dangling people with little link to the supportive networks – family,
> friends, school – that sustain some sense of purpose in life. We have witnessed
> the collapse of the spiritual communities that in the past helped Americans face
> despair, disease, and death and that transmit through the generations dignity
> and decency, excellence and elegance.

171

The result is lives of what we might call 'random nows,' of fortuitous and fleeting moments preoccupied with 'getting over' – with acquiring pleasure, property, and power by any means necessary. (This is not what Malcolm X meant by this famous phrase.) Postmodern culture is more and more a market culture dominated by gangster mentalities and self-destructive wantonness. This culture engulfs all of us – yet its impact on the disadvantaged is devastating, resulting in extreme violence in everyday life. Sexual violence against women and homicidal assaults by young black men on one another are only the most obvious signs of this empty quest for pleasure, property and power. (West 1993: 5)

In the British context Mirza makes a related point about the relation between postmodern theory and the reality of black women's lives:

To valorize our 'different' experience means we have to locate that experience in materiality. Holding on to the struggle against inequality and for social justice anchors the black feminist project. For it seems whatever the project of postmodern theorizing, black women remain subject to discrimination and exclusion. Black women remain preoccupied with their struggles against low pay, ill health and incarceration, and for access to care, welfare and education. In spite of postmodernism, little has changed for the majority of black women, globally and nationally. For them power is not diffuse, localized and particular. Power is centralized and secure as it always has been, excluding, defining and self-legitimating. (Mirza 1997b: 20)

There is a long way to go in transforming racist societies, yet postmodern theory arguably remains a useful tool for deconstructing the bases of existing hierarchies and enabling one to theorize and imagine how difference, identity and subjectivity might be realized otherwise in non-oppressive forms.

WOMEN OF COLOUR AND FEMINISM

A theory in the flesh, means one where the physical realities of our lives – our skin color, the land or concrete we grew up on, our sexual longings – all fuse to create a politics born out of necessity. Here, we attempt to bridge the contradictions in our experience:
We are the colored in a white feminist movement.
We are the feminists among the people of our culture.
We are often the lesbians among the straight.
We do this bridging by naming our selves and by telling our stories in our own words. (Moraga and Anzaldúa (eds) 1983: 23)

In the introduction to *This Bridge Called My Back* (1983), Cherríe Moraga and Gloria Anzaldúa describe how 'What began as a reaction to the racism of white feminists soon became a positive affirmation of the commitment of women of color to our *own* feminism' (1983: xxiii–xxiv). This concept of one's own feminism recognizes the specificity of different groups of women and the particular forms of power and oppression with which they are confronted. Central here are understandings of place, history, language and culture – that is questions of ethnic belonging – as well as the broader power structures of class, gender and race. Gloria Anzaldúa undertakes a journey into the history of her people and how this history has shaped the material conditions under which Chicanos and Chicanas live today in *Borderlands/La Frontera: The New Mestiza* (1987). This text argues that historically the territories north of the present-day Texan-Mexican border have passed from Native American to Spanish to white control. In the process the inhabitants became mixed, creating a new group of Chicanos and Chicanas who were dispossessed by whites. Their status is not only that of a distinct ethnic group but also of a racialized Other. As such they are the constant victims of oppressive racist practices while themselves often perpetuating patriarchal oppression. Chicana feminists thus have to be rooted in this broader history of ethnic and racist oppression while struggling to transform the patriarchal dimensions of Chicano culture from within.

For women of colour, questions of race and racism are often conflated with questions of ethnicity. Ethnicity is not the same thing as race, nor should it be collapsed into it. Ethnicity – the sense of belonging to a particular group, for example Italian Americans, the Welsh or Catalans – is a question of history, language, place and culture which affects white people as well as people of colour. Yet, where people of colour are concerned, there is a widespread tendency to make assumptions about ethnic identity on the basis of what people look like. White ethnocentrism and racism both structure the world which people of colour inhabit, causing crises of identity. As Nellie Wong put, it in her poem 'When I Was Growing Up':

> when I was growing up, I hungered
> for American food, American styles,
> coded: white and even to me, a child
> born of Chinese parents, being Chinese
> was feeling foreign, was limiting,
> was UnAmerican. (Wong 1983: 7)

The feeling of UnAmericanness expressed in this poem arises out of the dominant racist identification of Americanness with whiteness and of non-whiteness with an otherness which is by definition inferior. The tendency to

173

make assumptions about cultural identity on the basis of how a person looks is a particular problem in predominantly white societies with minorities of people of colour.

The collapsing of skin colour, phenotype and culture is both limiting and exclusive in its effects. In the Welsh context, for example, where conceptions of Welshness are linked to the Welsh language and a history of colonization by the English state, it is also assumed to be white. Yet in industrial South Wales, where the rise of the coal trade in the nineteenth century brought waves of immigrant settlers from all over the world, many people of mixed-race descent identify themselves as Welsh, challenging the exclusive equation of Welshness and whiteness. The identification of skin colour and phenotype with culture is a primary feature of racialized thinking and it permeates even potentially progressive movements like multiculturalism.[15] The fact that a person looks black or Asian does not mean that her identity and culture will necessarily be either. A mixed identity and bi- or multi-culturalism is just as possible; in some cases, even a white identity. Moreover the implicitly racialized hierarchization of different cultures within forms of multicultural-ism which continue to privilege whiteness and white culture compounds the problem faced by women and men of colour.

Respect for difference is central to the flourishing of multi-ethnic societies and this requires combating both racism and ethnocentrism. Maria Lugones offers a clear and uncompromising definition of ethnocentrism and its relation to racism:

> To speak another language and another culture are not the same as being racialized. One can be ethnocentric without being racist. The existence of races as the products of racialization presupposes the presence of racism, but the existence of different ethnicities does not presuppose ethnocentrism, even if ethnocentrism is universal. So we should conclude that ethnicity is not the same as race and ethnocentrism is not the same as racism.
>
> *Ethnocentrism*: the explicit and arrogantly held action-guiding belief that one's culture and cultural ways are superior to others; or the disrespectful, lazy, arrogant indifference to other cultures that devalues them through not seeing appreciatively *any* culture or cultural ways except one's own when one could do otherwise, or the disrespectful, lazy, arrogant indifference that devalues other cultures through stereotyping of them or through non-reflective, self-satisfied acceptance of such stereotypes. (Lugones 1990: 48)

MOVING BEYOND BINARIES

In us, intra- and cross-cultural hostilities surface in not so subtle put-downs. *Las no comprometidas, las que negan a sus gente. Fruncemos las caras y negamos toda responsabilidad*. Where some of us racially mixed people are stuck in now is denial and its damaging effects. Denial of the white aspects that we've been forced to acquire, denial of our sisters who for one reason or another cannot 'pass' as 100% ethnic – as if such a thing exists. Racial purity, like language purity, is a fallacy. Denying the reality of who we are destroys the basis needed from which to talk honestly and deeply about the issues between us. We cannot make any real connections because we are not touching each other. (Anzaldúa 1990c: 146)

Racist definitions of difference remain trapped within sets of binary oppositions in which one term is privileged over the other: white over black, First World over Third World. The oppositions also presuppose that a person is either one thing or the other. In recent writing, influenced by postmodern thinking, attempts have been made to deconstruct race and develop new ideas of hybridity as alternatives to the binary oppositions which structure racist ideas of difference. For example, Gloria Anzaldúa draws on her own experience, history and place, to suggest that 'new mestizas', women who are racially and ethnically mixed, are in a position to challenge and move beyond the binaries which structure racism, sexism, heterosexism and ethnocentrism:

José Vascocelos, Mexican philosopher, envisaged *una raza mestiza, una mezcla de razas afines una raza de color – la primera raza cósmica*, a fifth race embracing the four major races of the world[16] Opposite to the theory of the pure Aryan, and to the policy of racial purity that white America practices, his theory is one of inclusivity. At the confluence of two or more genetic streams, with chromosomes constantly 'crossing over', this mixture of races, rather than resulting in an inferior being, provides hybrid progeny, a mutable, more malleable species with a rich gene pool. From this racial, ideological, cultural and biological cross-pollinization, an 'alien' consciousness is presently in the making – a new *mestiza* consciousness, *una conciencia de mujer*. It is a consciousness of the Borderlands. (Anzaldúa 1987: 77)

As Anzaldúa describes her, this new *mestiza* calls into question borders and boundaries and the functioning of Western analytic reasoning which uses 'rationality to move towards a single goal'. She develops a 'tolerance for contradictions, a tolerance for ambiguity' (1987: 79):

The work of *mestiza* consciousness is to break down the subject–object duality that keeps her a prisoner and to show in the flesh and through images in her work how duality is transcended. The answer to the problem between the white race and the colored, between males and females, lies in healing the split that originates in the very foundation of our lives, our culture, our languages,

175

our thoughts. A massive uprooting of dualist thinking in the individual and collective consciousness is the beginning of a long struggle, but one that could, in our best hopes, bring us an end of rape, of violence, of war. (1987: 80)

This *mestiza* consciousness, which in some ways resembles Homi Bhabha's 'third space',[17] opens up a utopian vision of a world in which difference is valued and respected, not produced by hierarchical power relations which oppress. Other writers, particularly women of mixed heritage, children of one white and one black parent, have also argued for the need to challenge the binary oppositions which govern racialized thinking and force them to define themselves as only one thing.[18]

WHAT CAN WHITE WOMEN DO?

Racism is societal and institutional. It implies the power to implement racist ideology. Women of color do not have such power, but white women are born with it and the greater their economic privilege, the greater their power. This is how white middle class women emerge among feminist ranks as the greatest propagators of racism in the movement. Rather than using the privilege they have to crumble the institutions that house the source of their own oppression – sexism, along with racism – they often times deny their privilege in the form of 'down-ward mobility', or keep it intact in the form of guilt. Guilt is *not* a feeling. It is an intellectual mask to a feeling. Fear is a feeling – fear of losing one's power, fear of being accused, fear of a loss of status, control, knowledge. Fear is real. Possibly this is the emotional, non-theoretical place from which serious anti-racist work among white feminists can begin. (Moraga and Anzaldúa (eds) 1983: 62)

The main lesson of black feminism and feminisms of colour for white women is that they must take responsibility for racism. To refuse to acknowledge racialized difference, even for the best of motives, is an inadequate response, as is the tendency to see race and racism as black problems. To recognize the social and cultural status of the category 'white', which most often seems natural to white people, involves conscious effort on the part of white women. As Gloria Yamato argues, addressing 'whites who want to be allies to people of color':

You can educate yourselves via research and observations rather than rigidly, arrogantly relying solely on interrogating people of color. Do not expect that people of color should teach you how to behave non-oppressively. Do not give in to the pull to be lazy. Think, hard. Do not blame people of color for your frustration about racism, but do appreciate the fact that people of color will often help you get in touch with that frustration. Assume that your effort to be a good friend is appreciated, but don't expect or accept gratitude from people of color. Work on racism for your sake, not 'their' sake. Assume that you are needed and capable of being a good ally. Know that you'll make mistakes and commit yourself to correcting them and continuing on as an ally, no matter what. Don't give up. (1990: 23–4)

The important argument that white women need to work on racism for their own sakes is reiterated by Barbara Smith:

Let me make quite clear at this point, before going any further, something you must understand. White women don't work on racism to do a favor for someone else, solely to benefit Third World women. You have to comprehend how racism distorts and lessens your own lives as white women – that racism affects your chances for survival, too, and that it is very definitely your issue. Until you understand this, no fundamental change will come about. (Smith 1990: 26)

This understanding may well involve coming to terms with the anger and guilt which arise from the conflicting understandings produced by individual and structural analyses of white women's position:

It seems that much of our resistance to change comes from being angry at women of color. There are many times that white women are put in a real bind so that no matter what we do we are accused of being racist. There are times when racism is inappropriately used as an issue when the disagreements are clearly philosophical. But those, often very legitimate, resentments we have cannot become a justification for perpetuating our racism. The confusion we feel about when and how this movement is racist will not be cleared up until we understand racism as our issue and our responsibility and begin addressing it among ourselves rather than depending totally on Third World women to raise and clarify the issue for us. (Pence 1982: 46–7)

If feminism is to remain true to its original emancipatory, utopian vision, then it can neither afford to ignore the structural power relations which produce differences as inequalities, nor the implication of the individual woman in racialized power relations. In the words of Audre Lorde:

Ignoring the differences of race between women and the implications of those differences presents the most serious threat to the mobilization of women's joint power. (1984: 117)

CHAPTER 8
Beyond Eurocentrism: Feminism and the Politics of Difference in a Global Frame

What about the future? One of the things I have been most enlivened by is the fact that it is no longer strictly a Black feminist movement that I am part of, but a Third World feminist movement. And not only am I talking about my sisters here in the United States – American Indian, Latina, Asian American, Arab American – I am also talking about women all over the globe. I was fortunate enough to go to London twice this year for two book fairs, international events. We were talking about women's politics, not just publishing, and although we had never met one another, we basically agreed that we needed to talk about sexual, racial, class, anti-imperialist, antimilitaristic politics. I think Third World feminism has enriched not just the women it applies to, but also political practice in general. (Smith 1995: 27; original 1984)

Much of the theory discussed in the preceding chapters originates in Western societies, in Europe and the United States. Yet the project of feminism is far from restricted to women in the developed world. Not only do so-called Third World countries have active indigenous women's movements, but Third World women are increasingly making their voices heard in the realm of feminist theory and scholarship. In addition to analysing their own situations, Third World women are articulating powerful critiques of the Eurocentrism of much Western feminism and its tendency to reproduce colonial modes of representation.

From its inception in the early 1700s, feminism in the modern West has consistently held universalist aspirations. Liberal feminists have argued for three centuries for women's rights as human beings. A movement which began by representing the interests of white, Western, middle-class women has diversified to the point where human rights have been placed at the centre of the agenda for a global feminism. Reporting in *Signs* on the Fourth

World Conference on Women held in Beijing in 1995, Charlotte Bunch and Susana Fried recount how the conference:

> established clearly that women are a global force for the twenty-first century and that women's human rights are central to women's leadership for the future. Women's rights as human rights permeated debates and delegates' speeches at the official UN intergovernmental conference as well as at the parallel Non-Governmental Organization (NGO) Forum held some thirty miles away in Huairon, where it was a palpable presence in many sessions. The combined effect of these activities was a groundswell of support for making the entire platform (for Action) an affirmation of the human rights of women, including women's rights to education, health, and freedom from violence, as well as to the exercise of citizenship in all its manifestations. (Bunch and Fried 1996: 200)

Discourses of human rights have played an important role in progressive social movements in the modern period and remain central to politics in postmodernity, perhaps most visibly in the work of the United Nations. These discourses most often work by arguing for a fundamental sameness in the face of difference, for example, that women should have the same rights as men because they, too, are rational human beings. The political importance of discourses of human rights and equality remains compelling even in the face of poststructuralist critiques of sameness and identity, yet any adequate discourse of human rights must remain vigilant about its own partiality and limitations. As we saw in chapter 1, discourses of human rights for a long time excluded anyone who was not white, male and middle class and affirmed particular meanings and values as universal. Excluded groups have had to fight for centuries for inclusion within the liberal humanist project of liberty and equality. The history of contemporary feminism has made clear how important it is to pay attention to difference even in the interests of achieving rights for all. This is a key theme, too, in recent Third World feminist writing which both challenges the Eurocentric gaze and urges the value of Third World feminist perspectives to a global feminism.

One of the strengths of early second-wave feminism in the West was its emphasis on consciousness raising and the politics of the personal. Consciousness raising enabled women to re-examine and reinterpret their lives in the light of a new-found awareness of patriarchy as the effect of social relations rather than nature. Yet the emphasis on the personal as political could never be enough on its own. Consciousness raising which remained rooted solely in the reinterpretation of personal experience failed to address those forms of oppression not experienced directly by the mainly white, Western, middle-class and heterosexual women involved in early second-wave feminism. The forms of oppression to which other groups of women were subject, and which must necessarily be the focus of feminism as an effective political movement, received scant attention in the early years.

Since 1968, feminists have argued that theory and politics need to be integrally related. Much early second-wave feminist theory, like radical feminism today, privileged women's lives and experiences as the basis upon which to construct theory. Poststructuralist developments in feminist theory problematized this relationship by complexifying the categories of experience and subjectivity. In the realm of both politics and theory the increasingly audible voices of previously marginalized women, including Third World women, have demanded recognition for lives and experiences which long remained invisible in mainstream Western feminism. A complex understanding of experience remains central to those forms of feminist politics and theory which speak to the real conditions under which women live.

There remains a tension – often productive – in feminism between theory and politics, and conceptions of difference are one focal point of this tension. As has been shown in the preceding chapters, different types of feminism posit a variety of ways of understanding gender difference, which range from attempts to recover a non-patriarchal feminine, to positions which suggest that difference is always socially and culturally produced and in process. Approaches to gender difference become more complex once other social factors are taken into account, most centrally class, race, imperialism, ethnicity and sexuality. Each produces hierarchically structured forms of difference in historically, socially and culturally specific ways. These in their turn need to be located within the broader context of a white, Western hegemony which has the United States at its centre. Western hegemony is constantly reinforced both by widespread Eurocentrism and postmodern global and multinational capital. Eurocentrism, with its attendant racist dimensions, continues to define its Third World Others as different and inferior. Multi-national capitalism, like the colonialism that preceded it, continues to shape and reshape class relations on a global scale. The legacies of the slave trade and of the European empires have produced a range of diasporas. Postcolonial migrancy has fundamentally changed the composition of European countries, and the struggles of indigenous peoples and minorities of colour have challenged the hegemonic definitions of national identity and history in countries such as the USA, Canada, Australia and New Zealand.

Difference as inequality is produced by economic, political, social and cultural factors. In the global context these include the division of the world into radically different economic zones characterized by extremes of wealth and poverty. Factors which produce difference as oppression further include class, caste, colonial and racist practices, and heterosexism. Not all women experience difference as oppression. Not all women are subject to oppressive social relations. Even though most white, middle-class, heterosexual, Western women have some experience of sexism, they often remain unaware of the multiple forms of oppression – class, racism, heterosexism – that structure the lives of other women. Writing of racism in the United States, Cherríe Moraga and Gloria Anzaldúa, for example, state that:

> As Third World women we clearly have a different relationship to racism than white women, but all of us are born into an environment where racism exists. Racism affects all of our lives, but it is only white women who can 'afford' to remain oblivious to these effects. The rest of us have had it breathing or bleeding down our necks. (Moraga and Anzaldúa (eds) 1983: 62)

MODERN CERTAINTY VERSUS POSTMODERN PLAY

In the modern era approaches to difference have tended to categorize people on the basis of descriptions of biological, anatomical, social and cultural factors. Thus modern science in the nineteenth century sought to define racial and sexual differences via the categorization of bodies, heads and skulls. In the twentieth century science expanded to include, for example, genes and hormones. These categorization virtually always involved value judgements about the characteristics of the people who were classified as different from a white, Western, middle-class, male norm. Today, even in postcolonial, postmodern contexts – both global and national – the body remains central to gender oppression, Eurocentrism and racism. It continues to function as the guarantee both of what is naturally given and what natural differences mean. While feminists have either redefined the meaning of nature or rejected it altogether as a useful category for understanding difference, it remains a powerful concept in the wider world. The continuing role of the body in guaranteeing difference as inequality works against the transformation of oppressive relations and the realization of the postmodern project of celebrating and enjoying plurality and difference.

Feminists working within the Enlightenment tradition shifted the meanings ascribed to signifiers of difference, both refocusing attention on the social causes of inferiority and revaluing so-called natural differences. Postmodern theory has questioned the assumptions underpinning modern projects of mapping and describing the world. It has shown that there is no such thing as natural or transparent meaning. Meaning is always constructed within specific discourses and tied to particular social interests. The type of theory – modern or postmodern – which feminists use to understand difference and oppression implies related views of politics. Thus modern theories, such as Marxism, liberalism or radical feminism, tend to make definitive and often universal truth claims on which to ground feminist politics. As we saw in chapter 5, postmodern theories do away with this degree of certainty and are often accused of falling into the trap of politically bankrupt relativism. The debate between modern and postmodern theories touches all areas of feminist concern, both Western and Third World.

Many postmodern feminists have argued that relativism is not the only alternative to feminisms that are grounded in modern truth claims. Donna Haraway, for example, who has attempted to give feminist standpoint theory a postmodern inflection, suggests that 'the alternative to relativism is partial, locatable, critical knowledges sustaining the possibility of webs of connections called solidarity in politics and shared conversations in epistemology' (Haraway 1991b: 191; original 1988). Haraway sees a direct relation between traditional Enlightenment positions that claim objectivity on the one hand, and relativism on the other. Both, she suggests, deny the partial and located position of the knowing subject and it is in this partial and located position that she wants to locate a new conception of objectivity:

> Relativism is a way of being nowhere while claiming to be everywhere equally. The 'equality' of positioning is a denial of responsibility and critical inquiry. Relativism is the perfect mirror twin of totalization in the ideologies of objectivity; both deny the stakes in location, embodiment and partial perspective; both make it impossible to see well. Relativism and totalization are both 'god tricks' promising vision from everywhere and nowhere equally and fully, common myths in rhetorics surrounding Science. But it is precisely in the politics and epistemology of partial perspectives that the possibility of sustained, rational, objective inquiry rests. (1991b: 191; original 1988)

While Haraway wants to reclaim and redefine objectivity in the interest of feminist politics, most postmodern feminists are resigned or willing to do without it. Yet postmodern theory not only questions the status of knowledge and truth claims, but also the unified nature of the rational knowing subject. Poststructuralism posits a knowing subject who is both the agent and effect of discourse. Haraway sees the strength of the postmodern subject in its disunity which, she argues, can facilitate a plural vision and her more radical form of objectivity:

> The knowing self is partial in all its guises, never finished, whole, simply there and original; it is always constructed and stitched together imperfectly, and *therefore* able to join with another, to see together without claiming to be

another. Here is the promise of objectivity: a scientific knower seeks the subject position, not of identity, but of objectivity, that is partial connection. There is no way to 'be' simultaneously in all, or wholly in any, of the privileged (i.e. subjugated) positions structured by gender, race, nation and class. And that is a short list of critical positions. (1991b: 193; original 1988)

Haraway argues against the assumption in earlier feminist standpoint theory that oppression facilitates privileged access to truth, arguing instead for the idea of critical positioning which she equates with objectivity:

The search for such a 'full' and total position is the search for the fetishized perfect subject of oppositional history, sometimes appearing in feminist theory as the essentialized Third World Woman. Subjugation is not grounds for an ontology; it might be a visual clue. Vision requires instruments of vision, an optics is a politics of positioning. Instruments of vision mediate standpoints; there is no immediate vision from the standpoints of the subjugated. Identity, including self-identity, does not produce science; critical positioning does, that is, objectivity. (p. 193)

The important point here is that what Haraway calls 'instruments of vision' mediate standpoints. This is similar to the poststructuralist idea that discourses construct the meaning of the world. Yet whether or not feminism needs a new concept of objectivity grounded in standpoint theory is an ongoing debate. Just as poststructuralism has displaced the notion of any singular Truth, replacing it with competing discourses which make truth claims, objectivity, too, can no longer be seen as the guarantee of truth.

In the current climate of postmodern thinking and cultural practice, theories of difference are often linked to the Derridean idea of the free play of the signifier. For some, difference becomes a question of the market, consumption and performance in which it is suggested that we can choose our identities and be what we want to be. This reading of the postmodern condition is one that rests on white, middle-class, heterosexual privilege. From this standpoint, class, colonial modes of thinking and racism are not experienced as defining difference and limiting choice. Nor is heterosexuality experienced as the negation or marginalization of other forms of desire. Yet as Audre Lorde points out, hierarchically structured differences remain a central challenge for feminists:

Much of Western European history conditions us to see human differences in simplistic opposition to each other: dominant/subordinate, good/bad, up/ down, superior/inferior. In a society where the good is defined in terms of profit rather than in terms of human need, there must always be some group of people who, through systematized oppression, can be made to feel surplus, to occupy the place of the dehumanized inferior. Within this society, that group is made up of Black and Third World people, working-class people, older people, and women. (Lorde 1984: 114)

A key question in contemporary feminist writing is how to go beyond the limitations that come from one's location in a particular place at a particular moment in history and the experience derived from this. This transcending of ethnocentrism requires effort – the effort to listen to others, to learn about the histories of other women and the social and cultural conditions within which they are placed. It requires what bell hooks calls 'strategies of communication and inclusion that allow for the successful enactment of this feminist vision', that is a vision that takes diversity seriously (hooks 1989: 24). Writing of intersubjectivity in Gloria Anzaldúa's *Borderlands/La Frontera*, Diane L. Fowlkes suggests that what Seyla Benhabib (1986) has called 'a standpoint of intersubjectivity':

> provides a perspective from which people can recognize themselves and others as differently and complexly identified. From such a standpoint it is possible for people to recognize that by definition, they cannot effectively organize according to a single dimension and therefore need to build coalitions because of complex systems of oppression and privilege. (Fowlkes 1997: 107)

That inclusion remains a problem in all areas of feminism is clear from much black and Third World writing. Thus in the United States, where 'Third World' is used to signify not only people in the Third World but also minorities of colour in the West, many groups have to struggle to be heard. Writing in 1979, Barbara Cameron described how:

> At the Third World Bay Conference in October 1979, the Asian and Native American people in attendance felt the issues affecting us were not adequately included in the workshops. Our representation and leadership had minimal input which resulted in a skimpy educational process about our struggles. The conference glaringly pointed out to us the narrow definition held by some people that third world means black people only. It was a depressing experience to sit in the lobby of Harambee House with other Native Americans and Asians, feeling removed from other third world groups with whom there is supposed to be this automatic solidarity and empathy. The Indian group sat in my motel room discussing and exchanging our experiences within the third world context. We didn't spend much time in workshops conducted by other third world people because of feeling unwelcomed at the conference and demoralized by having an invisible presence. What's worse than being invisible among your own kind? (Cameron 1983: 50)

184

Many feminists argue that a politics of communication and inclusion requires not just knowledge of others but a working through at an individual and personal level of often unacknowledged assumptions and prejudices. It means a coming to terms with the contradictory nature of subjectivity, including individual women's often hidden complicity with oppression or perpetuation of oppressive practices:

> Within the women's movement, the connections among women of different backgrounds and sexual orientations have been fragile, at best. I think this phenomenon is indicative of our failure to seriously address ourselves to some very frightening questions: How have I internalized my own oppression? How have I oppressed? Instead, we have let rhetoric do the job of poetry. Even the word 'oppression' has lost its power. We need a new language, better words that can more closely describe women's fear of and resistance to one another; words that will not always come out sounding like dogma. (Moraga 1983b: 30)

Indeed Audre Lorde argues that 'the true focus of revolutionary change is never merely the oppressive situations which we seek to escape, but that piece of the oppressor which is planted deep within each of us, and which knows only the oppressor's tactics, the oppressor's relationships' (Lorde 1984: 123)

The recognition of difference and diversity requires the ability to acknowledge privileges which come from the structural power relations within which individuals are located, something that privileged women are rarely keen to do. As Gloria Anzaldúa explains in relation to different racialized positions:

> Often white-feminists want to minimize racial difference by taking comfort in the fact that we are all women and/or lesbians and suffer similar sexual–gender oppressions. They are usually annoyed with the actuality (though not the concept) of 'differences', want to blur racial difference, want to smooth things out – they seem to want a complete, totalizing identity. Yet in their eager attempt to highlight similarities, they create or accentuate 'other' differences such as class. These unacknowledged or unarticulated differences further widen the gap between white and colored. (Anzaldúa 1990b: xxi)

Anzaldúa explains how when white women do speak of differences, they often fall into the trap of alienating and marginalizing those defined as other:

> In the act of pinpointing and dissecting racial, sexual or class 'differences' of women-of-color, white women not only objectify these differences, but also

185

change those differences with their own white, racialized, scrutinizing and alienating gaze. Some white people who take up multicultural and cultural plurality issues mean well but often they push to the fringes once more the very cultures and ethnic groups about whom they want to disseminate knowledge. For example, the white writing about Native peoples or cultures displaces the Native writer and often appropriates the culture instead of proliferating information about it. The difference between appropriation and proliferation is that the first steals and harms; the second helps heal breaches of knowledge. (1990b: xxi)

The issues raised here in the North American context relate directly to current widespread debates in Third World feminism about the representation of women in the Third World.

IMPORTANCE OF HISTORY

The problems for feminism which arise from differences between women in Western societies produced by racism, class, heterosexism, ethnicity and a range of other cultural and religious factors take on new dimensions when placed in a global context. The relation of the West to the rest of the world has been profoundly shaped by colonialism and a lack of respect for difference. Yet this has remained a largely marginalized history.

To be without knowledge of history is to be without the knowledge that the present has been formed by the past and subsequent processes of change. Change is a key objective of feminist politics and since the late 1960s feminist scholars have been rewriting histories of the social, literature and the arts. Postmodernism has also been concerned with decentring History and in the process has created the space for multiple histories. Attention to the specific histories of marginalized and oppressed groups is a prerequisite for understanding the power relations of the present. Such analysis is also the basis for what Adrienne Rich has called 'the politics of location'.

In order to develop a feminism which can take due account of difference, individual history needs to be placed within the context of the often brutal history of colonialism and its role in shaping the modern world. Colonial exploitation was economic, but it also involved racist discourses, the legacy of which continues to affect the present. As Jean-Paul Sartre argued of Europeans and white Americans in 1961 in his Preface to Frantz Fanon's *The Wretched of the Earth*:

You know well enough that we are exploiters. You know too that we have laid hands on first the gold and metals, then the petroleum of the 'new continents,' and that we have brought them back to the old countries. This was not without excellent results, as witness our palaces, our cathedrals, and our great industrial cities; and then, when there was the threat of a slump, the colonial markets were there to soften the blow or to divert it. ... (Sartre 1968: 25)

The practices of colonialism were justified by a narrative of civilization in which Europe was defined by its difference from its colonies. Europe created what Sartre terms a racist humanism:

Chatter, chatter: liberty, fraternity, equality, love, honor, patriotism and what have you. All this did not prevent us from making anti-racial speeches about dirty niggers, dirty Jews, and dirty Arabs. High-minded people, liberal or just soft-hearted, protest that they were shocked by such inconsistency; but they were either mistaken or dishonest, for with us there is nothing more consistent than a racist humanism since the European has only been able to become a man through creating slaves and monsters. While there was a native population somewhere this imposture was not shown up; in the notion of the human race we found an abstract assumption of universality which served as cover for the most realistic practices. On the other side of the ocean there was a race of less-than-humans who, thanks to us, might reach our status a thousand years hence, perhaps . . . . (pp. 25–6)

This colonial history has formed the present and remains an issue which feminists in both the Third World and the West need to confront and explore. Thus Uma Narayan argues that:

Colonial history is the terrain where the project of 'Western' culture's self-definition became a project heavily dependent upon its 'difference' from its 'Others' both internal and external. The contemporary self-definitions of many Third-World cultures and communities are also in profound ways political responses to this history. Working together to develop a rich feminist account of this history that divides and connects us might well provide Western and Third-World feminists [with] some difficult but interesting common ground, and be a project that is crucial and central to any truly 'international' feminist politics. (Narayan 1997: 80)

FEMINISM AND THE COLONIAL LEGACY

In the 'dominant' phase of colonialism, European colonizers exercise direct control of the colonized, destroy the native legal and cultural systems, and negate non-European civilizations in order to ruthlessly exploit the resources of the subjugated with the excuse of attempting to 'civilize' them. Before the end of this phase, the natives internalize Western culture. By the time we reach the 'neocolonialist' phase, we've accepted the white colonizers' system of values, attitudes, morality, and modes of production. It is not by chance that in the more rural towns of Texas Chicano neighborhoods are called colonias rather than barrios.

There have always been those of us who have 'cooperated' with the colonizers. It's not that we have been 'won' over by the dominant culture, but that it has exploited pre-existing power relations of subordination and sub-jugation within our native societies. (Anzaldúa 1990c: 142–3)

Since the beginning of modern Western colonialism in the fifteenth century, Europeans and those people of European descent who settled in other parts of the world have defined themselves as different from and superior to the peoples of the five continents that they colonized. This project of establishing difference, which coincided in part with the growth of racial science, played a key ideological and moral role in justifying colonialism. In this narrative, colonized people became the 'white man's burden' and it was his Christian duty to bring 'civilization' to those thought either to lack it or to be trapped in outmoded forms of civilization. European colonial powers saw themselves as bearers of true religion, Enlightenment and modernization to the peoples that they were exploiting in the interests of the development of capitalism and industrialization at home. These colonial ways of thinking still shape attitudes in the West to Third World countries and Western models of progress are still widely assumed to be best. Indigenous cultures continue to be seen as different and often less valuable. Even Western feminist writings about Third World women share a marked tendency to view women from other societies through a Eurocentric gaze which privileges Western notions of liberation and progress and portrays Third World women primarily as victims of ignorance and restrictive cultures and religions.[1]

Both Third World and Western feminisms continue to be profoundly affected by the legacy of colonialism. The problems faced by Third World feminists in their own contexts, for example, include dismissive accusations of 'Westernization'. Writing of Indian feminism, Uma Narayan shows how anti-feminist forces in India use the notion of Westernization selectively to attack those aspects of modern Indian life and politics with which they disagree. Far from being an imitation of Western feminism, Narayan argues, Third World feminism, is very much a response to local issues in Third World countries (see figure 8.1).

Feminist movements in various parts of the world develop when historical and political circumstances encourage public recognition that many of the norms, institutions, and traditions that structure women's personal and social lives, as

188

8.1 Working women demonstrate in Delhi. Bedi workers from the Punjab, members of a trade union, demonstrate in Raj Pat, Delhi, November 1981. Photograph: Raissa Page/Format

well as the impact of new developments and social change, are detrimental to women's well-being, and enable political contestations in which the status quo is criticized and alternatives envisioned. Those in Third-World contexts who dismiss the politics of feminists in their midst as a symptom of 'Westernization' not only fail to consider how these feminists' experiences within their Third-World contexts have shaped and informed their politics, but also fail to acknowledge that their feminist analyses are results of political organizing and political mobilization, initiated and sustained within these Third-World contexts.

Issues that feminist groups in India have politically engaged with include problems of dowry-murder and dowry-related harassment of women, police rape of women in custody; issues relating to women's poverty, health and reproduction; and issue of ecology and communalism that affect women's lives. Indian feminist political activities clearly make feminists and feminism part of the *national political landscape* of many Third-World countries. I am arguing that Third-World feminism is not a mindless mimicking of 'Western' agendas' in one clear and simple sense – that, for instance, Indian feminism is clearly a response to issues specifically confronting many *Indian* women. (Narayan 1997: 13)

Narayan points out how 'Westernization' under colonialism served as a force against which to define an anti-colonial national identity based on particular constructions of traditional life which supported conservative gender politics:

In the Indian context, many nationalist women as well as men subscribed to a posited 'dichotomy between the "material West" and the "spiritual East",' within the terms of which nationalist women often embraced their roles as 'repositories of a national spiritual essence' who must remain untainted by 'Westernization' and its implied pollution. (p. 19)

In the postcolonial period accusations of 'Westernization' have continued to serve conservative gender interests:

The nationalist cultural pride that was predicated upon a return to 'traditional values' and the rejection of 'Westernization' that began under colonial rule thus reemerges today in a variety of postcolonial 'fundamentalist' movements, where returning women to their 'traditional roles' continues to be defined as central to preserving national identity and cultural pride. In such contexts, the fact that a number of Third-World feminists are middle-class urban women who have entered formerly male professional and political spheres, combined with the fact that they often demand greater equality and participation for women in various arenas of national life rather than a return to 'traditional roles', facilitates casting them and their political visions as embodiments of the demon 'Westernization'. Third-World women engaged in struggles over women-centred issues in Third-World contexts – women who are not urban or middle-class – are ignored and marginalised by an insistence on seeing only urban middle-class women as 'feminists'. As a result, Third-World feminist criticisms of practices and ways of life that are harmful and oppressive to women are depicted as mere symptoms of an antinationalist cultural disloyalty and as a form of 'cultural inauthenticity' rooted in an adoption of 'Western' ways and values.

The political location of many Third-World feminists makes it particularly clear that the scope of feminist struggles needs to include not only contesta-tions of *particular practices and institutions* detrimental to women, but additionally to include challenges to the larger pictures of Nation, National History, and Cultural Traditions that serve to sustain and justify these practices and institutions. These are often 'pictures of History' that *conceal their own historicity and their own status as representations* – suggesting that the nation and its culture are 'natural givens' rather than the *historical inventions and constructions* that they are. (Narayan 1997: 20–1)

The main problem with the approach of many Western feminists to Third World issues remains their lack of awareness of the persistence in their work of colonialist modes of representation. This problem is the subject of Chandra Mohanty's influential essay 'Under Western Eyes' (1991) in which she examines the work of Western feminists, in particular, certain books on Third World women's issues. Mohanty argues that:

Any discussion of the intellectual and political construction of 'third world feminisms' must address itself to two simultaneous projects: the internal critique of hegemonic 'Western' feminisms, and the formulation of autono-mous, geographically, historically, and culturally grounded feminist concerns and strategies. The first project is one of deconstructing and dismantling; the second, one of building and constructing. While these projects appear to be contradictory, the one working negatively and the other positively, unless these two tasks are addressed simultaneously, 'third world' feminisms run the risk of marginalization or ghettoization from both mainstream (right and left) and Western feminist discourses. (Mohanty 1991: 51)

Mohanty argues that much Western feminist writing about Third World women 'discursively colonize[s] the material and historical heterogeneities of the lives of women in the third world, thereby producing/re-presenting a composite, singular "third world woman" – an image which appears arbitrarily constructed, but nevertheless carries with it the authorizing signature of Western humanist discourse' (p. 53). The composite image which emerges from this writing is one of Third World women as victims of male control and of so-called traditional cultures and religions. Specificity, history and difference disappear and Western feminism functions as the norm against which the Third World is judged. The answer to representations of Third World women as passive victims lies in detailed attention to social relations in Third World contexts. Mohanty argues that Third World women, like Western women, are produced as subjects in historically and culturally specific ways by the societies in which they live and act as agents. Thus, for example, rather than portraying women as the victims and perpetrators of patriarchal practices such as genital mutilation, attention needs to be given to the specific contexts in which women live, the indigenous meaning of particular practices and how women in the Third World fight against them. Writing of the Sudan, Evelyne Accad explains how:

> Women who had been subjected to circumcision or who had witnessed the worst form of excision – infibulation – done on relatives or friends, not only voiced their opinion against it, but they are involved in a wide campaign and actions aimed at struggling to eradicate the practice. The struggle they described to me seemed quite remarkable. They go to the countryside with programs of hygiene and development. They explain the connection between diseases and infibulation which the people have no effort in making. They stage plays and have radio programs to teach the people about the disastrous consequences linked to the practice, and they also educate the midwives and lead them to other means of earning a living than performing these operations. (Accad 1996: 468)

This is a very different picture of Third World women's relation to genital mutilation than that found, for example, in Mary Daly's work (Daly 1979).

Similar points to Mohanty's are made by Uma Narayan in her critique of Mary Daly's treatment of *sati* in *Gyn/Ecology*. Narayan argues that 'while Daly's work addresses "Third-World women's issues," ... it does so in a manner that misrepresents what is at stake', and that 'these misrepresentations replicate some common and problematic Western understandings of Third-World contexts and communities' (1997: 45). Narayan identifies two key features of colonial modes of representation: the failure to give due attention to social and historical details and the failure to give due attention to context. Crucial is the absence of history and the representation of the Third World as static and timeless. Writing of Daly's account of *sati* and comparing it with her chapter on European witch burning, Narayan points to the absence of historical information provided on *sati*. She argues that Daly's account of *sati* renders its temporal and social context invisible, taking little or no account of differences of class, caste, religion or geographical location. Attending to detailed specificity of particular practices, she argues, works against the colonialist tendency to represent the Third World as lacking internal differences and complexity. There is, she suggests, a double standard in play in the work of many Western feminists who represent Western societies as complex and changing and the Third World as uniform and outside history. Moreover, given the history of these colonial modes of representation and 'its complex effects on Third-World subjects, it is hardly surprising that one can find "colonialist representations" produced by members of Third-World communities' (Narayan 1997: 45).

It is not only how one speaks of women in the Third World which is at issue in Third World feminism. Also important is the question of who speaks for whom. This issue was raised by Gayatri Spivak in her influential essay 'Can the Subaltern Speak?', in which she analyses 'the relations between the discourses of the West and the possibility of speaking of (or for) the subaltern woman' (1988: 271). Spivak is profoundly pessimistic about the possibility of giving voice to the subaltern woman:

> Reporting on, or better still, participating in, antisexist work among women of color or women in class oppression in the First World or the Third World is undeniably on the agenda. We should also welcome all the information retrieval in these silenced areas that is taking place in anthropology, political science, history and sociology. Yet the assumption and construction of a consciousness or subject sustains such work and will, in the long run, cohere with the work of imperialist-subject constitution, mingling epistemic violence with the advancement of learning and civilization. And the subaltern woman will be as mute as ever.
>
> In so fraught a field, it is not easy to ask the question of the consciousness of the subaltern woman; it is thus all the more necessary to remind pragmatic radicals that such a question is not an idealist red herring. Though all feminist and antisexist projects cannot be reduced to this one, to ignore it is an unacknowledged political gesture that has a long history and collaborates with a masculine radicalism that renders the place of the investigator transparent. In learning to speak to (rather than listen to or speak for) the historically muted subject of the subaltern woman, the postcolonial intellectual sytematically unlearns female privilege. This systematic unlearning involves learning to critique postcolonial discourse with the best tools it can provide and not simply substituting the lost figure of the colonized. (Spivak 1988: 295)

What Spivak terms the 'place of the investigator' is never transparent, a point made repeatedly in Third World critiques of Western feminism.

QUESTIONS OF GLOBAL FEMINISM, HYBRIDITY AND NON-HIERARCHICAL DIFFERENCE

As we saw earlier in this chapter, despite the challenge of postmodern thinking and its insistence on specificity rather than global theory, debate continues over 'global feminism'. The terrain, however, has shifted since the 1970s to models of global feminism which draw on Third World experience as well as on Western feminism. Indeed for some feminist writers and activists, Third World feminism has become a viable model for global feminism:

> Waging their struggle in the colonial environment, Third World feminist thinkers have achieved a multicultural ethical and intellectual formation and a plethora of experience relevant to the development of an internationally valid and effective discourse addressing women's condition on a global scale. The question is whether this foundation can become a springboard for a global discourse. By definition, such a discourse must transcend the boundaries of Christian, Jewish, Muslim, Buddhist, socialist, capitalist, or any other particular culture. It will be feminist rather than patriarchal, humane rather than ideological, balanced rather than extremist, critical as well as exhortatory. (Afkhami 1996: 525)

In its aspirations to global status, this approach affirms some of the most important insights of postmodern thinking on the repressive binary structuring of traditional models of difference: 'The global feminist discourse rejects the notion that "east" and "west" constitute mutually exclusive paradigms,' but in the name of a universal humanism rather than difference. Global feminist discourse 'looks at life as evolving for all and believes that certain humane and morally defensible principles can and should be applied in the west and in the east equally' (Afkhami 1996: 526). Yet hierarchical material difference affects the realization of this humanist project:

> At present, of course, reality belies the potential. The disparity in physical and material power between the developed and less-developed countries forces Third World women to withdraw to reactive positions, formulating their discourse in response to the west and its challenge. Consequently, they fail to think globally; that is, to move beyond the Indigenous culture they have objectively outgrown. Their discourse remains nationalistic, parochial, fearful, tradition-bound, and rooted in the soil of patriarchy. (Afkhami 1996: 526)

Yet in Afkhami's view, the postmodern tendency towards globalization can only help the realization of a global feminist humanism:

194

The world, however, is undergoing a qualitative change, an important aspect of which may be the tumbling of nation states qua culture boundaries. In the process, women may gain a chance to promote on a world scale the kinds of ideas that are applicable to women everywhere. If they do, Third World women will be able to critique women's condition in the west from a vantage point that transcends the cultures of Abraham, Buddha, and Confucius and thus will help the women of all 'worlds of development', including Iran. (p. 526)

Afkhani does not suggest that 'the west be taken as the standard for the evaluation of women's conditions in Iran' (p. 526). She suggests that many of the limitations of Western discourse can only be understood and addressed from a global feminist position.

The virtue of the global position is that it partakes of the wisdom of all cultures and that it accommodates differences in the levels of economic and social development without succumbing to either the normlessness of cultural relativism or the self-righteous parochialism of any particular culture. . . .

Non-western feminists can be instrumental in the development of a viable global feminism, despite their historical handicap. As the world moves from a disjointed society of nation-states to an increasingly interconnected economic and technological system, and as the symmetry of the enclaves of poverty and backwardness in the developed and developing countries is increasingly apparent, it becomes easier for Third World feminists to develop a sense of empathy with their sisters in other parts of the globe. Indeed, unless such empathy is effected and expanded, patriarchal norms, for all practical purposes, will not be transcended and feminism, global or otherwise, will not fully succeed. (pp. 526–7)

Thinking difference otherwise is one of the key objectives of Third World feminism both in the West and in the Third World. This is linked to the political project of creating a global climate in which difference can be lived as enriching and valuable rather than as the oppressive effect of hierarchical binary oppositions. Some recent writing by black and Third World women in the West has argued that the diasporic experience creates the conditions for breaking down traditional binary categories and liberating difference. This deconstruction of traditional binary oppositions is a move which also informs much postmodern culture. If respect for difference is one of the more positive aspects or aspirations of postmodernity, the challenging of boundaries is also integral to this project. This is a perspective developed by Gloria Anzaldúa in her writing:

Theorists-of-color are in the process of trying to formulate 'marginal' theories that are partially outside and partially inside the Western frame of reference (if that is possible), theories that overlap many 'worlds.' We are articulating new positions in these 'in-between,' Borderland worlds of ethnic communities and academies, feminist and job worlds. In our literature, social issues such as race, class and sexual difference are intertwined with the narrative and poetic elements of a text, elements in which theory is embedded. In our *mestizaje* theories we create new categories for those of us left out or pushed out of the existing ones. We recover and examine non-Western aesthetics; recover and examine non-rational modes and 'blanked-out' realities while critiquing Western aesthetics; recover and examine non-rational modes and 'blanked-out' realities while critiquing rational, consensual reality; recover and examine indigenous languages while critiquing the 'languages' of the dominant culture. And we simultaneously combat the tokenization and appropriation of our literatures and our writers/artists. (Anzaldúa 1990b: xxvi)

The idea of a cultural hybridity that can challenge existing binary oppositions and hierarchies is seen by many women of colour as a profound and empowering effect of diaspora experience. Thus black British feminist Heidi Safia Mirza writes:

Cultural hybridity, the fusion of cultures and coming together of difference, the 'border crossing' that marks diasporic survival, signifies change, hope of newness, and space for creativity. But in the search for rootedness – a 'place called home' – these women, in the process of self-identification, disidentify with an excluding, racist British colonizing culture. They articulate instead a multi-faceted discontinuous black identity that marks their difference. (Mirza 1997b: 16)[2]

One of the strengths of recent feminist thought is the possibilities that it offers for thinking difference differently. Much of this work is indebted both to women of colour in both the Third and First worlds and to the insights of poststructuralist theory. It is able to throw new light on the lived experience of women in postmodernity. While the struggle for equal rights remains an important dimension of feminist politics, it is no longer necessary, as it was in the liberal humanist tradition, to links rights to sameness. Instead of sameness, it is possible to imagine a world in which difference is celebrated and enjoyed free from the hierarchical structures of class, racial, sexual and gender power. Yet to move towards such a world continues to require the articulation of marginalized voices and the self-affirmation of oppressed groups as well as the recognition by white, Western, heterosexual, middle-class women of their structural privileges:

Moving from silence into speech is for the oppressed, the colonized, the exploited, and those who stand and struggle side by side a gesture of defiance

196

that heals, that makes new life and new growth possible. It is that act of speech, of 'talking back', that is no mere gesture of empty words, that is the expression of our movement from object to subject – the liberated voice. (hooks 1989: 211)

Both groups can contribute to making the existing social relations that produce hierarchical difference visible. Both can help bring about social change. This change requires the positive recognition of difference in the struggle to redefine its meaning and reshape its material effects. In the words of Audre Lorde:

The future of our earth may depend on the ability of all women to identify and develop new definitions of power and new patterns of relating across difference. The old definitions have not served us, nor the earth that supports us. The old patterns, no matter how cleverly rearranged to imitate progress, still condemn us to cosmetically altered repetitions of the same old exchanges, the same old guilt, hatred, recrimination, lamentation and suspicion. (Lorde 1984: 123).

Notes

Chapter 1: The Question of Difference

1 For more on multiculturalism and cultural diversity in cultural policy see Jordan and Weedon 1995, chs 2 and 13.

2 For an introductory history of the postmodern see Bertens 1995.

3 For an introduction to poststructuralism and its usefulness for feminism see Weedon 1996a.

4 See Anzaldúa 1990a and Bhabha 1990.

5 See Foucault 1981 and ch. 5 of this book.

6 Other books in the series included *What a Young Girl Ought to Know; What a Young Woman Ought to Know; What a Woman Over Forty-five Ought to Know*, and equivalent texts for boys and men. Each book contained substantial chapters on care of the body and reproduction.

7 For more on racial science see Gould 1981 and Harris 1968.

8 For more on racial science in the American context see Stanton 1960.

9 See Broverman et al. 1972.

10 For more on first-wave German feminism see Frederiksen 1981 and Gerhard 1990.

11 For more on wages for housework see Malos 1980.

12 For more on women in Eastern Europe see Tova Yedlin (ed.), *Women in Eastern Europe and the Soviet Union*, New York: Praeger, 1980 and Chris Corrin (ed.), *Superwomen and the Double Burden*, London: Scarlet Press, 1992.

13 For more on normative dualism see Jaggar 1983.

14 The Plebs League, founded in 1909, developed an extensive programme of adult education and became the National Council of Labour Colleges in 1921.

15 See Engels 1972 and Bebel 1971.

16 In the GDR literature was the main site where fundamental political issues could be discussed. In Western societies, the press and broadcasting usually provide this space.

In the GDR censorship precluded open discussion in the media of basic political issues. In women's writing, for example the work of Christa Wolf and Irmtraud Morger, fiction became a space for criticizing patriarchy. For more on this see Eva Kaufmann's essays in Weedon 1996b.

17 See Irigaray 1991b and Whitford 1991.
18 For more on the construction of black traditions see Christian 1980, Hull et al. 1982, Braxton and McLaughlin 1990, Carby 1990 and Gates 1990. For lesbian traditions see Smith (ed.) 1983a; Wolfe and Penelope 1993 and Jay and Glasgow (eds) 1992.
19 My translation. The original German reads:

> Warum wir Mädchen nichts lernten, weiß ich. Es wurde eben in den damaligen Mädchenschulen kaum etwas gelehrt, was über die Elementar-kenntnisse hinausging.
>
> Die Knaben hatten es gut: Sie turnten, sie exerzierten. Sie durften sich auf Straßen und Plätzen in Freiheit tummeln. Ihnen gehörten Schnee und Eis im Winter, das Wasser im Sommer.
>
> Wir Mädchen turnten nicht, wir schwammen nicht und ruderten nicht. Wir durften uns nicht mit Schneebällen werfen, ja nicht einmal schlittern. Denke doch, der Strickstrumpf florierte noch.

20 See for example Fuss 1991 and Butler 1993.

Chapter 2: Challenging Patriarchy, Decentring Heterosexuality: Radical and Revolutionary Feminisms

1 For more on the politics of women's bodies at the end of the nineteenth century see Bland 1995.
2 For examples of ecofeminism see Mies and Shiva 1993, Adams 1993, Gaard 1993 and Braidotti et al. 1994.
3 For more on political lesbianism see Bunch 1987 and Feminist Review (ed.) 1987.
4 For recent work on heterosexuality see Wilkinson and Kitzinger (eds) 1993 and Richardson 1996.
5 Heterosexuality: A Feminism and Psychology Reader was an expanded version of the Special Issue of the journal Feminism and Psychology 2 (3), 1992.
6 For more on this see Foucault 1981 and ch. 5 of this book.
7 For more on this see section 6 on 'Technologies' in Kemp and Squires 1997: 468–529.

Chapter 3: Lesbian Difference, Feminism and Queer Theory

1 See Kitzinger 1987.
2 Some writers are radically anti-essentialist. Monique Wittig is one writer who has challenged the assumption that lesbians are naturally women. For a discussion of Wittig see Butler 1990.

3 For more on the role of sex in lesbian relations see Ardill and O'Sullivan 1987.
4 See, for example, *Yours in Struggle*, Bulkin et al. 1984. Thanks to Alessandra Tanesini for drawing my attention to this text.
5 *Sula*, Toni Morrison, London: Triad Grafton Books, 1982.
6 *The Lesbian in America*, Donald Webster Cory, New York: Citadel Press, 1964.
7 For more on transgender practices see Garber 1992.

Chapter 4: Psychoanalysis and Difference

1 For examples of the application of psychoanalytic theory see Bhabha 1994.
2 Von Bischoff's work was subject to detailed deconstruction by the German feminist Hedwig Dohm in her 1874 text *Die wissenschaftliche Emanicipation der Frau*. See Dohm 1982 and Weedon 1994.
3 For more on feminist engagements with psychoanalysis see Wright 1984 and 1992.
4 For a brief introduction and bibliography on object relations theory see Kahane 1992.
5 For more on this see Kristeva 1984.
6 For more on femininity as masquerade see Fuss 1991.
7 See Butler 1993 and Grosz 1995.
8 Butler's critique of Kristeva can be found in Butler 1990: 86–8.

Chapter 5: The Production and Subversion of Gender: Postmodern Approaches

1 For accounts of nineteenth- and early twentieth-century sciences of racial and sexual difference see Gould 1981 and Sayers 1982.
2 Phrenology was first developed by the Austrian Joseph Gall. It became central to the American School of Anthropology in the 1830s and 1840s. A founder of this school was Samuel Morton, who collected skulls, categorized them according to a racial schema and published detailed studies of the supposed difference between the races. See Stanton 1960.
3 See ch. 4, pp. 89 to 93.
4 See in particular Derrida 1973 and 1976 and Foucault 1979 and 1981.
5 For recent examples of radical feminist critiques see Bell and Klein (eds) 1996.
6 For expositions of Derrida's theory and its relevance to feminism see Elam 1994.
7 For more on the importance of the category woman to feminist identity politics see Nicholson 1990, Elam 1994, Whelehan 1995, Bell and Klein (eds) 1996 and Jeffreys 1996.
8 See Braidotti 1991.
9 For discussions of feminist objections to Foucault's model of power see Nicholson 1990 and Fraser 1989.
10 For discussion of the Möbius strip see Grosz 1994.
11 Jeffreys has in mind the essays in *Inside/Out* (Fuss 1991).

12 Useful recent examples of radical feminist objections to postmodern theories can be found in the volume *Radically Speaking: Feminism Reclaimed* (Bell and Klein (eds) 1996).

13 For other clear discussions of Foucault's analytics of power see Foucault 1980 and 1981.

Chapter 6: Class

1   The 1960s and 1970s saw the growth of a large number of Maoist groups on the left both in Europe and the USA. They were attracted by the seemingly grass roots nature of Chinese communism during the Cultural Revolution. Similarly young black activists in the United States turned briefly to Maoism, partly on account of their perception of the Cultural Revolution and partly because Mao was non-white.

2   For example, the adult education organizations, the Plebs' League and the Workers' Educational Organisation with their respective journals *The Plebs* and *The Highway*. The Communist Party also provided education and published cultural journals the most important of which was *Left Review*.

3   For more on this see Weedon 1984.

4   See, for example, debates in the 1930s in *Left Review*.

5   See, for example, *Women Take Issue* (Women's Studies Group 1978).

6   Whereas the annual publication *Social Trends* (HMSO) categorizes by occupation, much sociology looks at lifestyle, taste etc.

7   See *Capital, Volume 1* (Marx 1976).

8   See, for example, Foreman 1977.

9   For more on Zetkin and other key socialist feminists in Germany at this time see Thönnessen 1976.

10 The Prussian Combination Laws were in force during the second half of the nineteenth century and were finally abolished in 1908.

11 See Malos 1980.

12 See ch. 1, n. 16.

13 See, for example, Judith Williamson's classic text *Decoding Advertisements: Ideology and Meaning in Advertising* (Williamson 1978).

14 See Feminist Review (ed.) 1987.

Chapter 7: Race, Racism and the Problem of Whiteness

1   Among the first and best known eighteenth-century attempts to produce a theory of racial difference was the work of the Swedish natural scientist Linnaeus who set out in the 1730s to classify the natural world and published his *Systema naturae* in 1735. Linnaeus not only classified different races but also organized them hierarchically as part of a 'Great Chain of Being'. His 1758 categorization of mankind consists of descriptions of both phenotypical features and of character types. Thus while Europeans are described among other things as 'gentle, acute, inventive' and

'governed by custom', Africans are 'phlegmatic, relaxed . . . crafty, indolent, negligent' and 'governed by caprice' (quoted in Jordan 1969: 221). Linnaeus's early attempt to develop a science of natural history was followed by a number of further influential works of classification such as Johann Blumenbach's *De generis humani varietate nativa* (1775) and Georges Louis Leclerc, Comte de Buffon's *Histoire Naturelle* (1749–1804).

2 Whereas racial difference was defined in terms of a hierarchical scale, eighteenth- and nineteenth-century racial scientists disagreed on whether this hierarchy was a natural God-given state of affairs or the effect of environmental differences. The environmentalists – who tended to be monogenesists, believing that God created a single human race – assumed that existing inequalities between the races could eventually be eradicated by the civilizing force of white Western culture. The polygenesists, on the other hand – who believed in separate creations – saw racial hierarchy as natural and unchangeable.

3 For more on the legacy of nineteenth-century racism in the present see Jordan and Weedon 1995: 249–314.

4 For more on primitivism see Jordan and Weedon 1995: 315–431.

5 The publications of far Right extremist groups often recycle classical nineteenth-century racist ideas and images. For a study of such publications see Daniels 1997.

6 See, for example, Frankenberg 1993 and Dyer 1997.

7 See Dyer 1997.

8 This response to discrimination against Irish people also referenced the ways in which nineteenth-century racial science was used to suggest that the Irish were an inferior race.

9 This point was made repeatedly by black British feminists in the 1980s. See, for example, political texts from the women's movement reprinted in sections 3 and 7 of Kanter et al. 1984.

10 For examples of texts recovering black feminist history and culture see ch. 1, n. 18.

11 This is a key theme, for example, in the work of bell hooks both in her historical study of feminism and racism and in her analyses of contemporary popular culture (see hooks 1986, 1989, 1991 and 1992). Among the recurrent images which black feminists have challenged are the ideas that black women are particularly sexual, unnaturally strong and matriarchal and that they pose a threat to black masculinity.

12 For more on Afrocentrism see Asante 1987. Examples of Afrocentric history include, for example, the work of Cheikh Anta Diop. See Diop 1974.

13 See the discussion of reverse discourse in ch. 5, pp. 119–20.

14 See Glenn Jordan's article 'Can the Postmodern Subject be Black' in *Postmodernism at the Century's End*, ed. Gerhard Hoffmann and Alfred Hornung, Heidelberg Universitätsverlag C. Winter, 1999. See also his forthcoming book, *Racism and the Black Subject: White Power, Black Bodies, Histories of the Present*, Oxford: Blackwell, 1999.

15 For more on this see Jordan and Weedon 1995, chs 10–13.

16 José Vascocelos, *La Raza Cósmica: Misión de la Raza Ibero-Americana*, México: Aguilar S. A. de Ediciones, 1961.

17 See also Bhabha 1990.
18 See, for example, writing on being 'mixed-race' in Mirza 1997a.

Chapter 8: Beyond Eurocentrism: Feminism and the Politics of Difference in a Global Frame

1 See, for example, Mohanty 1991 and Narayan 1997.
2 Similar points are made in the same anthology by Ahmed 1997, Ifekwunigwe 1997 and Rassool 1997.

BIBLIOGRaphy

Accad, Evelyne 1996: Truth versus Loyalty: In Bell and Klein (eds) 1996, pp. 465–9.

Adams, Carol J. (ed.) 1993: *Ecofeminism and the Sacred*. New York: Continuum.

Adler, Margot 1989: The Juice and the Mystery. In Plant (ed.) 1989, pp. 151–4.

Afkhami, Mahnaz 1996: Towards a Global Feminism: A Muslim Perspective. In Bell and Klein (eds) 1996, pp. 525–7.

Ahmed, Sara 1997: 'It's a Suntan Isn't It?' Autobiography as an Identificatory Practice. In Mirza (ed.) 1997a, pp. 153–67.

Althusser, Louis 1971: Ideology and Ideological State Apparatuses (Notes Towards an Investigation). In *Lenin and Philosophy*, London: New Left Books, pp. 152–73.

Anzaldúa, Gloria 1987: *Borderlands/La Frontera The New Mestiza*. San Francisco: Spinster/ Aunt Lute Books.

—— (ed.) 1990a: *Making Face, Making Soul. Haciendo Caras. Creative and Critical Perspectives by Feminists of Color*. San Francisco: Aunt Lute Books.

—— (1990b) Haciendo caras, una entrada. An introduction by Gloria Anzaldúa. In Anzaldúa (ed.) 1990a, pp. xv–xxviii.

—— (1990c) En rapport, In Opposition: Cobrando cuentas a las nuestras. In Anzaldúa (ed.) 1990a, pp. 142–8.

Appiah, Kwame W. and Henry Louis Gates (eds) 1995: Editors' Introduction: Multiplying Identities. In *Identities*, Chicago: University of Chicago Press.

Ardill, Susan and Sue O'Sullivan 1987: Upsetting an Applecart: Difference, Desire and Lesbian Sadomasochism. In Feminist Review (ed.) 1987, pp. 277–306.

Arnold, June 1976: Lesbian Fiction. *Sinister Wisdom*, 2, pp. 28–30.

Asante, Moleti Kete 1987: *The Afrocentric Idea*. Philadelphia: Temple University Press.

Astell, Mary 1986: *The First English Feminist Reflections upon Marriage and Other Writings*. Ed. Bridget Hill. Aldershot: Gower/Maurice Temple Smith.

—— 1996: *Political Writings*. Ed. Patricia Springborg. Cambridge: Cambridge University Press.

Barnes, Djuna 1972: *The Ladies' Almanach*. New York: Harper and Row.

Baudrillard, Jean 1981: *Simulacra and Simulations*. Trans. P. Foss, P. Patton and P. Beitchman. New York: Semiotext(e).

Bebel, August 1971: *Women and Socialism* (original 1878). Trans. D. de Leon. New York: Schocken Books.

Bell, Diane and Renate Klein (eds) 1996: *Radically Speaking: Feminism Reclaimed*. London: Zed Books.

Bellos, Linda 1984: For Lesbian Sex, Against Sadomasochism. In Kanter et al. (eds) 1984, pp. 190–7.

Benhabib, Seyla 1986: *Critique, Norm and Utopia: A Study of the Foundations of Critical Theory*. New York: Columbia University Press.

Benjamin, Jessica 1988: *The Bonds of Love: Psychoanalysis, Feminism and Problems of Domination*. New York: Pantheon.

Bertens, Hans 1995: *The Idea of the Postmodern: A History*. London and New York: Routledge.

Bhabha, Homi 1990: Interview with Homi Bhabha. The Third Space. In ed. Jonathan Rutherford, *Identity: Community, Culture, Difference*, London: Lawrence and Wishart, pp. 207–21.

—— 1994: *The Location of Culture*. London: Routledge.

Bland, Lucy 1995: *Banishing the Beast: English Feminism and Sexual Morality 1885–1914*. Harmondsworth: Penguin.

Bland, Lucy, Charlotte Brunsdon, Dorothy Hobson and Janice Winship 1978: Women 'Inside and Outside' the Relations of Production. In Women's Studies Group 1978, pp. 35–78.

Bloch, Iwan 1909: *The Sexual Life of Our Time*. London: Heinemann.

Bourne, J. 1987: Homelands of the Mind: Jewish Feminism and Identity Politics. *Race and Class*, 29 (1), pp. 1–24.

Brah, Avtar 1996: *Cartographies of Diaspora: Contesting Identities*. London and New York: Routledge.

Braidotti, Rosi 1991: *Patterns of Dissonance*. Oxford: Polity.

—— 1994: *Nomadic Subjects: Embodiment and Sexual Difference in Contemporary Feminist Theory*. New York: Columbia University Press.

Braidotti, Rosi, Ewa Charkiewicz, Sabine Häusler and Saskia Wieringa 1994: *Women, the Environment and Sustainable Development: Towards a Theoretical Synthesis*. London: Zed Books.

Braxton, Joanne M. and Andree Nicola McLaughlin (eds) 1990: *Wild Women in the Whirlwind: Afro-American Culture and the Contemporary Literary Renaissance*. London: Serpent's Tail.

Broverman, Inge K., Susan Raymond Vogel, Donald M. Broverman, Frank E. Clarkson and Paul S. Rosenkrantz 1972: Sex Role Stereotypes: A Current Appraisal. *Journal of Social Issues*, 28 (2) pp. 59–78.

Bryan, Beverley, Stella Dadzie and Suzanne Scafe 1985: *The Heart of the Race*. London: Virago.

Bulkin, Elly, Minnie Bruce Pratt and Barbara Smith 1984: *Yours in Struggle*. Ithaca, NY: Firebrand Publishers.

Bunch, Charlotte 1983: Not by Degrees: Feminist Theory and Education. In Bunch and Pollack (eds) 1983, pp. 248–60.

—— 1987: *Passionate Politics: Feminist Theory in Action. Essays 1968–1986*. New York: St Martin's Press.

205

Bunch, Charlotte and Susana Fried 1996: Beijing 95: Moving Women's Human Rights from Margin to Centre. *Signs*, 22 (1), 200–4.

Bunch, Charlotte and Sandra Pollack (eds) 1983: *Learning Our Way: Essays in Feminist Education*. New York: Crossing Press.

Butler, Judith 1990: *Gender Trouble*. New York and London: Routledge.

—— 1993: *Bodies That Matter*. New York and London: Routledge.

Cameron, Barbara 1983: Gee, You Don't Seem Like An Indian from the Reservation. In Moraga and Anzaldúa (eds) 1983, pp. 46–52.

Carby, Hazel V. 1982: White Woman Listen! Black Feminism and the Boundaries of Sisterhood. In Centre for Contemporary Cultural Studies 1982, pp. 212–35.

—— 1990: *Reconstructing Womanhood: The Emergence of the Afro-American Woman Novelist*. Oxford: Oxford University Press.

Centre for Contemporary Cultural Studies 1982: *The Empire Strikes Back: Race and Racism in 70s Britain*. London: Hutchinson.

Chodorow, Nancy 1974: Family Structure and Feminine Personality. In Rosaldo and Lamphère (eds) 1974, pp. 43–66.

—— 1978: *The Reproduction of Mothering*. Berkeley: University of California Press.

Christian, Barbara 1980: *Black Women Novelists: The Development of a Tradition 1892–1976*. Westport, C: Greenwood Press.

Cixous, Hélène 1987: Sorties. In Cixous and Clément 1987, pp. 63–130.

Cixous, Hélène and Catherine Clément 1987: *The Newly Born Woman*. Trans. Betsy Wing. Manchester: Manchester University Press.

Clark, Wendy 1987: The Dyke, the Feminist and the Devil. In Feminist Review (ed.) 1987, pp. 201–15.

Collins, Patricia Hill 1990: *Black Feminist Thought*. London: Unwin Hyman.

Combahee River Collective 1983: A Black Feminist Statement. In Moraga and Anzaldúa (eds) 1983, pp. 210–18.

Cooper, Anna Julia 1976: 1893 Speech. In *Black Women in Nineteenth-century American Life*, ed. Bert J. Loewenberg and Ruth Bogin, University Park: Pennsylvania State University Press, 1976, pp. 330–1.

Daly, Mary 1979: *Gyn/Ecology*. London: The Women's Press.

Daniels, Jessie 1997: *White Lies: Race, Class, Gender and Sexuality in White Supremacist Discourse*. New York and London: Routledge.

de Beauvoir, Simone 1972: *The Second Sex* (original 1949). Trans. and ed. H. M. Parshley. Harmondsworth: Penguin.

Deleuze, Giles 1968: *Différence et répétition*. Paris: Presses Universitaires de France.

—— 1978: Philosophie et minorité. *Critique*, 369, pp. 154–5.

Deleuze, Giles and Ferdinand Guattari 1977: *Anti-Oedipus: Capitalism and Schizophrenia*. Trans. R. Hurley, S. Seem and H. R. Lane. New York: Viking.

Derrida, Jacques 1973: *Speech and Phenomena*. Trans. D. Allison. Evanston, IL: Northwestern University Press.

—— 1976: *Of Grammatology*. Trans. G. Spivak. Baltimore, MD: The John Hopkins University Press.

—— 1979: *Spurs: Nietzsche's Style*. Trans. B. Harlow. Chicago: University of Chicago Press.

Di Stefano, Christine 1990: Dilemmas of Difference: Feminism, Modernity and Postmodernism. In Nicholson (ed.) 1990, pp. 63–82.

Dinnerstein, Dorothy 1976: *The Mermaid and the Minotaur: Sexual Arrangements and Human Malaise*. New York: Harper and Row.

Diop, Cheikh Anta 1974: *The African Origin of Civilization: Myth or Reality*. New York: Lawrence Hill.

Dohm, Hedwig 1982: *Emanzipation*. Zürich: Ala Verlag.

—— 1988: *Schicksale einer Seele* (original 1899). München: Verlag Frauenoffensive.

Drake, Emma F. Angell 1901: *What A Young Wife Ought to Know*. Philadelphia: The Vir Publishing Company.

Dreher, Sarah 1993: Waiting for Stonewall. In Wolfe and Penelope (eds) 1993, pp. 110–23.

Dyer, Richard 1997: *White*. London: Routledge.

Eisenstein, Hester and Alice Jardine (eds) 1985: *The Future of Difference*. New Brunswick and London: Rutgers University Press.

Elam, Diane 1994: *Feminism and Deconstruction*. London and New York: Routledge.

Ellis, Havelock 1934: *Psychology of Sex*. London: Heinemann.

Engels, Frederick 1972: *The Origin of the Family, Private Property and the State* (original 1884). London: Lawrence and Wishart.

Faderman, Lillian 1981: *Surpassing the Love of Men: Romantic Friendship and Love Between Women from the Renaissance to the Present*. New York: William Morrow.

—— 1991: *Odd Girls and Twilight Lovers: A History of Lesbian Life in Twentieth-Century America*. Harmondsworth: Penguin.

Fanon, Frantz 1968: *The Wretched of the Earth*. New York: Grove Press.

Feminist Review 1979 –. London: Routledge.

Feminist Review (ed.) 1987: *Sexuality: A Reader*. London: Virago.

Filser, Franz (ed.) 1977: *Die Frau in der Gesellschaft*. Stuttgart: Reclam.

Firestone, Shulamith 1972: *The Dialectic of Sex: The Case for Feminist Revolution* (original 1970). London: Paladin.

Flax, Jane 1985: Mother–Daughter Relationships: Psychodynamics, Politics, and Philosophy. In Eisenstein and Jardine 1985, pp. 20–40.

Forel, Auguste Henri 1908: *The Sexual Question: A Scientific, Psychological, Hygienic and Sociological Study*. Trans. C. F. Marshall. New York: Physicians and Surgeons Book Company.

Foreman, Ann 1977: *Femininity as Alienation: Women and the Family in Marxism and Psychoanalysis*. London: Pluto.

Foucault, Michel 1979: *Discipline and Punish*. Harmondsworth: Penguin.

—— 1980: *Power/Knowledge, Selected Interviews and Other Writings 1972–77*. Ed. Colin Gordon. Trans. C. Gordon, L. Marshall, J. Mepham and K. Soper. Brighton: The Harvester Press.

—— 1981: *The History of Sexuality, Volume One. An Introduction*. Harmondsworth: Penguin.

—— 1991: *Remarks on Marx: Converations with Duccio Trombadori*. Trans. R. J. Goldstein and J. Cascaito. New York: Semiotext(e).

Fowlkes, Diane L. 1997: Moving from Identity Politics to Coalition Politics Through a Feminist Materialist Standpoint of Intersubjectivity in Gloria Anzaldúa's *Borderlands/La Frontera: The New Mestiza*. *Hypatia A Journal of Feminist Philosophy*, 12 (2), pp. 105–24.

207

Frankenberg, Ruth 1993: *White Women, Race Matters: The Social Construction of Whiteness.* Minneapolis: University of Minnesota Press.

Fraser, Nancy 1989: *Unruly Practices: Power, Discourse and Gender in Contemporary Social Theory.* Cambridge: Polity.

Frederiksen, Elke (ed.) 1981: *Die Frauenfrage in Deutschland: Texte und Documente.* Stuttgart: Reclam.

Freud, Sigmund 1975a: Some Psychical Consequences of the Anatomical Distinction Between the Sexes (original 1925). In Strouse (ed.) 1975, pp. 27–38.

—— 1975b: Female Sexuality (original 1931). In Strouse (ed.) 1975, pp. 53–72.

—— 1975c: *The Psychopathology of Everyday Life* (original 1901). Harmondsworth: Penguin.

—— 1976: *The Interpretation of Dreams* (original 1900). Harmondsworth: Penguin.

Friedan, Betty 1965: *The Feminine Mystique* (original 1963). Harmondsworth: Penguin.

Fuss, Diane 1991: *Inside/out: Lesbian Theories, Gay Theories.* New York and London: Routledge.

Gaard, Greta (ed.) 1993: *Ecofeminism, Women, Animals, Nature.* Philadelphia: Temple University Press.

Gallop, Jane 1988: *Thinking Through the Body.* New York: Columbia University Press.

Garber, Majorie 1992: *Vested Interests: Cross-Dressing and Cultural Anxiety.* Harmondsworth: Penguin.

Gates, Henry Louis (ed.) 1990: *Reading Black, Reading Feminist.* New York and London: Meridean.

Gerhard, Ute 1990: *Unerhört: Die Geschichte der deutschen Frauenbewegung.* Reinbek bei Hamburg: Rowohlt.

Gill, Rosalind and Rebecca Walker 1993: Heterosexuality, Feminism, Contradiction: On Being Young, White, Heterosexual Feminists in the 1990s. In Wilkinson and Kitzinger (eds) 1993, pp. 68–72.

Gilligan, Carol 1982: *In A Different Voice: Women's Conceptions of the Self and Morality.* Cambridge, MA: Harvard University Press.

Gough, Kathleen 1975: The Origin of the Family. In *Towards an Anthropology of Women,* ed. Rayna Reiter. New York: Monthly Review Press.

Gould, Stephen Jay 1981: *The Mismeasure of Man.* New York and London: W. W. Norton.

Greer, Germaine 1970: *The Female Eunuch.* London: MacGibbon and Kee.

Griffin, Susan 1984: *Woman and Nature: The Roaring Inside Her* (original 1978). London: The Women's Press.

Grosz, Elizabeth 1994: *Volatile Bodies: Towards a Corporeal Feminism.* Bloomington and Indianapolis: Indiana University Press.

—— 1995: *Space, Time and Perversion.* New York and London: Routledge.

Gutman, Herbert 1976: *The Black Family in Slavery and Freedom, 1750–1925.* New York: Random House.

Hall, Radclyffe 1982: *The Well of Loneliness* (original 1928). London: Virago.

Haraway, Donna J. 1990: A Manifesto for Cyborgs: Science, Technology and Socialist Feminism in the 1980s (original 1985). In Nicholson (ed) 1990, pp. 190–233.

—— 1991a: *Simians, Cyborgs, and Women: The Reinvention of Nature.* London: Free Association Books Ltd.

—— 1991b: Situated Knowledges: The Science Question in Feminism and the Privilege of Partial Perspective (original 1988). In Haraway 1991a, pp. 183–202.

Harding, Sandra 1997: Comment on Hekman's 'Truth and Method: Feminist Standpoint Theory Revisited': Whose Standpoint Needs the Regimes of Truth and Reality? *Signs*, 22 (2), pp. 382–91.

Harding, Sandra and Merrill Hintikka (eds) 1983: *Discovering Reality: Feminist Perspectives on Epistemology, Metaphysics, Methodology, and the Philosophy of Science.* Dordrecht: Reidel.

Harris, Marvin 1968: *The Rise of Anthropological Theory.* New York: Harper and Row.

Hartsock, Nancy 1983a: *Money, Sex and Power.* New York: Longman.

—— 1983b: The Feminist Standpoint: Developing the Ground for a Specifically Feminist Historical Materialism. In Harding and Hintikka (eds) 1983, pp. 283–310.

—— 1990: Foucault on Power: A Theory for Women? In Nicholson (ed.) 1990, pp. 157–75.

Hawthorne, Susan 1996: From Theories of Indifference to a Wild Politics. In Bell and Klein (eds) 1996, pp. 483–501.

Hekman, Susan 1997: Truth and Method: Feminist Standpoint Theory Revisited. *Signs*, 22 (2), pp. 341–65.

Herskovits, Melville J. 1958: *The Myth of the Negro Past* (original 1941). Boston, MA: Beacon Press.

Hervé, G. 1881: Du poids de l'encéphale. *Revue d'Anthropologie*, 2nd series, 4, pp. 681–98.

Hirsch, Marianna 1992: Object-relations Orientated Criticism. In Wright (ed.) 1992, pp. 280–4.

Hoagland, Sarah Lucia and Julia Penelope (eds) 1988: *For Lesbians Only: A Separatist Anthology.* London: Onlywomen Press.

hooks, bell 1986: *Ain't I a Woman: Black Women and Feminism* (original 1982). London: Pluto Press.

—— 1989: *Talking Back: Thinking Feminist Thinking Black.* Boston, MA: South End Press.

—— 1991: *Yearning: Race, Gender and Cultural Politics.* London: Turnaround.

—— 1992: *Black Looks: Race and Representation.* London: Turnaround.

Hull, Gloria T., Patricia Bell Scott and Barbara Smith (eds) 1982: *All the Women Are White, All the Blacks Are Men, But Some of Us Are Brave: Black Women's Studies.* New York: The Feminist Press at the City University of New York.

Hunt, Margaret 1990: The De-Erotization of Womens Liberation: Social Purity Movements and the Revolutionary Feminism of Sheila Jeffreys. *Feminist Review* 34 (1990), pp. 23–46.

Hypatia A Journal of Feminist Philosophy 1986 –. Bloomington and Indianapolis: Indiana University Press.

Ifekwunigwe, Jayne 1997: Diaspora's Daughters, Africa's Orphans?: On Lineage, Authenticity and 'Mixed Race' Identity. In Mirza (ed.) 1997a, pp. 127–52.

Irigaray, Luce 1985: *This Sex Which is Not One* (original 1977). Trans. C. Porter and C. Burke. New York: Cornell University Press.

—— 1991a: *The Irigaray Reader*, ed. Margaret Whitford. Oxford: Blackwell.

—— 1991b: Women-mothers, the Silent Substratum of the Social Order. In Irigaray 1991a, pp. 47–52.

—— 1993: *An Ethics of Sexual Difference* (original 1984). Trans. C. Burke and G. C. Gill. London: The Athlone Press.

—— 1994: *Thinking the Difference: For a Peaceful Revolution* (original 1989). Trans. K Montin. London: The Athlone Press.

Jaggar, Alison 1983: *Feminist Politics and Human Nature*. Brighton: Harvester.

Jameson, Fredric 1984: Postmodernism or the Cultural Logic of Late Capitalism. *New Left Review*, 146, pp. 53–93.

Jay, Karla & Joanne Glasgow (eds) 1992: *Lesbian Texts and Contexts: Radical Revisions*. London: Onlywomen Press.

Jeffreys, Sheila 1990: *Anticlimax: A Feminist Perspective on the Sexual Revolution*. London: The Women's Press.

—— 1996: Return to Gender: Post-modernism and Lesbianandgay Theory. In Bell and Klein (eds) 1996, pp. 359–74.

Jordan, Glenn and Chris Weedon 1995: *Cultural Politics: Class, Gender, Race and the Postmodern World*. Oxford: Blackwell.

Jordan, Winthrop 1969: *White Over Black: American Attitudes Towards the Negro 1550–1812*. Baltimore, MA: Penguin Books.

Kahane, Claire 1992: Object-relations Theory. In Wright (ed.) 1992, pp. 284–90.

Kahn, Karen (ed.) 1995: *Front Line Feminism, 1975–1995: Essays from* Sojourner's *First 20 Years*. San Fransisco: Aunt Lute Books.

Kanter, Hannah, Sarah Lefanu and Carole Spedding (eds) 1984: *Sweeping Statements: Writings from the Women's Liberation Movement 1981–83*. London: The Women's Press.

Kelly, Mary 1983: *Post Partum Document*. London: Routledge and Kegan Paul.

—— 1987: Mary Kelly. Interviewed by Terence Maloon. In Robinson (ed.) 1987, pp. 72–9.

Kemp, Sandra & Judith Squires (eds) 1997: *Feminisms*. Oxford: Oxford University Press.

Kitzinger, Celia 1987: *The Social Construction of Lesbianism*. London: Sage.

—— 1994: Problematising Pleasure: Radical Feminist Deconstructions of Sexuality and Power. In *Power/Gender: Social Relations in Theory and Practice*, ed. H. Lorraine Radtke and Henderikus J. Stam, London: Sage.

Krafft-Ebing, Richard 1882: *Psychopathia Sexualis*. Trans. M. E. Wedneck. New York: Putnams.

Kristeva, Julia 1982: *Desire in Language: A Semiotic Approach to Literature and Art*. Trans. T. Gora, A. Jardine and L. S. Roudiez. Oxford: Blackwell.

—— 1984: *Revolution in Poetic Language*. Trans. M. Waller. New York: Columbia University Press.

—— 1986a: *The Kristeva Reader*. Ed. Toril Moi. Oxford: Blackwell.

—— 1986b: Revolution in Poetic Language. In Kristeva 1986a, pp. 90–136.

—— 1986c: Stabat Mater. In Kristeva 1986a, pp. 160–87.

—— 1986d: A New Type of Intellectual: The Dissident. In Kristeva 1986a, pp. 292–300.

Lacan, Jacques 1977: The Mirror Phase as Formative of the Function of the I (original

1949). In *Écrits*, trans. A. Sheridan, London: Tavistock, pp. 1–7.

Lange, Helene 1977: Intellektuelle Grenzlinien zwischen Mann und Frau [Intellectual Boundaries Between Man and Woman] (original 1899). In Filser (ed.) 1977, pp. 46–52.

Le Bon, Gustave 1879: Recherches anatomiques et mathématiques sur les lois des variations du volume du cerveau et sur leurs relations avec l'intelligence. *Revue d'Anthropologie*, 2nd series, 2, pp. 27–104.

Leeds Revolutionary Feminist Group 1981: *Love Your Enemy? The Debate Between Heterosexual Feminism and Political Lesbianism* (original 1979). London: Onlywomen Press.

Linnaeus, Carl 1735: *Systema naturae*. Apud Theodorum Haak: Lugduni Bavatorum.

Lorde, Audre 1984: *Sister Outside*. Freedom, CA: The Crossing Press.

Lovelock, Molly 1995: Wages for Housework: The Idea's Everywhere (original 1978). In Kahn (ed.) 1995, 77–9.

Lugones, Maria 1990: Hablando cara a cara/Speaking Face to Face: An Exploration of Ethnocentric Racism. In Anzaldúa (ed.) 1990a, pp. 46–54.

Lyotard, Jean François 1984: *The Postmodern Condition: A Report on Knowledge*. Manchester: Manchester University Press.

M/F 1978: London.

MacCowan, Lyndall 1992: Re-collecting History, Renaming Lives: Femme Stigma and the Feminist Seventies and Eighties. In Nestle (ed.) 1992, pp. 299–328.

Malos, Ellen (ed.) 1980: *The Politics of Housework*. London: Allison and Busby.

Marx, Karl 1970: *The German Ideology* (original 1845). London: Lawrence and Wishart.

—— 1975: *Eighteenth Brumaire of Louis Bonaparte* (original 1852). New York: International Publishers.

—— 1976: *Capital, Volume 1* (original 1867). Harmondsworth: Penguin.

Marx, Karl and Frederick Engels 1969: *Manifesto of the Communist Party* (original 1848). Moscow: Progress Publishers.

Melucci, A. 1989: *Nomads of the Present: Social Movements and Individual Needs in Contemporary Society*. London: Radius.

Menschik, Jutta (ed.) 1976: *Grundlagentexte zur Emanzipation der Frau*. Köln: Pahl-Rugenstein.

Merchant, Carolyn 1982: *The Death of Nature*. London: Wildwood House.

Mies, Maria and Vandana Shiva 1993: *Ecofeminism*. London: Zed Books.

—— 1997: Ecofeminism. In Kemp and Squires (eds) 1997, pp. 497–502.

Mill, John Stuart 1984: On the Subjection of Women (original 1869). In *Collected Works of John Stuart Mill*, ed. John M. Robson, London: Routledge and Kegan Paul, pp. 259–340.

Millett, Kate 1971: *Sexual Politics*. London: Rupert Hart-Davies.

Minh-ha, Trinh T. 1989a: *Woman, Native, Other: Writing Postcoloniality and Feminism*. Bloomington: Indiana University Press.

—— 1989b: 'Outside In Inside Out'. In *Questions of Third Cinema*, ed. Jim Pines and Paul Willeman, London: BFI Publishing, pp. 133–49.

—— 1990: Not You/Like You: Post-colonial Women and the Interlocking Questions of Identity and Difference. In Anzaldúa (ed.) 1990a, pp. 371–5.

Mirza, Heidi Safia (ed.) 1997a: *Black British Feminism: A Reader*. London and New York: Routledge.

—— 1997b: Introduction: Mapping a Genealogy of Black British Feminism. In Mirza (ed.) 1997a, pp. 1–28.

Mitchell, Juliet 1975a: *Psychoanalysis and Feminism*. Harmondsworth: Penguin.

Mitchell, Juliet 1975b: On Freud and the Distinction Between the Sexes. In Strouse (ed.) 1975, pp. 39–52.

Mohanty, Chandra Talpade 1991: Under Western Eyes: Feminist Scholarship and Colonial Discourse. In Mohanty et al. (eds) 1991, pp. 51–80.

Mohanty, Chandra Talpade, Ann Russo and Lourdes Torres (eds) 1991: *Third World Women and the Politics of Feminism*. Bloomington and Indianapolis: Indiana University Press.

Moraga, Cherríe 1983a: Refugees of a World on Fire. Foreword to the Second Edition of *This Bridge Called My Back*. In Moraga and Anzaldúa (eds) 1983, pp. i–iv.

—— 1983b: La Güera. In Moraga and Anzaldúa (eds) 1983, pp. 27–34.

Moraga, Cherríe and Gloria Anzaldúa (eds) 1983: *This Bridge Called My Back: Writings by Radical Women of Color*. New York: Kitchen Table: Women of Color Press.

Morgan, Robin (ed.) 1970: *Sisterhood is Powerful: An Anthology of Writings from the Women's Liberation Movement*. New York: Random House.

—— 1993: *The Word of a Woman: Selected Prose 1968–1992*. London: Virago.

Mulvey, Laura 1987: *Post Partum Document* by Mary Kelly. In Robinson (ed.) 1987, pp. 100–1.

Narayan, Uma 1997: *Dislocating Cultures: Identities, Traditions and Third World Feminism*. New York and London: Routledge.

Nestle, Joan 1987: *A Restricted Country: Essays and Short Stories*. London: Sheba Feminist Publishers.

—— (ed.) 1992: *The Persistent Desire: A Femme-Butch Reader*. Boston, MA: Alyson Publications.

Nicholson, Linda (ed.) 1990: *Feminism/Postmodernism*. New York and London: Routledge.

Norcross, Paul 1996: Deconstruction. *A Dictionary of Cultural and Critical Theory*, ed. Michael Payne, Oxford: Blackwell, pp. 136–9.

Nott, Josiah C. M.D. 1844: *Two Lectures on the Natural History of the Caucasian and Negro Races*. Mobile, AL: Dade and Thompson.

O'Brien, Mary 1981: *The Politics of Reproduction*. London: Routledge and Kegan Paul.

Ortner, Sherry 1974: Is Female to Male as Nature is to Culture? In Rosaldo and Lamphère (eds) 1974, pp. 67–88.

Pence, Ellen 1982: Racism – A White Issue. In Hull et al. (eds) 1982, pp. 45–7.

Plant, Judith (ed.) 1989: *Healing the Wounds: The Promise of Ecofeminism*. Toronto: Between the Lines.

Plebs Magazine 1909–19, continued as *The Plebs* 1919 –: London: Plebs League.

Radcliffe Richards, Janet 1982: *The Sceptical Feminist*. Harmondsworth: Penguin.

Radicalesbians 1988: The Woman Identified Woman (original 1970). In Hoagland and Penelope (eds) 1988, pp. 17–22.

Rassool, Naz 1997: Fractured or Flexible Identities: Life Histories of 'Black', Diasporic Women in Britain. In Mirza (ed.) 1997a, pp. 187–204.

Raymond, Janice G. 1982: *The Transsexual Empire: The Making of the Shemale* (original 1979). Boston, MA: Beacon Press.

Reich, June L. 1992: Genderfuck: The Law of the Dildo. *Discourse*, 15 (1), pp. 112–27.

Rich, Adrienne 1977: *Of Woman Born: Motherhood as Experience and Institution*. London: Virago.

—— 1984: Compulsory Heterosexuality and Lesbian Existence. In Snitow et al. (eds) 1984, pp. 212–41.

Richardson, Diane (ed.) 1996: *Theorising Heterosexuality*. Buckingham: Open University Press.

Riley, Joan 1987: *Waiting in the Twilight*. London: The Women's Press.

Riviere, Joan 1986: Womanliness as a Masquerade (original 1929). In *Formations of Fantasy*, ed. Victor Burgin, James Donald and Cora Kaplan, London and New York: Methuen, pp. 35–61.

Roberts, Michèle 1984: *The Wild Girl*. London: Methuen.

Robinson, Hilary (ed.) 1987: *Visibly Female: Feminism and Art Today, An Anthology*. London: Camden Press.

Rodgerson, Gillian and Elizabeth Wilson (eds) 1991: *Pornography and Feminism: The Case Against Censorship*. London: Lawrence and Wishart.

Rosaldo, Michelle Zimbalist and Louise Lamphère (eds) 1974: *Woman, Culture and Society*. Palo Alto, CA: Stanford University Press.

Rowland, Robyn and Renate Klein 1996: Radical Feminism: History, Politics, Action. In Bell and Klein (eds) 1996, pp. 9–36.

Rubin, Gayle 1992: Of Catanites and Kings: Reflections on Butch, Gender and Boundaries. In Nestle (ed.) 1992, pp. 466–82.

Sandoval, Chela 1991: US Third World Feminism: The Theory and Method of Oppositional Consciousness in the Postmodern World. *Genders*, 10, pp. 1–24.

Sartre, Jean-Paul 1968: Preface. In Fanon 1968, pp. 7–31.

Sayers, Janet 1982: *Biological Politics*. London: Tavistock.

Schopenhauer, Arthur 1977: Über die Weiber [On Women] (original 1851). In Filser (ed.) 1977, pp. 28–31.

Schwichtenberg, Cathy (ed.) 1993: *The Madonna Connection: Representational Politics, Subcultural Identities, and Cultural Theory*. Boulder, CO: Westview Press.

Showalter, Elaine (ed.) 1986: *The New Feminist Criticism*. London: Virago.

Signs 1975–: Chicago: University of Chicago Press.

Smith, Barbara (ed.) 1983a: *Home Girls: A Black Feminist Anthology*. New York: Kitchen Table: Women of Color Press.

—— 1983b: From a talk given at the National Women's Studies Association Conference, May 1978, published in *Frontiers*, 5 (1), 1980, quoted in Moraga and Anzaldua (eds) 1983, pp. 61–2.

—— 1986: Towards a Black Feminist Criticism (original 1977). In Showalter (ed.) 1986, pp. 168–95.

—— 1990: Racism and Women's Studies. In Anzaldua (ed.) 1990a, pp. 25–8.

—— 1995: Black Feminism: A Movement of Our Own (original 1984). In Kahn (ed.) 1995, pp. 22–7.

Smitherman, Geneva 1977: *Talkin' and Testifyin': The Language of Black America*. Boston, MA: Houghton Mifflin.

Smyth, Ailbhe 1992: A (Political) Postcard from a Peripheral Pre-Post-Modernist State of

Mind or How Alliteration can Knock you down Dead in Women's Studies. *Women's Studies International Forum*, 15, pp. 331–7.

Snitow, Ann, Christine Stansell and Sharon Thompson (eds) 1984: *Desire: The Politics of Sexuality*. London: Virago.

Sobel, Mechal 1979: *Trabelin' On: The Slave Journey to an Afro-Baptist Faith*. Princeton, NJ: Princeton University Press.

Spivak, Gayatri 1988: Can the Subaltern Speak? In *Marxism and the Interpretation of Culture*, eds Cary Nelson and Lawrence Grossberg, London: Macmillan, pp. 271–313.

—— 1990: *The Post-Colonial Critic Interviews, Strategies, Dialogues*. Ed. Sarah Harasym. New York and London: Routledge.

Spretnak, Charlene 1989: Towards an Ecofeminist Spirituality. In Plant (ed.) 1989, pp. 127–32.

Stanton, William 1960: *The Leopard's Spots: Scientific Attitudes Towards Race in America 1815–59*. Chicago: University of Chicago Press.

Stanworth, Michelle 1997: Reproductive Technologies: Tampering with Nature? In Kemp and Squires (eds) 1997, pp. 474–86.

Starhawk 1989: Feminist Earth-based Spirituality and Ecofeminism. In Plant (ed.) 1989, pp. 174–88.

Stimpson, Catherine R. 1981: Zero Degree Deviancy: The Lesbian Novel in English. *Critical Inquiry* 8 (2), pp. 363–80.

Strouse, Jean (ed.) 1975: *Women and Analysis: Dialogues on Psychoanalytic Views of Femininity*. New York: Dell.

Sudarkasa, Niara 1981: Interpreting the African Heritage in Afro-American Family Organization. In *Black Families*, ed. Harriette Pipes McAdoo, Beverly Hills, CA: Sage, pp. 37–53.

Thönnessen, Werner 1976: *The Emancipation of Women: The Rise and Decline of the Women's Movement in German Social Democracy 1863–1933*. Trans. J. de Bres. London: Pluto.

Topinard, P. 1888: Le poids de l'encéphale d'après les registres de Paul Broca. *Mémoires Société d'Anthropologle Paris*, 3rd series, 2, pp. 658–91.

Webber, Thomas L. 1978: *Deep Like the Rivers*. New York: W. W. Norton.

Weedon, Chris 1984: *Aspects of the Politics of Literature and Working-class Writing in Interwar Britain*. Ph.D. thesis, Centre for Contemporary Cultural Studies, University of Birmingham.

—— 1994: The Struggle for Women's Emancipation in the Work of Hedwig Dohm. *German Life and Letters* 47, pp. 182–92.

—— 1996a: *Feminist Practice and Poststructuralist Theory*. Second edn. Oxford: Blackwell.

Weedon, Chris (ed.) 1996b: *Postwar Women's Writing in German*. Oxford and Cambridge, MA: Berghahn.

West, Cornel 1982: *Prophesy Deliverance! An Afro-American Revolutionary Christianity*. Philadelphia: The Westminster Press.

—— 1993: *Race Matters*. Boston, MA Beacon Press.

Whelehan, Imelda 1995: *Modern Feminist Thought: From the Second Wave to 'Post-Feminism'*. Edinburgh: Edinburgh University Press.

Whitford, Margaret 1991: *Luce Irigaray: Philosophy in the Feminine*. London and New York: Routledge.

Wilkinson, Sue and Celia Kitzinger (eds) 1993: *Heterosexuality: A Feminism and Psychology Reader*. London: Sage.

Wilkinson, Sue and Celia Kitzinger 1996: The Queer Backlash. In Bell and Klein (eds) 1996, pp. 375–82.

Williams, Raymond 1976: *Keywords*. London: Fontana.

Williamson, Judith 1978: *Decoding Advertisements: Ideology and Meaning in Advertising*. London: Marion Boyars.

Wolfe, Susan J. and Julia Penelope (eds) 1993: *Sexual Practice, Textual Theory: Lesbian Cultural Criticism*. Oxford: Blackwell.

Wollstonecraft, Mary 1975: *A Vindication of the Rights of Woman* (original 1792). Harmondsworth: Penguin.

Women's Studies Group, Centre for Contemporary Cultural Studies 1978: *Women Take Issue: Aspects of Women's Subordination*. London: Hutchinson.

Wong, Nellie 1983: When I Was Growing Up. In Moraga and Anzaldúa (eds) 1983, pp. 7–8.

Woodley, Karin 1987: The Inner Sanctum: *The Dinner Party*. In Robinson (ed.) 1987, pp. 97–9.

Wright, Elizabeth 1984: *Psychoanalytic Criticism: Theory in Practice*. London: Methuen.

—— (ed.) 1992: *Feminism and Psychoanalysis: A Critical Dictionary*. Oxford: Blackwell.

Yamato, Gloria 1990: Something About the Subject Makes It Hard to Name. In Anzaldúa (ed.) 1990a, pp. 20–4.

Zetkin, Clara 1976: Die sozialdemokratische [proletarische] Frauenbewegung [The Social Democratic [proletarian] women's movement]. In Menschik (ed.) 1976, pp. 52–61.

—— 1977: Was die Frauen Karl Marx verdanken [What Women Owe Karl Marx]. In Filser (ed.) 1977, pp. 57–9.

Zimmerman, Bonnie 1993a: What Has Never Been: An Overview of Lesbian Feminist Criticism. In Wolfe and Penelope (eds) 1993, pp. 33–35.

—— 1993b: Perverse Reading: The Lesbian Appropriation of Literature. In Wolfe and Penelope (eds) 1993, pp. 135–49.

INDEX